Microsoft Security, Compliance, and Identity Fundamentals Exam Ref SC-900

Familiarize yourself with security, identity, and compliance in Microsoft 365 and Azure

Dwayne Natwick

BIRMINGHAM—MUMBAI

Microsoft Security, Compliance, and Identity Fundamentals Exam Ref SC-900

Group Product Manager: Vijin Boricha
Publishing Product Manager: Mohd Riyan Khan
Senior Editor: Shazeen Iqbal
Content Development Editor: Rafiaa Khan
Technical Editor: Arjun Varma
Copy Editor: Safis Editing
Project Coordinator: Shagun Saini
Proofreader: Safis Editing
Indexer: Sejal Dsilva
Production Designer: Jyoti Chauhan
Marketing Coordinator: Hemangi Lotlikar

First published: June 2022

Production reference: 1020522

Published by Packt Publishing Ltd.
Livery Place
35 Livery Street
Birmingham
B3 2PB, UK.

978-1-80181-599-4

www.packt.com

To my wife, Kristy, for being my loving and supportive partner throughout our journey together, and for my three wonderful children that make us so proud.

– Dwayne Natwick

Foreword

What comes to mind if I mention *security*?

Is it phishing attempts on the unsuspecting elderly, stereotypical hackers with black hoodies staring at screens of code, or defiant security operation centers responding to malware infections? All of these portray aspects of security, but security is so much more than this. Security is in everything.

We used to secure an organization's data by keeping it behind firewalls, accessible only on the corporate network from managed computer systems with disabled USB ports. That model no longer works for employees who expect to work from anywhere, at any time, from any device. Now, your security posture must encompass devices, networks, user credentials, multi-factor authentication, certificates, encryption, information protection and many other terms, often historically reserved for the most regulated of industries such as finance, healthcare, and government. Data breaches are common news headlines and a thriving industry for bad actors, who also prey on the smallest insecure technology environments to hold them to ransom.

This requires technology professionals across a spectrum of titles – developers, systems administrators, data scientists, systems architects, security professionals, and so on – to build solutions with security in mind, take advantage of security capabilities, and detect and respond to security events. Don't expect the responsibility of security to fall only one dedicated department.

Industry, national, and international regulations set the guidelines for technology solutions to be considered compliant with defined standards. Identity administration has evolved beyond just requiring a complex password. A user's identity is now the main security perimeter, allowing or denying access to an organization's confidential information. When you put it all together, it can be overwhelming to think of this bigger security picture.

This book is a great introduction to industry-standard security concepts. You'll learn about concepts such as defense-in-depth, zero trust, and where responsibility lies between your organization and Microsoft, across on-premises and cloud services. Then, you'll explore the capabilities of Microsoft's identity and access management solutions, security products, and compliance solutions, including Microsoft Azure and Microsoft 365. You'll understand how to limit access, secure authentication, monitor and respond to security incidents, and protect system configurations and information. Hopefully, you'll be inspired to test your knowledge with the SC-900 – Microsoft Security, Compliance, and Identity Fundamentals exam and earn your certification.

Regardless of your job role or career path, understanding the fundamental components of security, identity, and compliance will arm you with a security mindset in everything you do. It will broaden your knowledge of how you can improve your organization's security posture. And it may surprise you how far we've come from isolating physical network segments and blocking USB ports. The threats may have become more sophisticated, but we have a few defensive tricks up our sleeves too.

You're in good hands with the author Dwayne Natwick's experience as a Microsoft Certified Trainer, and I wish you the very best on your learning journey.

Sonia Cuff

Senior Cloud Advocate of Modern Infrastructure at Microsoft

Contributors

About the author

Dwayne Natwick is a senior product manager for migration and security service lines at Cloudreach, an Atos company, and a Microsoft expert CSP. He has been in IT, security design, and architecture for over 35 years. His love of teaching led him to become a **Microsoft Certified Trainer (MCT)**, a Regional Lead, and a **Microsoft Most Valuable Professional (MVP)**.

Dwayne has a master's degree in business IT from Walsh College, the CISSP from ISC2, and 18 Microsoft certifications, including Identity and Access Administrator, Azure Security Engineer, and Microsoft 365 Security Administrator. Dwayne can be found providing and sharing information on social media, industry conferences, his blog site, and his YouTube channel.

Originally from Maryland, Dwayne currently resides in Michigan with his wife and three children.

About the reviewers

Shabaz Darr is a master at Netcompany, based in the UK, and has over 15 years of experience in the tech industry. He currently works for Netcompany as an infrastructure master, where his main areas of focus are Microsoft Endpoint Manager, Azure IaaS, and Azure Virtual Desktop.

Shabaz has co-authored a book on the SC-400 – Microsoft Information Protection exam study guide and individually authored a book on the AZ-140 – Azure Virtual Desktop exam study guide.

Finally, Shabaz has his own YouTube channel called *IAmITGeek*, where he creates community content on Microsoft and Azure cloud services.

> *I would like to thank Packt for the opportunity to be part of this amazing project and also say well done and thank you to the author, Dwayne Natwick, for allowing me to be part of this journey. It has been an honor and a privilege to review this book.*

Prashant Khaire is a security technologist with over 24 years of experience in various verticals of information security and IT. Currently, he is a lead security professional for a large retail company in the US. Prashant has a broad knowledge of securing the digital assets of organizations. He holds an MS in cybersecurity and information assurance and several industry-recognized certifications, including CISSP, CISM, CCSP, CCSK, CEH, Azure Security, and AWS Certified Solutions Architect. Prashant is a firm believer in a continuous learning approach to the information security technologies he pursues daily. He tweets at @pkhaire22.

> *I want to thank God first for his almighty guidance on whatever decisions I made and my family for their daily support and patience. I'd also like to thank Packt Publishing for the opportunity to review this excellent book.*

Table of Contents

3

Understanding Key Security Concepts

4

Key Microsoft Security and Compliance Principles

Section 3: The Microsoft Identity Management Solutions

5

Defining Identity Principles/Concepts and the Identity Services within Azure AD

6

Describing the Authentication and Access Management Capabilities of Azure AD

7
Describing the Identity Protection and Governance Capabilities of Azure AD

Section 4: The Microsoft Security Solutions for Microsoft 365 and Azure

8
Describing Basic Security Services and Management Capabilities in Azure

9

Describing Security Management and Capabilities of Azure

10

Describing Threat Protection with Microsoft 365 Defender

11

Describing the Security Capabilities of Microsoft Sentinel

12

Describing Security Management and the Endpoint Security Capabilities of Microsoft 365

Section 5: The Microsoft Compliance Monitoring Capabilities within Microsoft 365 and Azure

13

Compliance Management Capabilities in Microsoft

14

Describing Information Protection and Governance Capabilities of Microsoft 365

15

Describing Insider Risk, eDiscovery, and Audit Capabilities in Microsoft 365

16

Describing Resource Governance Capabilities in Azure

17

Final Assessment/Mock Exam

Index

Other Books You May Enjoy

Preface

This book simplifies **identity and access management (IAM)** concepts to help you pass the SC-300 certification exam. Packed with practical examples, you'll gain hands-on knowledge to drive strategic identity projects while modernizing identity solutions, implementing hybrid identity solutions, and monitoring identity governance.

Who this book is for

This book is for cloud security engineers, Azure administrators, Microsoft 365 administrators, Microsoft 365 users, Azure security engineers, Microsoft identity administrators, and anyone who wants to learn about IAM and gain the SC-900 certification. You should have a basic understanding of the fundamental services within networking, virtualization, Microsoft 365, Azure, and Azure Active Directory before getting started with this Microsoft book.

What this book covers

Chapter 1, *Preparing for Your Microsoft Exam*, provides guidance on getting prepared for the Microsoft exam, along with resources that can assist in your learning plan. This includes helpful links along with steps on how to gain access to a trial Microsoft 365 subscription for hands-on practice.

Chapter 2, *Describing Security Methodologies*, covers the methodologies that you should know when planning and architecting a good security posture for your company to properly protect identities and information.

Chapter 3, *Understanding Key Security Concepts*, provides some basis for common security concepts and the types of threats that may affect your users and information. This chapter provides a high-level overview of how encryption can be used to protect that information.

Chapter 4, *Key Microsoft Security and Compliance Principles*, focuses on Microsoft's principles and guidelines for protecting the privacy of their customers. This includes the information that is provided in the Service Trust Portal for customers to find information on these principles and compliance reports on Microsoft data centers.

Chapter 5, Defining Identity Principles/Concepts and the Identity Services within Azure AD, covers the concept of identity protection. This includes how authentication and authorization work along with common identity attacks. It also introduces Azure Active Directory and describes identity providers.

Chapter 6, Describing the Authentication and Access Management Capabilities of Azure AD, covers identity management with Azure Active Directory. This includes the protection of identities for cloud and hybrid applications and how to use external users and groups for collaboration.

Chapter 7, Describing the Identity Protection and Governance Capabilities of Azure AD, discusses the different ways to utilize the services within Azure AD to govern and protect identities. This includes access reviews, PIM, and Conditional Access policies.

Chapter 8, Describing Basic Security Services and Management Capabilities in Azure, describes the various security services within Azure for network, compute, and data protection. This includes perimeter and application security services.

Chapter 9, Describing Security Management and Capabilities of Azure, describes the capabilities within Azure to manage, monitor, and protect against security threats and vulnerabilities within your infrastructure.

Chapter 10, Describing Threat Protection with Microsoft 365 Defender, describes the threat protection services within Microsoft 365 Defender for the protection of cloud and hybrid applications. This defines the various services that make up the Defender suite of products environment.

Chapter 11, Describing the Security Capabilities of Microsoft Sentinel, describes the capabilities of a modern security operations center and how Microsoft Sentinel can be used for SIEM and SOAR capabilities for integrated threat management.

Chapter 12, Describing Security Management and Endpoint Security Capabilities of Microsoft 365, describes the security management capabilities within Microsoft 365. This includes how to use Microsoft 365 Defender for security posture and incident management.

Chapter 13, Compliance Management Capabilities in Microsoft, describes how to use the Microsoft compliance center to access and manage security best practices and regulatory compliance with your Microsoft 365 connected applications.

Chapter 14, Describing Information Protection and Governance Capabilities of Microsoft 365, describes the information protection and governance capabilities within Microsoft 365. This includes how to use these services for the protection and retention of data.

Chapter 15, Describing Insider Risk, eDiscovery, and Audit Capabilities in Microsoft 365, describes the services that allow protecting barriers, auditing, and putting a hold on data for the purposes of review and investigation.

Chapter 16, Describing Resource Governance Capabilities in Azure, describes the governance capabilities within Azure to maintain baselines and consistency within our resources. This includes how to prevent unauthorized changes, create a standard for deployment, and create policies to govern cost and security. This chapter closes with an overview of the Cloud Adoption Framework.

Chapter 17, Final Assessment/Mock Exam, provides a final assessment and mock exam questions to complete the final preparations to take the SC-900 exam.

To get the most out of this book

This book explores configuring a tenant for the use of Microsoft 365 and Azure. There are exercises that require access to Azure Active Directory. *Chapter 1, Preparing for Your Microsoft Exam,* provides directions for creating a trial license of Microsoft 365 and a free Azure account.

Software/hardware covered in the book	OS requirements
Azure Active Directory	Windows, macOS, or Linux (any)
Microsoft 365 Business trial	Windows, macOs or Linux (any)
Azure free account	Windows, macOs or Linux (any)

Download the color images

We also provide a PDF file that has color images of the screenshots/diagrams used in this book. You can download it here: `https://static.packt-cdn.com/downloads/9781801815994_ColorImages.pdf`.

Conventions used

There are a number of text conventions used throughout this book.

`Code in text`: Indicates code words in text, database table names, folder names, filenames, file extensions, pathnames, dummy URLs, user input, and Twitter handles. Here is an example: "To configure the host side of the network, you need the `tunctl` command from the **User Mode Linux (UML)** project."

Bold: Indicates a new term, an important word, or words that you see onscreen. For example, words in menus or dialog boxes appear in the text like this. Here is an example: "Once someone has authenticated to the systems that they are attempting to access, then authorization takes place. **Authorization** verifies the permissions for that user and determines what they are allowed to do when accessing the company systems."

> **Tips or Important Notes**
> Appear like this.

Get in touch

Feedback from our readers is always welcome.

General feedback: If you have questions about any aspect of this book, mention the book title in the subject of your message and email us at customercare@packtpub.com.

Errata: Although we have taken every care to ensure the accuracy of our content, mistakes do happen. If you have found a mistake in this book, we would be grateful if you would report this to us. Please visit www.packtpub.com/support/errata, selecting your book, clicking on the Errata Submission Form link, and entering the details.

Piracy: If you come across any illegal copies of our works in any form on the Internet, we would be grateful if you would provide us with the location address or website name. Please contact us at copyright@packt.com with a link to the material.

If you are interested in becoming an author: If there is a topic that you have expertise in and you are interested in either writing or contributing to a book, please visit authors.packtpub.com.

Share Your Thoughts

Once you've read *Microsoft Security, Compliance, and Identity Fundamentals Exam Ref SC-900*, we'd love to hear your thoughts! Scan the QR code below to go straight to the Amazon review page for this book and share your feedback.

https://packt.link/r/1801815992

Your review is important to us and the tech community and will help us make sure we're delivering excellent quality content.

Section 1: Exam Overview

This section will focus on the objectives of this book and an overview of what to expect in the exam.

This part of the book comprises the following chapter:

- *Chapter 1, Preparing for Your Microsoft Exam*

1
Preparing for Your Microsoft Exam

You have decided to take the steps to get **Microsoft certified**. The **SC-900** exam focuses on *Security*, *Compliance*, and *Identity Fundamentals*. This chapter will help you prepare for the Microsoft exam, along with the resources that can assist you with your learning. This will include helpful links, along with steps on how to gain access to a trial **Microsoft 365** subscription and a month of free **Microsoft Azure** access for hands-on practice.

Once you have completed this chapter, you will become familiar with the tools that enable you to know what is needed to prepare for the exam, follow this book, and begin your journey within a security, compliance, and/or identity role.

In this chapter, we're going to cover the following main topics:

- Preparing for the Microsoft exam
- Resources available and accessing Microsoft Learn
- Creating a Microsoft 365 trial subscription
- Setting up a free month of Azure services
- Exam objectives
- Who should take the SC-900 exam?

Technical requirements

To follow along and complete the exercises within this book, you will need to have access to security, compliance, and identity services within **Microsoft 365** and **Azure**. This can be accomplished by getting a trial subscription for Microsoft 365 and a free month of Azure. Advanced security services will also require an **Enterprise + Mobility** license. The steps to set up these licenses will be covered later in this chapter.

Preparing for the Microsoft exam

There are multiple aspects of preparing for the Microsoft exam. These include the resources available to prepare for the exam, the ability to access a subscription for hands-on learning, and how you are going to take your exam. If this is your first Microsoft exam, understanding the format that most of these exams will follow is important.

Let's take a closer look at each of these areas.

Resources to prepare for the exam

There are many resources available that can help you prepare for most Microsoft exams. This includes pre-recorded content from learning companies, live courses from *Microsoft Learning Partners*, and content that's been posted by the community and Microsoft blog articles. Each of these resources is helpful, but the pre-recorded content and live courses will come at a price. This may not be within your budget. Community and Microsoft blog articles generally provide a level of direction regarding where you need to go for each topic, but they do not get into specifics.

One of the best resources is Microsoft itself. Microsoft provides detailed documentation about each of their services via *Microsoft Docs*, which allows you to search freely and find the information that you need. This information is publicly available and free. Microsoft Docs is tied very closely to Microsoft Learn's content, which will be discussed later in this chapter.

To access and search Microsoft Docs, simply go to https://docs.microsoft.com.

Access to a subscription

When preparing for the Microsoft exam, it is highly recommended that you have had some level of hands-on experience with the services within the objectives. For fundamental-level exams, with the SC-900 being a fundamental-level exam, hands-on experience is extremely helpful in reinforcing your understanding. Microsoft courses have a *GitHub* repository for labs that are recommended and available to the public.

The lab guides can be found at this link: `http://www.microsoft.com/learning`.

Microsoft offers trial subscriptions for both Azure and Microsoft 365. The process of creating these trials will be covered later in this chapter.

Where to take the exam

Part of the preparation process of taking the exam includes where you are going to take it. Traditionally, there has only been the option to take these exams at a proctored exam site. Some may prefer this method because it is a controlled environment. Understanding the location and setup of the site can help lower your level of stress on the day of the exam. Making a trip to the site before your exam date can avoid any potential surprises on the day.

When the role-based exams became available, Microsoft provided an additional option of taking the exam remotely from your home or office by using a **remote proctor**. This may be your preferred option if you are more comfortable using your own equipment and environment. If you do not have this choice when scheduling your exam, then this option has not been made available to your region. If it is available, you will see options similar to the following:

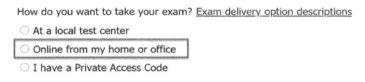

Figure 1.1 – Selecting a location when scheduling the exam

There are some important steps to prepare for the remote proctor. From an equipment standpoint, you must have a device with a webcam, microphone, and speakers. You can only use one monitor, so ensure that you have a high resolution to avoid any issues when viewing the exam. It is highly recommended that you test your equipment before the day of the exam to avoid any issues with anti-malware software.

The location that you are going to take the exam in must be cleared of any papers, books, pens, and pencils. It must also be a quiet environment where no one will enter while you are taking the exam. You will be required to photograph the location and surrounding area when checking in. Valid identification is required as well. During the exam, you must remain within the view of the camera. This may feel intrusive and may not be a manner that is comfortable for some, but others may prefer being within their own environment.

Exam format

Microsoft exams are typically made up of 4-6 question types. These are case studies, multiple-choice, drag and drop, true/false, drop-down fill-in, and best answer scenarios. Let's provide some additional details about what each of these means, as follows:

- **Case study** questions provide a hypothetical company setting within the current environment, proposed future environment, and the technical and business requirements. From this scenario, 6-8 questions are asked that may cover multiple objective areas of the exam. In most associate-level exams, you could see 1-3 of these case studies.

- **Multiple-choice** questions are straightforward questions. Some multiple-choice questions may have more than one answer. Microsoft is generally transparent on how many correct answers need to be chosen for the question, and you will be alerted if you do not choose the correct number of selections.

- **Drag-and-drop** questions are usually based on the steps of a process to test your knowledge of the order of operations to deploy a service. You are given more selections than needed and need to move the steps that apply to the question to the right-hand column in the proper sequence.

- The next type of question is a modified type of **true/false** question. In these questions, you are usually provided with some exhibits or screenshots from within the Microsoft portals or tables that show what has been configured. There are then 3-4 statements about this information, where you need to select yes or no for each statement based on whether the statement is correct based on the information provided.

- **Drop-down fill-in** questions are usually where you will find PowerShell or Azure CLI code. You will be asked to complete certain steps within a string of code where the blank sections provide drop-down selections to choose from.

- The **best answer scenario** questions test your understanding of an objective area. Microsoft will warn you when you get to this section as you will no longer have the option to navigate back to the other questions. You will be provided a specific scenario that needs to be solved, along with a proposed solution. The requirement is to determine whether that solution is the best solution to solve the scenario at hand. After selecting yes or no, you may see the same scenario again with a different solution, where you must select yes or no again.

Each of these exam question types tests your level of understanding in different ways, and all of them are weighted against the exam objectives, which will be discussed later in this chapter.

With that, we have covered how to determine an exam's location and the types of questions that you may expect. The next few sections will cover the resources that will help you learn about the topics within the exam, as well as how to gain access to the solutions so that you can follow along with the exercises in this guide.

Resources available and accessing Microsoft Learn

Earlier in this chapter, some of the resources that are available for preparing for the exam were mentioned. **Microsoft Learn** was mentioned, along with Microsoft Docs, but Microsoft Learn requires its own section due to the amount of free content that it provides to help you prepare for the exam.

Accessing Microsoft Learn

Microsoft Learn is a great resource to get your learning path started. All the content on Microsoft Learn is free. When you create an account on Microsoft, your learning progress is tracked and you can acquire badges along the way. In addition, Microsoft creates learning challenges periodically with prizes, such as free exam vouchers. Creating a free account can be done by selecting the icon at the top right of the page and selecting **Sign in**, as shown in the following screenshot:

Figure 1.2 – Microsoft Learn site profile – Sign in

You can sign in with an existing Microsoft account or create one to get started, as indicated here:

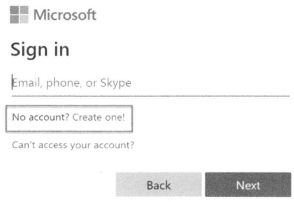

Figure 1.3 – Create or sign in to a Microsoft account

You can get to Microsoft Learn by going to the following link: `https://www.microsoft.com/learn`.

Finding content on Microsoft Learn

Content on Microsoft Learn can be found in various ways. You can search for specific products, roles, or certifications. These options can be found on the selection ribbon at the top of the **Learn** home page, as shown in the following screenshot. The home page also provides several recommendations so that you can start your learning journey:

Figure 1.4 – Learn content navigation

From the Learn content navigation tabs, select a drop-down arrow to filter for content in the specific **Products**, **Roles**, or **Certifications** areas:

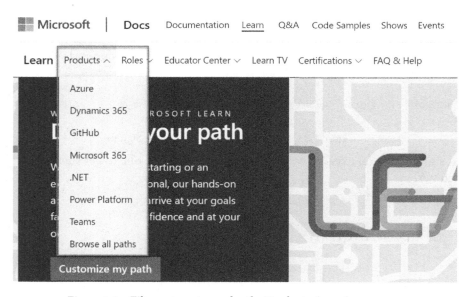

Figure 1.5 – Filter categories under the Products drop-down menu

Once you have selected an area of interest, or simply chosen **Browse all paths**, you can search for specific topics and filter for individual courses or learning paths, as shown in the following screenshot:

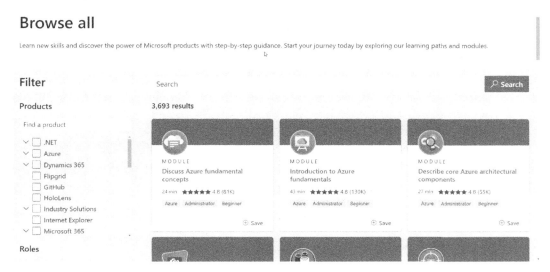

Figure 1.6 – Browse all content in Microsoft Learn

This section has shown you how to access Microsoft Learn and browse for modules and learning paths. The next section will assist you in finding content specific to the SC-900 exam.

Exam pages on Microsoft Learn

Another common area within Microsoft Learn is the **exam pages**. For any exam provided by Microsoft, there is an exam page and a certification page that is located within Microsoft Learn. These pages provide an overview of the exam or certification, the roles of individuals that may be interested in the exam, the objective areas for the exam, scheduling the exam, and the Microsoft Learn learning path to prepare for the exam. These pages are extremely helpful when you are preparing for an exam rather than just learning to gain general technical knowledge. The following screenshot shows us searching for the SC-900 exam, where you can see sc-900 being typed in the search box:

Figure 1.7 – Browse for the SC-900 exam

The following screenshot shows the exam page for the SC-900 exam:

Docs / Learn / Browse Certifications / Microsoft Security, Compliance, and Identity Fundamentals - Learn

Exam SC-900: Microsoft Security, Compliance, and Identity Fundamentals

The content of this exam was updated on July 26, 2021. Please download the skills measured document below to see what changed.

This exam is targeted to those looking to familiarize themselves with the fundamentals of security, compliance, and identity (SCI) across cloud-based and related Microsoft services.

This is a broad audience that may include business stakeholders, new or existing IT professionals, or students who have an interest in Microsoft security, compliance, and identity solutions.

Candidates should be familiar with Microsoft Azure and Microsoft 365 and want to understand how Microsoft security, compliance, and identity solutions can span across these solution areas to provide a holistic and end-to-end solution.

Part of the requirements for: Microsoft Certified: Security, Compliance, and Identity Fundamentals
Related exams: none
Important: See details
Go to Certification Dashboard

Schedule exam

Exam SC-900: Microsoft Security, Compliance, and Identity Fundamentals

United States	∨

$99 USD*

Price based on the country in which the exam is proctored.

Languages: English, Japanese, Chinese (Simplified), Korean, French, Spanish, Portuguese (Brazil), Russian, Arabic (Saudi Arabia), Indonesian (Indonesia), German, Chinese (Traditional), Italian

This exam measures your ability to describe the following: concepts of security, compliance, and identity; capabilities of Microsoft identity and access management solutions; capabilities of Microsoft security solutions; and capabilities of Microsoft compliance solutions.

For non-students interested in technology

Schedule with Pearson VUE >

For students or instructors

Schedule with Certiport >

Official practice test for Microsoft Security, Compliance, and Identity Fundamentals
All objectives of the exam are covered in depth so you'll be ready for any question on the exam.

⊕ Save

Skills measured

- The content of this exam was updated on July 26, 2021. Please download the exam skills outline below to see what changed.
- Describe the concepts of security, compliance, and identity (10-15%)
- Describe the capabilities of Microsoft identity and access management solutions (30-35%)
- Describe the capabilities of Microsoft security solutions (35-40%)
- Describe the capabilities of Microsoft compliance solutions (25-30%)

⤓ Download exam skills outline

Figure 1.8 – SC-900 exam page

As you continue to prepare for the SC-900 exam, it is recommended that you use this exam page as a reference.

You should now have access to log in and browse the content on Microsoft Learn. The next section will show you how to sign up for a trial subscription to Microsoft 365 services and sign up for a month of free Azure services.

Creating a Microsoft 365 trial subscription

If you are new to Microsoft 365 and Azure, getting hands-on experience is important – not just for exam preparation, but also for professional development. If you are getting certified to open doors to new job opportunities, you must understand the administration portals and how to work within them. This book will provide some exercises that will get you familiar with how to work within Microsoft 365, advanced security and compliance solutions, and Azure Active Directory. To follow along, it is recommended that you have a subscription to Microsoft 365 and Enterprise + Mobility. The steps to create these when using a 30-day trial are provided in the following sections.

Office 365 or Microsoft 365 trial subscription

Many of the features and capabilities discussed within the exam objectives require you to have an enterprise-level license within Microsoft 365. The available enterprise licenses are the *E3* and *E5* licenses. Microsoft offers 30-day trial licenses for these, so as you prepare for the exam, you can create a trial subscription and be able to follow along with the exercises.

To get started, as shown in the following screenshot, navigate to `https://www.microsoft.com/en-us/microsoft-365/enterprise/compare-office-365-plans` and select **Try for free** under the **Office 365 E5** plan:

Office 365 E5

All the features of Office 365 E3 plus advanced security, analytics, and voice capabilities[1].

$35.00 user/month
(annual commitment)

Buy now

Try for free >

Contact sales >

Learn more >

Figure 1.9 – Signing up for an Office 365 trial subscription

Follow the steps provided to create an account, as shown in the following screenshot. If you have already created an account, you may need to use a different email address to obtain the free trial:

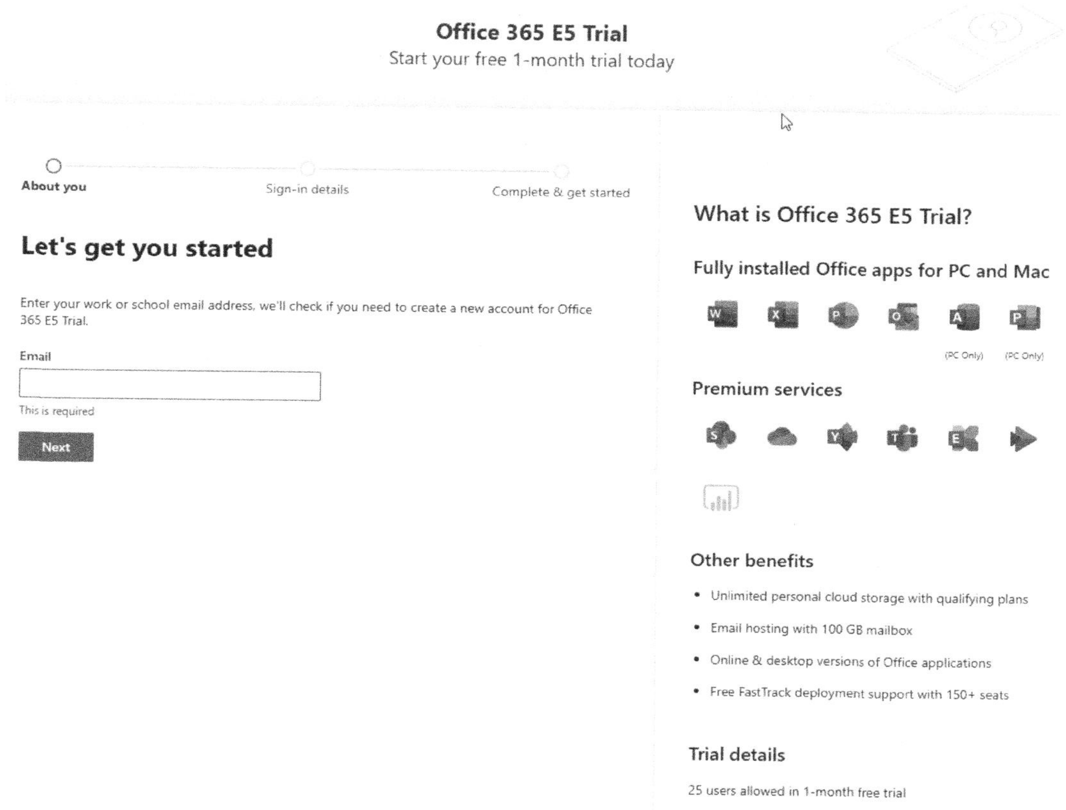

Office 365 E5 Trial

Start your free 1-month trial today

○————————○————————○
About you   Sign-in details   Complete & get started

Let's get you started

Enter your work or school email address, we'll check if you need to create a new account for Office 365 E5 Trial.

Email

[   ]

This is required

[Next]

What is Office 365 E5 Trial?

Fully installed Office apps for PC and Mac

(PC Only)   (PC Only)

Premium services

Other benefits

* Unlimited personal cloud storage with qualifying plans

* Email hosting with 100 GB mailbox

* Online & desktop versions of Office applications

* Free FastTrack deployment support with 150+ seats

Trial details

25 users allowed in 1-month free trial

Figure 1.10 – Office 365 E5 subscription sign-up form

After completing the form and creating your Microsoft 365 tenant, you will have access to Microsoft 365's services and the administration panel. The next section will show you how to sign up for an additional add-on service that will be required to follow the exercises in this book, as well as gaining full hands-on preparation for your exam.

Enterprise Mobility + Security subscription

In addition to the Office 365 E5 trial subscription, you will need access to advanced security and compliance features, as well as an Azure Active Directory Premium license for many of the solutions and services that will be discussed within the exam objectives. The best way to obtain these features is through an **Enterprise Mobility + Security E5** license. Microsoft also offers this as a 30-day free trial:

1. To get started, navigate to this link: `https://www.microsoft.com/en-us/microsoft-365/enterprise-mobility-security/compare-plans-and-pricing`.

2. Then, select **Try now** under the **Enterprise Mobility + Security E5** plan, as shown in the following screenshot:

$14.80
user/month
(annual commitment)

Enterprise Mobility + Security E5

Try now >

Buy E5

Figure 1.11 – Signing up for an EMS E5 trial subscription

This is an add-on license to Microsoft 365, so you should enter the same email address that you used to sign up for the Office 365 E5 subscription in the box shown in the following screenshot:

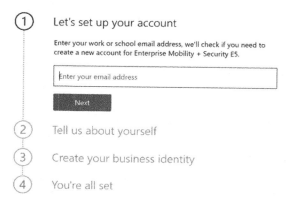

Figure 1.12 – EMS E5 subscription sign-up form

You should now have everything that you need for your hands-on exam preparation and to follow the exercises in this book. The next section will provide an overview of the objectives that will be covered in the exam and throughout this book.

Free month of Azure services

Since this exam includes security, compliance, and identity services for Microsoft 365 and Azure, it is recommended that you have access to Azure as well. Microsoft offers a free month of services from Azure. If you have not taken advantage of this offer previously, you can sign up at this link: `https://azure.microsoft.com/`.

Once you've done that, you can select **Free account** at the top right or **Get started for free** in the middle of the page, as shown in the following screenshot:

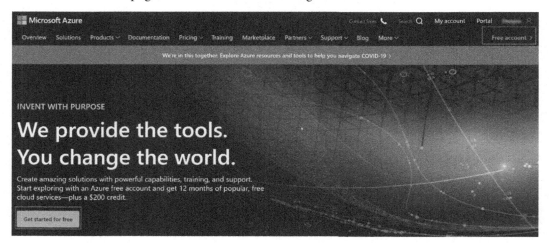

Figure 1.13 – Microsoft Azure sign-up page

Once you have created these trial subscriptions as described, you will be ready to follow the exercises in this book. Hands-on learning is an important tool for understanding topics, so it is highly recommended that you complete the steps within this section and follow along. The next section will discuss the structure of the exam and its objectives.

Exam objectives

This book will cover the specific objectives of the SC-900 Microsoft Security, Compliance, and Identity Fundamentals exam. The structure of this book follows these objectives closely. However, there is an added section on monitoring and management that provides additional emphasis on furthering your career within the areas of security, compliance, and identity.

As is the case with all Microsoft exams, each objective area is weighted differently. The weight of each objective is meant to be used as a guide to help you understand the potential number of questions to expect in these areas for the exam. The objectives that are covered within the SC-900 exam are shown in the following table:

Objective	Weight
Describe the concepts of security, compliance, and identity	5-10%
Describe the capabilities of Microsoft identity and access management solutions	25-30%
Describe the capabilities of Microsoft security solutions	30-35%
Describe the capabilities of Microsoft compliance solutions	25-30%

Additional details on the topics that make up these objectives can be found at this link: `https://query.prod.cms.rt.microsoft.com/cms/api/am/binary/RE4Myp5`.

Note that the weights do not mean that if an objective is weighted at 10%, you will only get 5 questions out of 50 on this area. Microsoft exams use a scoring scale of 1,000 based on the type of question and the objectives that are covered within the question. Many questions may have elements of multiple objectives, so they get working into percentages. The weights of the objectives can help you understand the level of importance that is being placed on the objective.

Now that you know the objective areas that are covered in this exam, you may be wondering how this exam and certification can assist in professional development and career advancement. The next section will provide some insight into the types of roles that this exam highlights.

Who should take the SC-900 exam?

Now that you understand more about Microsoft exams, paths to learning, and the specific areas covered in the SC-900 exam, it is important to think about the roles that someone should have or want before preparing for this exam. The SC-900 exam is the Security, Compliance, and Identity Fundamentals exam, so it covers a broad range of services and solutions for maintaining security and compliance within Microsoft 365, Azure, and hybrid infrastructures. Anyone that wishes to work with Microsoft cloud technologies will benefit from learning the objectives of this exam.

This exam will also help you obtain a role in security, compliance, or identity administration within Microsoft 365 or Azure. This exam is a starting point that helps determine your areas of interest while providing you with a rounded understanding of the broad range of security, compliance, and identity services and solutions within Microsoft's cloud technologies.

Summary

In this chapter, we covered the areas that will prepare you for the Security, Compliance, and Identity Fundamentals exam and the setup required to follow along with the exercises covered within this book. We also provided an overview of what to expect when taking the Microsoft exam.

The next chapter will discuss the various concepts that make up the foundation of security, compliance, and identity.

Section 2: The Key Concepts of Security, Compliance, and Identity

This section will cover the key concepts of security, compliance, and identity. This will include the planning and approaches to take to protect your company.

This part of the book comprises the following chapters:

- *Chapter 2, Describing Security Methodologies*
- *Chapter 3, Understanding Key Security Concepts*
- *Chapter 4, Key Microsoft Security and Compliance Principles*

2
Describing Security Methodologies

The previous chapter covered the necessary preparation for the **SC-900** *Security, Compliance, and Identity Fundamentals exam*. This chapter will discuss the key methodologies for security, shared responsibility, and identity protection. Once you have completed this chapter, you will have a solid understanding of the foundational methods and principles that Microsoft 365 and Azure solutions follow for security, compliance, and identity protection.

In this chapter, we're going to cover the following main topics:

- Describing and using a defense-in-depth security strategy
- Understanding shared responsibility within cloud security
- Using and implementing the principles of the zero-trust methodology

Describing and using a defense-in-depth security strategy

When protecting the cloud and hybrid infrastructure, many aspects need to be considered. As you go through the various solutions offered within **Microsoft 365** and **Azure**, these methodologies and principles play a key role in the process of protecting resources, identity, and data. One of the primary strategies in which to protect your company is through **defense in depth**. However, before we dive into the full use of the defense-in-depth strategy, it is important to understand the *cyber-attack kill chain*, as this correlates to your protection strategy of defense in depth.

Understanding the cyber-attack kill chain

There are many ways in which an attacker can attempt to access resources within a company. How they gain this access and what they attempt to accomplish once they have gained access is the foundation of a cyber attack. We will examine each of these areas and discuss how we can protect them using the cyber-attack kill chain. *Figure 2.1* shows the stages of a cyber attack in a linear format:

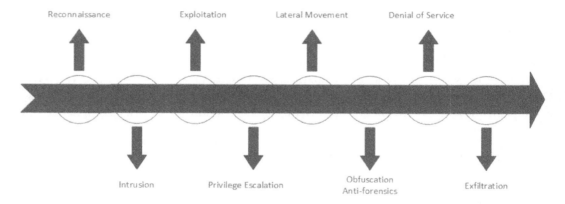

Figure 2.1 – The stages of a cyber attack

In the majority of cases, an attacker attempts to enter and carry out some level of damage at one of these stages. Sophisticated attackers might go through every one of these stages in order to gain full access to resources and increase the amount of damage they can do to a company. Let's define each of these stages in order to gain a better understanding:

1. **Reconnaissance**: This is the planning stage of the attack. The attacker is gathering any information they can find regarding the company, or companies, that they will be targeting. This could be through social media, websites, phishing, or the social engineering of personnel within the company. Another aspect of this stage is the port scanning of known management ports, such as **Remote Desktop Protocol (RDP)** port 3389 or **Secure Shell (SSH)** port 22. At this stage, the goal is to find ways to access the systems.

2. **Intrusion**: Once the reconnaissance is successful, the attacker will have found a way to access a system or systems within the company network. Now they will use that knowledge to get into those systems. One type of intrusion is a brute-force attack.

3. **Exploitation**: The attacker has gained access to a system on the company network, and now they want to exploit that system. This is where the attacker begins to show malicious intent. They will begin to use this access to deliver malware across the network.

4. **Privilege Escalation**: Once the attacker has gained access to a system, they will want to gain administrator-level access to the current resource along with additional resources on the network. If they have gained access to a virtual machine on the network, they could also have administrative login privileges to other virtual machines and resources on the network.

5. **Lateral Movement**: Companies that use the same administrator username and password could allow the attacker to gain access to other systems across the network. This lateral movement could lead the attacker from a system without sensitive information to one that has extremely sensitive information.

6. **Obfuscation/Anti-forensics**: As is the case with any attack or crime, the person, or people, involved do not want to be found or traced. Therefore, they attempt to keep their access anonymous. If they have gained access through someone's credentials within the company, this could help to decrease their traceability.

7. **Denial of Service**: When an attacker cuts off access to resources, this is a denial of service. This might be through an attack such as a SYN flood in which a large number of requests are sent to a company's public IP address, which cannot be processed quickly enough. This flood of requests blocks legitimate requests from being able to access resources.

8. **Exfiltration**: The final aspect of a cyber attack is exfiltration. This is where the attacker has gained access to sensitive information, and they are able to remove that information to do harm in some way. For instance, this could be banking information, personnel, customer **personal identifiable information (PII)**, or other valuable data.

The ability to protect against each of these aspects of the *cyber attack* is our kill chain. Having a strong defense-in-depth security posture addresses these areas of the kill chain. In the next section, we will discuss the concept of building a defense-in-depth security posture.

Building a defense-in-depth security posture

In order to protect your company against cyber attacks, you should have controls in place that address the stages of a cyber attack and maintain a defense-in-depth security posture. When planning for security on information technology resources, protecting one aspect is not enough, as every aspect of the infrastructure should have *security controls* in place to protect at all levels. Controls are those services or solutions that we have in place to properly secure and protect the resources at that level of defense.

Each of these levels of defense is important since attackers look for various entry points into a company's network. The levels of defense in depth are shown in *Figure 2.2*:

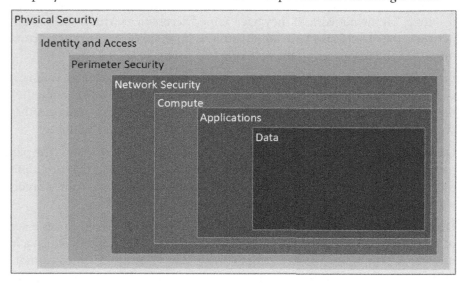

Figure 2.2 – Levels of defense-in-depth security

Now that you know why defense in depth is important, let's discuss each of these areas and provide an example of a control that can be used to protect resources.

Physical

The **physical** level of defense includes the actual hardware technology and spans the entire data center facility. This includes the compute, storage, and networking components, rack spaces, power, internet, and cooling. Additionally, it includes the room in which that equipment is housed, the building's location and surroundings, and the people who have access to these locations.

Protecting the physical level of defense in depth encompasses how we create redundancy and resiliency in the previously mentioned systems, along with how we capture and audit who accesses the building and systems. This could include gated fences, guard stations, video surveillance, logging visitors, and background checks. These physical controls should be in place for any company that utilizes its own private data center.

When utilizing Microsoft cloud services, the physical controls are Microsoft's responsibility. In the next section, we will discuss shared responsibility for cloud security.

Identity and access

Since within cloud services, the provider is responsible for the physical controls, **identity and access** are the first line of defense that a customer can use to configure and protect against threats. This is why statements such as *Identity is the new control plane* or *Identity is the new perimeter* have become popular when discussing cloud security. Even if your company maintains a private data center for its primary business applications, there is still a good chance that you are consuming a cloud application that uses your company identity. For this reason, having the proper controls in place, such as **multi-factor authentication (MFA)**, **conditional access policies**, or **Azure Identity Protection**, will help to decrease any vulnerabilities and recognize potential threats before a widespread attack can take place.

Perimeter security

Within a private data center, where the company controls the internet provider connection terminations and has their *firewall appliances, intrusion detection*, and *protection* solutions, along with DDoS protection in place and fully configured, the protection of the perimeter is a straightforward architecture.

When working within cloud providers, **perimeter security** takes on a different focus. The cloud providers have agreements with the internet providers that provide services to their data centers, and these providers terminate these connections with their hardware. The company's perimeter security then becomes more of a virtual perimeter to their tenant rather than a physical perimeter to the data center's network facilities. The company now relies on the provider's ability to protect against DDoS attacks at the internet perimeter.

Within Microsoft, *DDoS protection* is a free service, since Microsoft wants to avoid a DDoS attack that could bring down a large number of their customers within a data center. For additional perimeter protection, the company can implement virtual firewall appliances to protect the tenant perimeter, such as blocking port-level and packet-level attacks, and additional solutions, such as Application Gateway with a **Web Application Firewall (WAF)** to protect against application-layer attacks.

Network security

The perimeter and **network security** layers work closely together. Both layers focus on the network traffic aspect of the company infrastructure. Where perimeter security handles the internet traffic that is entering the tenant, or data center, network security solutions protect how and where that traffic can be routed once it passes through the perimeter. If we go back to the cyber-attack kill chain discussed in the previous section, once an attacker is able to gain access to a system on the network, they want to find ways to move laterally within the network infrastructure. Having a proper IP address and network segmentation on the network can protect against this lateral movement taking place.

On a private data center network, this can be accomplished via switch ports with virtual LANs, or *VLANs*, being configured to block traffic between network segments. In a cloud provider infrastructure, virtual networking, or VNETs, can accomplish similar network segmentation. Additionally, in an Azure infrastructure, network security groups and application security groups can be configured on network interfaces with additional port, IP address, or application layer rules for how traffic can be routed within the network.

Compute

After network security, we begin to get into the resources that hold our data. The first of these is our **compute** resources. In order to maintain clarity, we will generalize the compute layer as devices with an operating system, such as **Linux** or **Windows**. Within your own private data center with equipment that you own, protecting the host equipment and avoiding exposure by hardening the virtual hypervisor is necessary. In the public cloud, Microsoft or another cloud provider will be responsible for this. Our responsibility on virtual machines relies on maintaining the proper patching of updates and security, to avoid having exploit vulnerabilities within the operating system. In addition, encrypting virtual machine operating systems and disks with Azure Disk Encryption will protect the virtual machine image from being exposed.

A common attack at the compute layer is scanning and gaining access to management ports on devices. Not exposing these ports, for example, 3389 for the Windows RDP and 22 for the Linux SSH *protocol*, to the internet will provide a layer of protection against these attacks. Within Microsoft Azure, this can be accomplished with network security group rules, removing public IP addresses on virtual machines, *Bastion hosts*, and/ or utilizing *just-in-time virtual machine access*. Many of these security options will be discussed later in this book.

Applications

The layer of defense that is closest to our data is our **applications**. Applications present data to users through our internet websites, intranet sites, and line-of-business applications that are used to perform our day-to-day business. Protecting against common threats, such as cross-site scripting on our websites. To protect against these common threats, a WAF can be used to properly evaluate the traffic that is accessing our applications. Utilizing *secure transport layer (TLS) protocols* that are encrypted can also help to avoid the exposure of sensitive data to unauthorized individuals.

Prior to an application being moved to production, it should be properly tested to make sure that there are no open management ports and that all API connections have also been secured.

If the application references connections to databases and storage accounts, the secrets and keys should not be exposed. Additionally, a key management solution, such as *Azure Key Vault*, should be in place for the proper rotation of secrets, keys, and certificates. Properly securing these areas of our applications will help to avoid the exposure of sensitive data to those who are not authorized to view it.

Data

Always at the center of our defense-in-depth security posture is our **data**. Data is the primary asset of our company. This includes the business and financial data that is necessary for the company's survival and the personal information of our employees and customers. Exposure or theft of this information can, potentially, have catastrophic effects on the company's ability to continue. These effects could be both financial losses and reputational losses.

As a security professional, you need to protect data from intentional and accidental exposure to those that are not authorized to view it. Data resides in various areas within our technology infrastructure. Primarily, data can be found in different storage accounts, such as blob containers or file shares, and within relational and non-relational databases. The common practice with which to accomplish this is through *encryption*.

Encryption makes data unreadable to those who are not properly authenticated and authorized to view that data. Encryption can be used in a variety of different ways. First, there is encrypting data at rest, which is when it is simply stored and not accessed. Next, there is encryption in transit or while it is being delivered from where it is stored to the person requesting access. Finally, there is encryption in use, which maintains the encryption of the data within the application throughout the time that it is being viewed. This is the more complex of the types of data encryption since it requires the application to have the capability to present the encrypted data. Microsoft provides options for these encryption types, and they will be discussed later in this book.

Encrypting data in our storage accounts and databases decreases the potential of this data being exposed to those that are not authorized. Additionally, requiring verification through authentication and authorization maintains the protection of the data. This includes avoiding anonymous access to storage accounts and masking sensitive data within our databases. The most important aspect in protecting our data is knowing where our sensitive data is located and planning proper steps in which to avoid it being exposed to the unauthorized.

Maintaining a proper security posture across all of the defense-in-depth layers is the best way to protect our company from loss or exposure across the cyber-security kill chain. As security professionals, it is important that we take ownership in the planning, execution, monitoring, and management of all of these layers. Additionally, we need to work with other stakeholders at each of these layers to maintain the overall security posture for the company.

Special considerations and understanding need to be accounted for within this security posture when utilizing public cloud services. In the next section, we will discuss how this shared responsibility for cloud services requires possible adjustments to our defense-in-depth security approach.

Understanding a shared responsibility in cloud security

Shared responsibility focuses on who has the ownership to interact at a specific level of protection. This might be the physical ownership of equipment or administrative ownership to enable various controls. The level of ownership between the company using the service and the cloud provider changes depending on the type of service that is being consumed by the company.

Before going any further with cloud security and shared responsibility, it is important to understand some terminology. You might have already gained some knowledge of these terms if you previously worked within cloud technologies or have read or taken an **Azure Fundamentals** or **Microsoft 365 Fundamentals** course. However, if you have not, and since this is a security, compliance, and identity fundamentals course, you might not be completely familiar with some of the terminology or how we arrived at the *cloud*. So, let's provide some of this base knowledge before discussing shared responsibility as it pertains to cloud services.

Evolution to the cloud and cloud services

For someone new to technology, the *cloud* might be a difficult concept to grasp. You might ask yourself questions regarding where your data is going or how it is separated from other customers. These are valid questions, and we can help to answer them with a simple journey through the evolution of computer networking. The following sections will discuss how we started and where we are today in terms of connecting to servers to access our applications and data.

Mainframes and supercomputers

The beginning of application server computing began in the 1970s and 1980s with mainframes and then supercomputers. The graphic in the following diagram does not do the size of these machines justice as they could take up entire rooms. Think of the movie *War Games* and the size of that single computer named *Joshua*, which was processing the game *Global Thermal Nuclear War*.

As you can imagine, these *computers* were extremely expensive and most of them were leased to enterprise organizations by **IBM** at the time due to the high costs.

Primarily, mainframes were used for government applications or line-of-business applications for large enterprise businesses, such as **General Motors** or **Ford Motor Company**, for example.

Figure 2.3 provides a visual depiction that suggests these mainframes and supercomputers wouldn't be something that you would want to carry around. They had limited flexibility, and once they were in place, they were going to stay there:

Figure 2.3 – Large mainframes and supercomputers

With the evolution of supercomputers, there was more cost flexibility, but they were still expensive and primarily used for single-use applications. Users connected to these servers using computer terminals. These terminals rarely had any internal memory or processing power because this was done by the server. From a security perspective, the network was highly secure, since it was rarely accessed outside the walls of the company, and the devices accessing the server had no local information stored on them.

Client-server computers

The 1990s began to see the personal computer becoming more accessible to both consumers and businesses with the release of **Windows 3.1**. This hardware was far more portable than a mainframe, with most servers being similar in size to a desktop personal computer, as shown in *Figure 2.4*:

Figure 2.4 – Client-server computers

Now, users could access the *internet* through a dial-up modem and communicate with others through *email*.

Twisted-pair cabling and network switch technology made it cost-effective for organizations to *network* their offices and use computers, known as *servers*, to deliver line-of-business applications and company email applications for better inter-office communication.

These personal computers now had their own memory and processing power in which to install and run local applications. For business applications, local data existed but the computers connected to the servers in order to get up-to-date information, such as customer information or the inventory of a retail business. This allowed companies more flexibility in how they were able to carry out their business. As more applications were added to a company, more servers were also added, increasing the capital expense toward technology and the amount of space required for the hardware.

Client-server computing required some additional security considerations. The computing devices that were initially connecting to company applications were now storing data and connecting to the internet. Appliances known as firewalls became necessary to create rules to block unwanted traffic from the company network.

Virtualization

As more applications became server-based, companies were seeing the amount of space required and the financial cost of hardware increase. This led to the growth of virtualization at the turn of the century, or around 2000. Companies began to combine applications onto a single server *host* by partitioning the memory and processing to each application by creating virtual servers on the host. **VMware** and **OpenStack** created management interfaces on these hosts that allowed for the creation and monitoring of these virtual servers. You could simply adjust the memory and processing power to these virtual servers as needed.

Thus, hardware needs began to decrease as did the size of the hardware, as shown in *Figure 2.5*:

Figure 2.5 – The virtualization of servers

Virtualization decreased the amount of capital expense and space needed in data centers since a single powerful host could manage multiple applications on multiple virtual machines. During this time, networks and internet connections also evolved and high-speed connections became more affordable to companies. Companies could now have a single centralized data center for their headquarters and branch offices, with high-speed internet connections between them, without a noticeable drop in productivity. This geographic expansion of connections created new security concerns. Malware and viruses planted by attackers to cause harm to companies required more sophisticated firewall devices that could perform deep packet inspection to keep unauthorized transmissions away from the network.

Hyperscalers

Virtualization and high-speed internet signified a major change in how we were able to interact and communicate. Around 2010, we began to see a shift in how consumers, and then businesses, were able to access software.

Online shopping was becoming more popular, and software was now available in a subscription format rather than having to purchase the software and maintenance for updates.

With Office 365, consumers and businesses could now access productivity software and email online without ever being concerned that their software was out of date.

In addition, **AWS** and **Microsoft** built data centers with massive compute and storage resources to support the expanding online shopping market and the Office software business, respectively.

Then, they began to rent the excess capacity to businesses to use their virtual server environments for development. This made it easy to create environments and break them down when done. This approach costs a small fraction compared to asking the company to invest in a server that will be strictly used for development purposes.

Now that we were in the cloud, there was no longer any need to purchase and maintain expensive hardware, freeing up the company capital and decreasing maintenance. *Figure 2.6* depicts this weight being lifted off the company's shoulders:

Figure 2.6 – Hyperscalers for global access

As this use of subscription servers began to grow and gain confidence, organizations found that they could expand their enterprise faster by moving production workloads to these *hyperscaler* clouds.

The last point to take away from this section is that as server hardware became smaller, the ability to process more information increased. *Figure 2.7* brings together the changes and evolution of server hardware and its use over the past decades to where we are today with the use of cloud provider technologies for our server infrastructure. Although many companies might still have a private data center with virtualized servers used together with cloud solutions in a hybrid infrastructure, today, we don't see many single-use servers for applications in data centers:

Figure 2.7 – The evolution to the cloud

This allowed the entry into server technologies to be far more accessible to businesses, no matter what their size, and provided users with more and more flexibility in how they worked.

Cloud providers, such as Microsoft, now provide business and personal consumers with access to virtual servers, web application platforms, and software subscriptions without the need to purchase expensive equipment. All that we require is an internet connection. These virtual machines (**Infrastructure as a Service** or **IaaS**), web application platforms (**Platform as a Service** or **PaaS**), and software subscriptions (**Software as a Service** or **SaaS**) have security requirements and controls that are either the responsibility of the cloud provider or the customer. To make sure that you understand these three services within a hyperscaler infrastructure, we will provide a clarifying definition of each.

IaaS

IaaS is the most flexible of the services within a cloud provider, such as Microsoft. With IaaS, the customer creates and manages the virtual machines, networking, applications, identity, and access. IaaS is the most similar to on-premises virtualization. The customer does not have access to the hypervisor host or the physical components, but they must still continue to manage the operating systems.

PaaS

PaaS is primarily used for application development and database services within a cloud provider. These services provide the customer with the most stable operating system to utilize for their development of applications without any concern for managing patches and updates to the operating systems. PaaS provides the platforms in which to develop applications and create databases to support these applications without the management overhead.

SaaS

SaaS is a ready-to-use application that is purchased on a per-user licensing basis. Microsoft 365 and the applications that are provided in the suite are all SaaS applications. There is no management for the applications within SaaS. The customer can manage the users that have access, and the customer decides how the data is handled.

In the next section, we will discuss the concept of shared responsibility and how it pertains to security.

Shared responsibility comparison

As technology has evolved and more resources have a level of exposure to external internet connections, the attack surface that is potentially vulnerable also increases. We need to understand this and know what our responsibilities are for each of the areas within our defense-in-depth security approach.

Shared responsibility refers to the relationship between the customer and the cloud provider at each of the layers of defense in depth. This relationship is different depending on the technology that is being consumed. It is important for a customer, or company, to understand this relationship to properly protect and secure their environment on the cloud. *Figure 2.8* shows how a customer has full responsibility for their equipment on-premises and how the level of responsibility decreases as the type of cloud service changes:

Responsibility	On-Premises	IaaS	PaaS	SaaS
Data governance and Rights Management	Customer	Customer	Customer	Customer
Client endpoints	Customer	Customer	Customer	Customer
Account and access management	Customer	Customer	Customer	Customer
Identity and directory infrastructure	Customer	Customer	Microsoft/Customer	Microsoft/Customer
Application	Customer	Customer	Microsoft/Customer	Microsoft
Network controls	Customer	Customer	Microsoft/Customer	Microsoft
Operating system	Customer	Customer	Microsoft	Microsoft
Physical hosts	Customer	Microsoft	Microsoft	Microsoft
Physical network	Customer	Microsoft	Microsoft	Microsoft
Physical datacenter	Customer	Microsoft	Microsoft	Microsoft

Figure 2.8 – Shared responsibility for security

Let's discuss each of these services and the level of security responsibility beyond *Table 2.1*. As you move through this book, and the services that Microsoft provides for security, you should think back to how it pertains to the shared responsibility model and defense-in-depth security approach.

On-premises responsibility

On-premises infrastructure is synonymous with a private data center. This is the equipment and infrastructure that the company owns. Therefore, the responsibility of security controls across every level of defense in depth is the company's responsibility. We have yet to consume any cloud services, so there is no responsibility for the cloud provider.

IaaS shared responsibility

IaaS is the service that is the most like a private data center. The primary difference between IaaS infrastructure and an on-premises data center is that the cloud provider is responsible for the physical security of the data center, physical network equipment, and the hosts that provide our virtual servers. The customer is responsible for putting all of the security controls in place to protect and patch the operating system, create rules and infrastructure services such as firewalls to protect the network, manage and protect our applications from common threats, protect identities and control access, and patch and protect the endpoint devices. Additionally, the customer is always responsible for the protection and governance of their data.

PaaS shared responsibility

PaaS removes the customer responsibility of maintaining the operating system. The cloud provider now handles all of the security patches and updates required to avoid vulnerabilities and zero-day threats. In general, platform services also have a level of baseline security controls in place for the network, applications, and identity infrastructure. These are in place to mainly protect against threats that could affect multiple customers that are utilizing these platform services. These baseline controls might not be seen as enough for some companies, so options to increase these controls are in place and are the customer's responsibility to turn on. Many of these capabilities will be discussed later in this book. Within PaaS, the responsibility of access management, endpoint protection, and data protection and governance remains the sole responsibility of the customer.

SaaS shared responsibility

SaaS provides an application where you purchase a license on a per-user basis, log in to that application, and you are able to use it immediately. This simplifies these services to the consumer level, as there is a level of configuration that takes place for business applications. Microsoft 365 is an example of a SaaS application. The suite of software, Office, Exchange, SharePoint, Teams, and more, is available to use when you assign a license to a user. The cloud provider, in this case, Microsoft, has all of the security controls in place to protect the application, network, operating system, and physical environment. The customer only needs to configure the identity and access control, endpoint protection, and data protection and governance.

Note that in *Table 2.1*, there is a shared responsibility for the identity infrastructure. Microsoft does provide a level of security controls to protect user identities as a baseline, but the customer is responsible for increasing that level of protection. Here, an example would be turning on MFA. It is provided by Microsoft, but the customer needs to enable the service for some or all of their users.

Many companies continue to have this private infrastructure while also utilizing public cloud services. These hybrid infrastructures have a mix across all of the areas of responsibilities to account for their overall security posture. As we continue through this book, the services that are discussed fall into one of the three main categories of IaaS, PaaS, or SaaS; however, they might also have a hybrid component to support on-premises.

You now should have a strong understanding of defense-in-depth security and shared responsibility in the cloud. Note that the shared responsibility of securing the account, data, and access management is an area of customer responsibility no matter what service is being consumed.

In the next section, we will discuss a methodology where we will address account identity and access management for our users and administrators.

Using and implementing the principles of the zero-trust methodology

In the previous section, we mentioned that the responsibility of securing the physical infrastructure for cloud services is provided by the cloud provider, Microsoft. Since Microsoft is responsible for the first layer of defense in our defense-in-depth security posture, the first layer that we are responsible for as a company is the identity and access layer. Therefore, the statements of *identity is the new perimeter* and *identity is the new control plane* have become extremely important in securing a cloud infrastructure. In *Chapter 5, Defining Identity Principles/Concepts and the Identity Services within Azure AD*, we will discuss the role of identity and access management within a cloud and hybrid infrastructure and the services that Microsoft provides to protect resources at this layer. It is important to understand the core concept that a company should adhere to when securing identity and access. This concept is the zero-trust methodology.

The **zero-trust methodology** is a process of continuously requiring someone on the network to verify that they are who they say they are. The concept appears to be straightforward and simple, but if you were to constantly ask users to enter their username and password, they would get frustrated. To avoid this frustration, zero-trust implementation utilizes various signals that alert potential anomalous behavior, leaked credentials, or insecure devices that trigger the need for a user to reverify their identity. These signals lead to a decision regarding what is needed to provide access to applications, files, or websites. This workflow is shown in *Figure 2.9*:

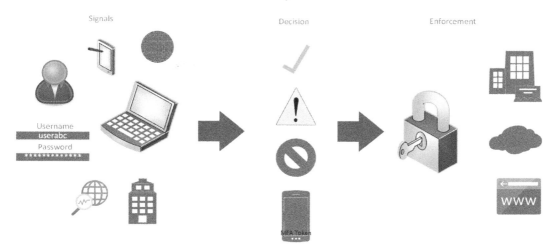

Figure 2.9 – The zero-trust model workflow

The next sections will describe each of these components of the workflow in more detail.

Signal

As stated in the previous section, the signal is the state that the user or device is in that triggers a potential need for a user to reverify their identity. This state could be that the user has been identified at risk of having a compromised password, that they are using an IP address that has been flagged as vulnerable, or that their device is not compliant with current security patches. These are only a few examples of the signals that might be reviewed to trigger a decision to invoke the need for more information. Microsoft utilizes several tools within Azure and Microsoft 365 to identify the vulnerabilities and risks to users and devices that create these signals. Once a signal has been created to require more information to verify a user's identity, then a decision is made as to what happens next.

Decision

As stated in the previous section, when a signal is triggered, a decision is made regarding what we are going to require or allow to provide access to the resources that have been requested. There are several options here, and this is where a company creates policies on how zero trust is going to be handled depending on the resource being request access. This could include a user reverifying whether they have been compromised by requiring MFA before they are given access. The policies might limit or block access to that application entirely until the user or device changes the status or location that they are requesting access to. The least likely policy decision is to allow access if a user or device is detected as being at risk. Generally, the allow access decision is used in a policy that identifies a user or device as being in a trusted location. Once the decision is made within the policy, the policy then enforces the workflow.

Enforcement

Enforcement refers to the action of the decision based on the user or device signal as defined by the company policy. As discussed in the previous section, there are multiple enforcement actions that could take place. The level of access and enforcement of zero trust is usually dependent on the application and information that is being accessed. If the application contains highly sensitive information that the company cannot have exposed, the level of zero-trust enforcement should be at the highest level, by either blocking access, limiting the level of access, or requiring additional verification from the user, such as MFA and/or a password reset. The ability of a company to identify the risks and vulnerabilities of the users and determine a plan to protect access to their applications is a critical factor to the success of implementing a zero-trust model for identity and access management.

As mentioned earlier, the principles of zero trust are an important aspect in which to protect access to applications within a cloud and hybrid infrastructure. The decreased access and ability to protect physical access and the increased access to applications from various locations across public internet connections require a company to do their due diligence to identify the various scenarios that users might request access to company resources and the numerous devices that they might use to access. Policies that identify the potential vulnerabilities and threats that can make the correct decision regarding how to enforce zero trust will protect the company while maintaining a positive user experience.

Summary

In this chapter, we covered various security concepts and methodologies. These include the defense-in-depth security posture to counteract and protect against a cyber-attack, the evolution to the cloud and the shared responsibility to protect our infrastructure between the company and the cloud provider, and the zero-trust model to protect our access to data and applications now that identity has become our first level of defense within cloud technologies.

These will be the foundation of the security, compliance, and identity solutions provided by Microsoft that will be discussed throughout this book.

In the next chapter, we will discuss the various threats to our cloud and hybrid infrastructure and the role and ways in which encryption can be utilized.

3
Understanding Key Security Concepts

The previous chapter discussed and described security methodologies that can be used for security, compliance, and identity protection. This chapter will continue to build on those methodologies and how they are used within **key security concepts** for protecting our data and identities. Once you have completed this chapter, you will have an understanding of how to identify common threats and the concepts of encryption to protect against exposure of data.

In this chapter, we're going to cover the following main topics:

- Describing common threats
- Describing encryption

Describing common threats

This section is going to cover some of the *common threats* that you should maintain an awareness of within your technology infrastructure. Before we discuss those common threats, it's important to understand how to identify a threat.

What is a threat?

As we discussed in the previous chapter, there are many stages of a cyberattack, and we protect against them by incorporating a **defense in depth** security posture. The reason that we do this is to decrease vulnerabilities within our infrastructure. A threat is created when an attacker takes advantage of a vulnerability. As security professionals, it is our responsibility to identify and respond to threats within our company infrastructure.

Threats can be *internal* or *external*. They are also not always intentional or malicious, nor necessarily meant to cause harm to the organization. We will discuss this in more detail as we identify some of these threats in the next sections. The threats listed are examples of internal and external threats and are not expected to be an exhaustive list.

Let's start by discussing *internal* threats.

Internal threats

Internal threats are caused when a vulnerability is exposed by an internal user or resource. As stated previously, these are not always malicious or meant to cause harm – they could be accidental and created due to a lack of education. In some cases, these internal threats can become vulnerabilities that become causes of external attacks as well. We will expand on this in some of the following examples.

Shadow IT

Shadow IT is extremely common within companies. This is caused when people within the organization utilize applications that are not tested and approved by the company. Not all shadow IT causes a threat to the company, but not properly monitoring these applications could create vulnerabilities within the company IT infrastructure. One way to discourage shadow IT is to have company policies in place regarding the use of third-party applications that are not approved on devices that access company resources. Additionally, utilizing mobile device or mobile application management can also deter the use of these applications by blocking access to them with device policies and conditional access. Educating users is another valuable aspect to preventing shadow IT from becoming prevalent within the company.

The life cycle of monitoring and preventing shadow IT within your company is shown in the following diagram:

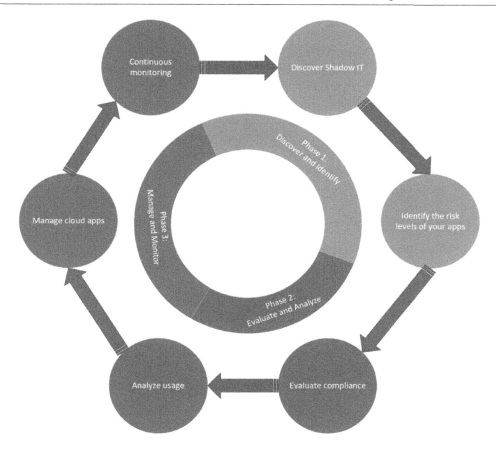

Figure 3.1 – Shadow IT prevention life cycle

Next, we will discuss patch vulnerabilities as an internal risk.

Patch vulnerabilities

Patch vulnerabilities are another internal threat to a company. These vulnerabilities can be created by users that defer the patch installation and restarting of their devices due to inconvenience. The most frequent patches that are provided for device operating systems are security patches. Therefore, if these patches are not installed company-wide in a timely manner, the entire company is vulnerable to a potential exploit. As was the case with shadow IT, a way to discourage deferring patch installation is through educating users on the risks that avoiding these updates pose to the company and their own devices. Automating patch updates and turning off the ability to defer them through mobile device management is also an option for companies to mitigate this threat.

Elevated privileges

Elevated privileges are created when users have administrative rights to resources within the IT environment that may not be required for them to complete their job tasks. A user that has these privileges is actually both an internal and an external threat. As an external threat, if a user's credentials are compromised, then an attacker could gain access to sensitive information. As an internal threat, someone that has elevated privileges that allows them to access information that they are not required to view for their job could create a privacy concern for the company. Therefore, it is important to review and audit user access and exercise due diligence so that sensitive information is only available to those who are required to access it.

Developer backdoors

When developing applications, access to the application infrastructure may be provided through an open port or service path that is open to the public. While the application is in development and isolated from the production infrastructure and data, this access helps developers gain access and build and test the application. However, if these **developer backdoors** are left in place after production, this could allow access to sensitive data and even access to application code that could be altered. Similar to privileged access, this could be thought of as an internal and an external threat. The exposure of these backdoors becomes a vulnerability that can be leveraged by attackers. It is an internal threat for the reason that it is created through the internal application development process.

Data exposure

Data exposure is another threat that could fall into both the internal and external categories. It is imperative that companies protect their sensitive data from being exposed to those that are not authorized to access it. Not having proper controls in place to protect access to sensitive data through authentication, and authorization could lead to exposure from either internal or external sources. Therefore, masking data from unauthorized users can protect from this exposure of data.

Perimeter threats

Perimeter threats are considered internal because they are created by having inadequate controls in place to protect the internal infrastructure. Perimeter threats could be caused by allowing users to access resources through insecure open ports or transferring data through unencrypted transmission channels. IT professionals should have proper controls in place to avoid these threats and to monitor who is accessing data from inside and outside the company firewall.

As stated in the previous sections, the examples of internal threats can also become external vulnerabilities if not properly addressed with controls. It is an IT professional's responsibility to exercise care and due diligence to protect the company.

Now that we have discussed some potential internal threats, let's review some potential external threats.

External threats

The previous section focused on threats that are created internally by users, developers, or IT staff that could cause data exposure to unauthorized personnel or allow external attackers into the company infrastructure. In this section, we will discuss external threats that are initiated by external sources. These external threats can cause disruption to the company and customers, causing decreases in efficiency and revenue.

Denial of Service attacks

Denial of Service (DoS) attacks are a very common external threat to companies. Also referred to as **Distributed Denial of Service**, or **DDoS**, these attacks flood your **internet service provider (ISP)** with thousands of requests to overwhelm the ISP and company infrastructure to the point where real users attempting to access resources cannot get through and their requests time out. A DDoS attack is not a threat that is based on theft, and no personal or company data is at risk during these types of attacks. These attacks are damaging to a company from a revenue and efficiency standpoint. Remote internal users may not be able to access the resources that they require to perform their tasks. Additionally, customers may not be able to access the company website to browse and order products or services, costing the company in revenue.

Figure 3.2 shows how these attacks threaten the ability of a real user to access a system:

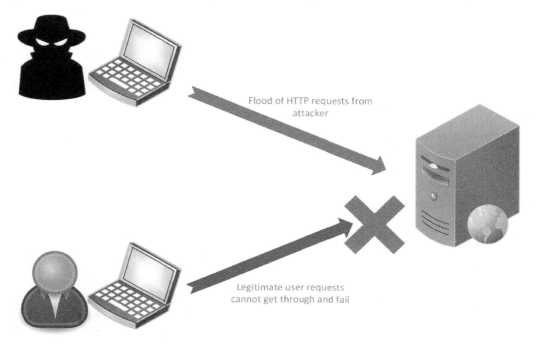

Flood of HTTP requests from attacker

Legitimate user requests cannot get through and fail

Figure 3.2 – DoS attack

The more time that a company is under these types of attacks, the more that it will cost them in lost revenue and time. Therefore, it is important that a company monitors for these attacks and can block the source of them quickly to minimize the impact.

Next, we will look at brute force attacks.

Brute force attacks

In contrast to a DDoS attack, where there is not a threat of personal or company data being stolen, this is not the case with a **brute force attack**. A brute force attack is an attack where the primary purpose is to gain access to a company's systems to digitally burglarize data. Brute force attack threats are commonly tied to some of the internal threats mentioned previously within this chapter. These types of threats attempt to gain access to the company systems by finding a point of entry and then, as the name suggests, using brute force to access them. These attacks are carried out through scanning for ports that are open to the internet, finding those systems that have public internet addresses on those ports, and then using commonly used usernames and passwords on systems to gain access.

Figure 3.3 shows how an attacker utilizes multiple systems and attempts to gain access to systems:

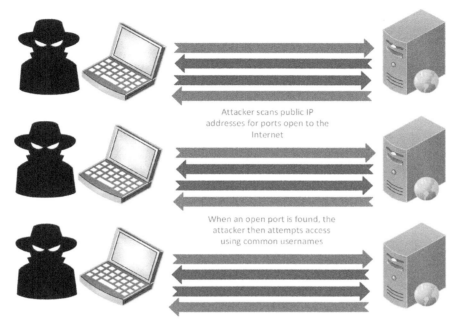

Figure 3.3 – Brute force attack

When a brute force attack is successful, the company is now exposed to potential theft of sensitive personal or company data that may be on that system, or other databases and file shares that are accessible from that system.

Now, let's look at threats from vulnerability exploits.

Vulnerability exploits

Vulnerability exploits are external threats where attackers take advantage of some of the controls that are not in place to protect the company. Some of these vulnerabilities can be caused by the internal threats that were mentioned within the previous section, such as development backdoors and patch vulnerabilities. Improperly securing application APIs also creates a vulnerability that an attacker can exploit. The threat of vulnerability exploits can lead to a brute force attack where an attacker could gain access to sensitive information and applications.

Many vulnerability exploits are caused by operating system code that an attacker has found could be exploited. These are called **zero-day exploits** and are the most common widespread threats to systems.

Figure 3.4 shows the life cycle of a zero-day threat from an attack through to the patching of the system:

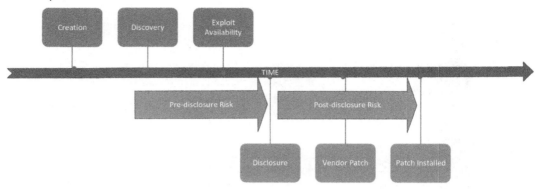

Figure 3.4 – Vulnerability exploit life cycle

Next, we will look at IP and identity spoofing.

IP or identity spoofing

An **IP spoofing** or **identity spoofing** threat comes from an attacker pretending to be someone within the company or utilizing an IP address that is seen by systems as internal. Attackers that leverage these vulnerabilities have most likely gathered information on the company through some kind of phishing campaign that has allowed them to identity usernames, passwords, and IP addresses that have access to systems.

Figure 3.5 shows an attacker that has gained access to an authorized user's identity to gain access to another user:

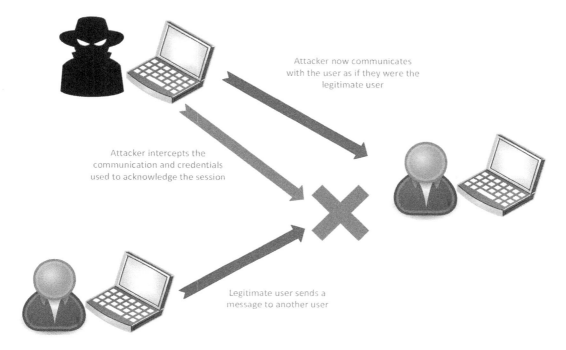

Attacker now communicates
with the user as if they were the
legitimate user

Attacker intercepts the
communication and credentials
used to acknowledge the session

Legitimate user sends a
message to another user

Figure 3.5 – Identity spoofing

Proper education of users on phishing email campaigns and having a zero-trust model for user authentication and access will help to protect against these types of attacks.

Next, let's discuss injection attacks as an external threat.

Injection attacks

Injection attacks are a threat primarily to databases that are connected to our applications. These threats are similar to a brute force attack as they are making an active effort to gain access to systems. The manner in which injection attacks gain access is through sending a command or query to a database, taking advantage of a known flaw in that database. This command code or query is then executed without proper authorization, allowing the attacker to gain access to sensitive data.

Figure 3.6 illustrates the process of how this attack may take place on an SQL database:

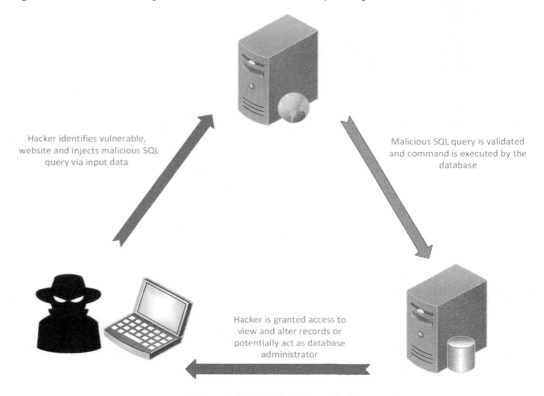

Figure 3.6 – SQL injection attack

The possibility of this injection attack is caused mainly by poor authentication and monitoring controls in place for the database.

Next, we will discuss cross-site scripting.

Cross-site scripting

Similar to injection attacks that take advantage of security flaws within databases, **cross-site scripting** threats take advantage of insecure code and validation within a website. Attackers will use the lack of security to create a redirection from the secure website to an insecure website created by the attacker. These attacks are used primarily to gain access to the device that is accessing the website and execute malicious scripts and malware that could gain access to sensitive personal information on the device.

Figure 3.7 shows the process of how the attacker gains access to the user's session cookie:

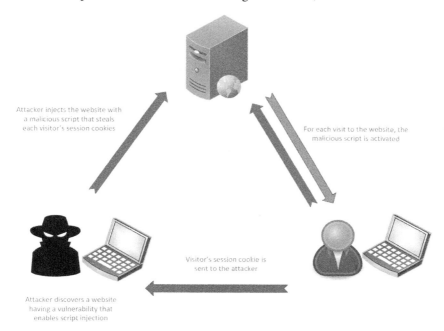

Figure 3.7 – Cross-site scripting attack

The visitor to the website has no knowledge that their session cookie has been intercepted and that they have been redirected. This allows the attacker to interact with the user's device and activate malicious code and malware.

Others

New external threats to companies and users are always evolving. A great resource to keep up with the most current risks is the *OWASP Top Ten Web Application Security Risks*: `https://owasp.org/www-project-top-ten/`.

Now that we have discussed some of the common threats to our company data and personal information, let's talk about how we analyze the impact of these threats and determine the feasibility of putting security controls in place to mitigate them.

Threat analysis

Threat analysis is a process that every company should go through in order to properly understand the vulnerabilities within their systems and the potential threat to the company if that vulnerability is exploited.

Understanding threat analysis is not an assessed learning objective of the SC-900 exam, but as we discuss the security, compliance, and identity solutions that are available from **Microsoft 365** and **Azure**, you should understand the basics of how to determine whether to utilize these solutions.

When conducting a threat analysis, you need to take into account the perceived risk to an asset. To accomplish this, you must consider the combination of the cost of the asset along with any vulnerabilities that may create the loss of the asset, and the potential threat that the vulnerability will be exploited. As an equation, this would look like this:

Asset (A) + Vulnerability (V) + Threat (T) = Risk (R)

The assessment of the risks to assets can be categorized by the various levels of risk, as shown in the following diagram:

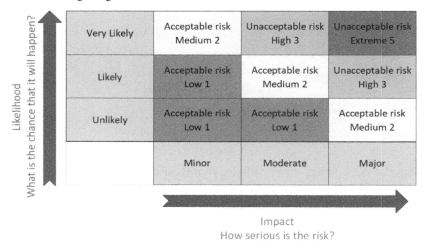

Figure 3.8 – Risk assessment matrix

Identifying the company assets and then assessing the risk should be done at both a business and technical level to have a proper understanding and perception across departments.

Once all of the assets and levels of risk have been identified, then the analysis of financial exposure needs to be determined. This is accomplished by determining the following criteria for each asset:

- **Exposure factor (EF)**: This is the impact that is measured by the percentage of loss of an asset if the risk is realized.

- **Single loss expectancy (SLE)**: This is the value of the asset multiplied by the exposure factor. This is going to place a financial value on the asset loss when exposed.

- **Annualized rate of occurrence (ARO)**: This places the possible number of times that this risk may be exploited over the course of the year.

- **Annualized loss expectancy (ALE)**: This is the combined financial impact of the SLE multiplied by the ARO, providing an annual cost of loss to the asset.

Calculating the ALE for all of the company's digital assets places a tangible value on those assets and then allows a company to evaluate the cost of investing in the controls needed to mitigate or avoid that risk. If a company is not going through these steps, it is not exercising due care and diligence in protecting company assets.

Another point to make here is that this is placing a financial value on assets and not reputational value. The reputational impact of data exposure or data loss can be much more damaging to a company from its customers' point of view than the perceived financial value of the assets. Companies should take this into consideration when determining investment in security controls as well.

The following link provides a good resource if you would like to learn more about cyber threat analysis:

```
https://cyberexperts.com/cyber-threat-analysis-a-complete-
overview/#:~:text=%20Components%20of%20the%20Cyber%20Threat%20
Analysis%20Process,In%20this%20phase%2C%20the%20analysts%20
test...%20More%20
```

Throughout this book, we will discuss multiple solutions and controls that address the mitigation of the threats discussed within this chapter. The next section will focus on the concept of encryption and how it can protect against the exposure of data.

Describing encryption

This section discusses **encryption** and how it is used to protect against data exposure. Encryption is used to stop plain text data from being accessed by those not authorized to. In the next sections, we will discuss how this is accomplished and the ways that data is encrypted.

What is encryption?

As stated previously, using encryption avoids data from being exposed in plain text. Encryption converts the plain text to a cipher-text code that is unreadable without the proper authorization keys to decrypt the data back into plain text. The users that have access to that data have been authorized through their login credentials or by accessing the data through a secure encrypted channel in order to view it. If an unauthorized user attempts to access the same data through unencrypted channels, it will be shown as unreadable letters and numbers.

The next sections will discuss the various types of encryption and how they are used to protect unauthorized access to data.

Encryption-at-rest

Encryption-at-rest protects the data when it is in the state of being stored. This is the data that resides in a database or a storage account. Having this data encrypted, even though it is not being used or transmitted, is important. If someone is able to gain access to a database or storage account and copy this data to a local source, unencrypted data could then be read and exposed. If this data is encrypted at rest, it will be unreadable when copied to another source by an unauthorized user because they will not have the key needed to decipher the data back into its plain-text form.

The process of how the data can then be accessed through the use of its encryption key can be seen in the following diagram:

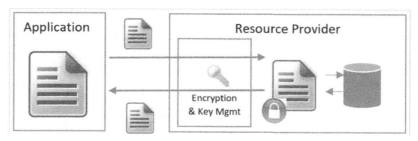

Figure 3.9 – Accessing data encrypted-at-rest

As you can see in *Figure 3.9*, the application is required to authenticate with the key before accessing the data that is stored in its encrypted state.

Now, let's look at encryption-in-transit and how it protects data that is being transmitted.

Encryption-in-transit

Encryption-in-transit protects data from being exposed when it is being transmitted over the internet. This is accomplished mainly by using an encrypted and secured transmission channel that uses **Transport Layer Security 1.2 (TLS 1.2)** (previously **Secure Sockets Layer (SSL)**). When accessing a website, you will know that it is over an encrypted channel when it is using *HTTPS* rather than *HTTP*. This is extremely important on shopping sites where you may be required to enter personal information, such as addresses and bank card details. The access to this information is protected through the use of your local browser and the data is encrypted during transmission rather than plain text. Therefore, information within the browser is not readable by outside sources that are not logged into the browser session with your credentials.

TLS 1.2 utilizes a handshake process between the client browser and the server to pass the key and encrypt/decrypt the data, as shown in the following diagram:

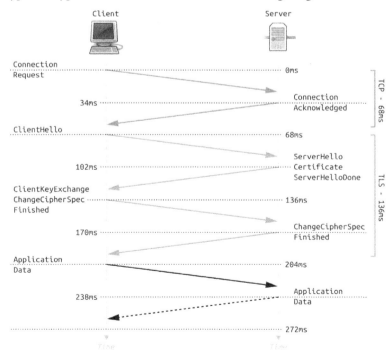

Figure 3.10 – TLS 1.2 handshake process

Now that we know about encryption-at-rest and encryption-in-transit, let's look at the third encryption type, encryption-in-use.

Encryption-in-use

In the context of encryption, encryption-at-rest and in-transit are the most commonly used types. However, it is important not to underestimate the importance of **encryption-in-use**. Encryption-in-use is the more complex of the three types to implement but when the applications that users are accessing contain high levels of personal or sensitive data, having it in place can avoid exposure. Encryption-in-use is commonly used when accessing databases from within an application and would require additional levels of authentication to view sensitive data. Authorized users would be allowed to view the data, while unauthorized users would have that sensitive data masked or blocked from view. In order for encryption-in-use to be effective, the application must require constant authorization of the user when they access the data. This will avoid data being exposed from an unauthorized user physically accessing an authorized user's device.

Summary

In this chapter, we covered some common threats to companies and users and discussed both internal and external threats. We also showed some ways to analyze the threats to company assets to provide a cost analysis to justify the implementation of solutions to mitigate and avoid threats from being realized. Finally, we discussed the key aspects of protecting data with encryption.

The next chapter will discuss the key principles that Microsoft adheres to for *security*, *compliance*, and *privacy*.

4
Key Microsoft Security and Compliance Principles

The previous chapters discussed and described important security methodologies, key security concepts, and potential security threats that companies should consider within their security, compliance, and identity protection strategies. This chapter will discuss the key security, privacy, and compliance principles that **Microsoft** follows when providing its customers with cloud services and solutions. Once you have completed this chapter, you will understand these principles and where to access documents that define them for Microsoft customers.

In this chapter, we're going to cover the following main topics:

- Microsoft's privacy principles
- Service trust portal offerings

Microsoft's privacy principles

Microsoft provides its customers with access to and details of its privacy principles. There are six privacy principles that Microsoft focuses on, and they are *control*, *transparency*, *security*, *strong legal protection*, *no content-based targeting*, and *benefits to you*. The full details of Microsoft's privacy principles can be found here: `https://privacy.microsoft.com`. The following sections will go into further detail about each of these principles and how they would pertain to you and your company.

Control

The *principle of control* is that Microsoft does not control the privacy of you or your company – it allows you to control your own privacy with Microsoft's tools and allows you to make clear choices. This control over the access to your data allows companies to manage their own risks and protect their own data. However, Microsoft provides companies with guidance and tools that allow companies to make good decisions based on best practices through security recommendations.

Transparency

Microsoft makes very clear the level of responsibility that it takes and the degree to which it handles any data collected on its cloud platforms. This provides transparency to companies and regulatory standards bodies on how the company accesses any data that is collected. This level of transparency is important for the privacy of users and gives companies visibility of any breaches to their data, as well as how litigation is handled in regard to data that is held within Microsoft's infrastructure.

Security

The *principle of security* is that Microsoft will maintain minimum encryption levels for data stored on Microsoft platforms. A best practice is that data is encrypted at rest. All data is encrypted at rest by default within Microsoft's services, and this will not change unless the customer explicitly requests or makes this change themselves. If the customer does make this change, any liability for data exposure would fall on the customer and not on Microsoft.

Strong legal protections

Microsoft follows all local jurisdictions as they pertain to privacy. This is Microsoft's *principle of strong legal protections*. Many countries have laws and standards in place that protect privacy as a basic human right, and Microsoft adheres to this when handling data. All data is governed and protected by the legal protections of the local laws and regulatory standards.

No content-based targeted marketing

Social media and content-based marketing are very popular for providing focused advertising to potential customers. Microsoft's privacy principles state that it will not use any customer data or communications for the use of targeted ads to users and companies. This is an extremely strong stance to take, as many social media and cloud-based companies use these tactics to target new business.

Benefits to you

The *benefits to you* principle states that when Microsoft does collect data from any communication with you or your company, it will only be used to benefit you. In other words, Microsoft will take your feedback to product owners and use that information to make the product and experience better for its customers.

Microsoft stands behind these principles, and the Microsoft privacy website referenced earlier in this section provides further details and definitions of the types of data used to benefit products and service offerings to Microsoft customers.

For full transparency, Microsoft also provides access to its privacy statement, privacy report, and a list of privacy **frequently asked questions** (**FAQs**).

Now, let's expand on Microsoft's privacy and compliance information by exploring the Service Trust Portal offerings.

Service Trust Portal offerings

The **Microsoft Service Trust Portal** provides valuable information for customers based on the policies and controls for security, privacy, and compliance for the physical infrastructure of Microsoft's cloud services. Companies that are using Microsoft's cloud services require information about this layer of the infrastructure to maintain their own compliance and to perform audits to maintain their adherence to industry and regulatory standards. This documentation is easily accessible within the Service Trust Portal. More information on the Service Trust Portal can be found here: `https://servicetrust.microsoft.com/`.

The following sections will discuss the documents available within the various sections of the Service Trust Portal.

Compliance manager

When navigating to the Service Trust Portal link (provided in the previous section), you will see multiple navigation tabs across the top of the page. Each of these tabs serves a purpose and directs you to the documentation that you need. The first of these is the link to **Microsoft Compliance Manager**, as shown in *Figure 4.1*:

Figure 4.1 – Microsoft Service Trust Portal navigation and Compliance Manager

This is the only link within the navigation that redirects to your **Microsoft 365** tenant, as shown in *Figure 4.2*:

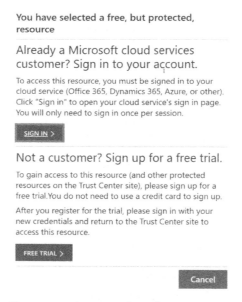

Figure 4.2 – Accessing Compliance Manager

Compliance Manager is located within the Microsoft 365 compliance center portal to show the overall company compliance score, which includes the company's level of compliance combined with Microsoft's, categorized by the type of services and shared responsibility (**shared responsibility** was discussed in detail in *Chapter 2, Describing Security Methodologies*. The **Overview** dashboard for Compliance Manager with the Compliance Score is shown in *Figure 4.3*:

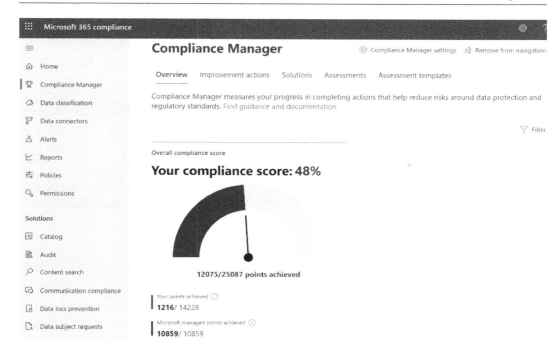

Figure 4.3 – The compliance score in Compliance Manager

We will discuss Compliance Manager in further detail when we explore Microsoft's compliance services in *Chapter 12, Describing Security Management and the Endpoint Security Capabilities of Microsoft 365*.

Now, let's review the other navigation tabs and the documentation that is available within each one, starting with the **Trust Documents** tab.

The Trust Documents tab

As stated at the beginning of this section, the Service Trust Portal provides documentation to support the security and compliance attestations that Microsoft has received on its physical infrastructure to support its cloud services. Customers that require audits for regulatory and/or standards compliance will need to provide this documentation to show the full end-to-end compliance of the physical infrastructure, controls, and processes that they maintain in order to meet all requirements.

The **Trust Documents** tab is the first place to go to find these documents. As you can see in *Figure 4.4*, this navigation provides access to audit reports, data protection documentation, the **Azure Security and Compliance Blueprint**, and **Azure Stack** documents:

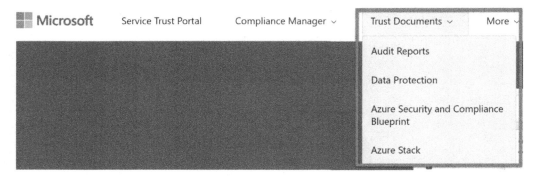

Figure 4.4 – The Trust Documents tab

Let's look at each of these individually. The **Audit Reports** web page documents the list of reports that Microsoft has completed on its physical infrastructure, and Microsoft makes them available for access and download to assist in your own audits. As you can see in *Figure 4.5*, these include compliance guides, **Security Operations Center** (**SOC**) reports, FAQs and white papers, and various audit reports for specific compliance standards, such as **Enterprise Network Services** (**ENS**), FedRAMP, **Governance Risk and Compliance** (**GRC**), **International Standards Organization** (**ISO**), and **Payment Card Industry Data Security Standard** (**PCI DSS**). Each of these sections can be used to gather the information needed to support a customer's audit for these standards:

New and Archived Audit Reports

Use these reports to stay current on the latest privacy, security, and compliance-related information for Microsoft's cloud services.

| Select start date | to | Select end date | | Document Type | Cloud Service | Industries |

☐ Sign in with your Microsoft Account to access locked files and save to your library.

Compliance Guides   ENS Audit Reports and Certificates   FAQ and White Papers   FedRAMP Reports   GRC Assessment Reports   ISO Reports   PCI DSS   SOC Reports

Figure 4.5 – New and Archived Audit Reports

In addition, the Trust Documents tab also provides access to the **Data Protection Resources** page. This page has the documentation specific to the relevant controls and the testing that has taken place to protect customer data. As *Figure 4.6* shows, this includes audited controls, compliance guides, pen test and security assessments, security and vulnerability assessments, and additional white papers, FAQs, and reports. These documents may be needed for certain audits and can also provide guidance on the protection of data within your Microsoft tenant:

Figure 4.6 – The Data Protection Resources page

The next page in the Trust Documents tab is the **Azure Security and Compliance Blueprint** page. This page has documents for each of the standards to provide guidance for you on the controls required to maintain proper levels of security and compliance. You can access this information from this page, or you can go directly to the **Microsoft Docs** page that has the most recent documentation by following this link: https://docs.microsoft.com/azure/governance/blueprints/samples/.

The final navigation page under the **Trust Documents** tab is the **Azure Stack** page. This page provides documentation specifically tailored for customers that are utilizing Azure Stack in their on-premises infrastructure. Since Azure Stack still falls under the defense in depth level of the physical responsibility of Microsoft, it provides the documentation relevant to the physical controls and audits that Azure Stack has gone through for standards and regulatory compliance. *Figure 4.7* provides a screenshot of this page:

Azure Stack

These documents provide security and compliance solutions and support, tailored to the needs of Azure Stack customers.

| Select start date | to | Select end date | Document Type ∨ | Cloud Service ∨ | Industries ∨ |

🔒 **Sign in** with your Microsoft Account to access locked files and save to your library.

Azure Stack

	Title	Series	Description
☐	Azure Stack – Cloud Security Alliance (CSA) Cloud Control Matrix (CCM) v. 3.0.1 Assessment Report ↓		This document reports on the assessment performed by a third-party assessor on Azure Stack against the Cloud Security Alliance Cloud Control Matrix (CSA CCM) v. 3.0.1. It... Show more

Figure 4.7 – The Azure Stack page

Many of the documents that are necessary for audits can be found within the **Trust Documents** navigation tab. The additional navigation tabs also provide more directed navigation for specific needs. Let's look at them more closely next.

Industries and regions

The industries and regions tab is where the **Trust Documents** navigation tab takes us to audit documents and data protection documents specific to various global regions and targeted industries, such as financial. These documents are all for Microsoft's own documentation, and they are not specific to any industry or region. Therefore, they may require some filtering to find what you need for your own industry or location. The **Industries & Regions** tab provides that filtering of documentation for you. *Figure 4.8* shows that you have the drop-down navigation that allows you to go directly to an industry or region of interest:

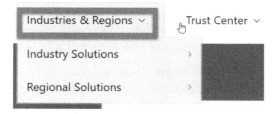

Figure 4.8 – The Industries & Regions tab

Currently, the **Industry Solutions** section only has a page for financial services. Within this page, you can find compliance offerings, FAQs, and success stories for this specific industry. The **Regional Solutions** section provides specific guidance and information for multiple regions. The current list is shown in *Figure 4.9*:

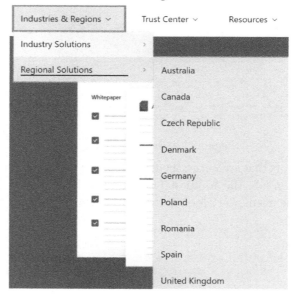

Figure 4.9 – List of regions

The region pages contain documents that relate specifically to that region's policies and regulations. This includes solutions blueprints for guidance in configuring Microsoft services when operating in these regions. *Figure 4.10* shows the navigation tabs to access this documentation:

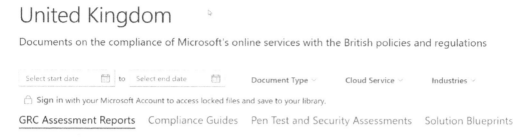

Figure 4.10 – Regional documentation

Next, let's look at the documentation that can be found within the **Trust Center** navigation tab.

The Trust Center tab

The next tab that we find as we navigate across the Service Trust Portal menu is the **Trust Center** tab. The **Trust Center** tab provides us with navigation directly to pages that Microsoft has put together for **Privacy**, **Security**, and **Compliance** pages, as shown in *Figure 4.11*:

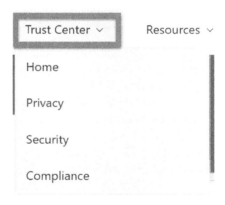

Figure 4.11 – The Trust Center tab

Unlike the previous navigation tabs, the **Trust Center** tab does not take you directly to specific documentation, but to other sites that provide a full page of resources, FAQs, case studies, reports, and documents that can be used for not just proof of compliance, but also for marketing and customer support. If you are in need of Microsoft's full documentation and position on one of these areas, then navigating to the **Trust Center** tab is where you should start.

Now, let's look at another navigation option that provides us with guidance, the **Resources** tab.

The Resources tab

Similar to the **Trust Center** tab, the **Resources** tab provides us with more documentation on Microsoft's controls, position, and direction for support through the **Security and Compliance Center**, **Microsoft Global Datacenters**, and **Frequently Asked Questions**, as shown in *Figure 4.12*:

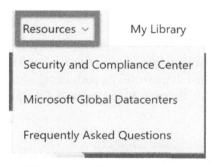

Figure 4.12 – The Resources tab

Each of these sections directs you to a page that provides Microsoft's specific documentation and position. The **Security and Compliance Center** page focuses content on Microsoft's protection of data, personal information, and **General Data Protection Regulation (GDPR)**. The **Microsoft Global Datacenters** page provides information about Microsoft's datacenters and a link to more information regarding its global infrastructure. Finally, the **Frequently Asked Questions** page provides the answers to some commonly asked questions about the Service Trust Portal, Compliance Manager, and privacy and GDPR.

Now, let's discuss the final section of the Service Trust Portal navigation, the **My Library** tab.

The My Library tab

The **My Library** tab is the final navigation menu option on the Service Trust Portal. This is a link that allows you to customize the documentation that you have found in the **Trust Documents** and **Industries & Regions** tabs and save them for future access:

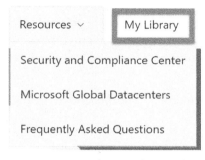

Figure 4.13 – The My Library tab

When logging in with your customer information, you can save documents that you have found in the **Trust Documents** and **Industries & Regions** tabs to the **My Library** tab.

Figure 4.14 shows how this is done with an audit report by going to the end of the row, selecting the **...** drop-down icon, and selecting **Save to Library**:

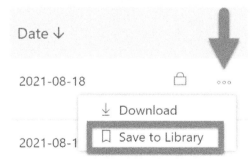

Figure 4.14 – Selecting Save to Library

This is helpful to gather documentation that is necessary and relevant to your own standards and regulatory compliance. Keep in mind that the documentation that you save may become out of date, so you should review this regularly for new reports that Microsoft may publish.

This concludes our exploration of the navigation menu and the information that can be accessed within the Microsoft Service Trust Portal. Next, we will summarize the topics that we have discussed in this chapter.

Summary

In this chapter, we covered Microsoft's privacy principles and the Microsoft Service Trust Portal. This included going through some of the information that is provided on Microsoft's websites on how Microsoft protects customer information and the security and compliance controls that are in place for its physical infrastructure. We discussed each of the sections of the Service Trust Portal and how to access information that may be necessary for your own compliance audits, and how to save that information to your library for quick access.

The next chapter will discuss identity concepts and principles, and **Azure Active Directory Identity Services**.

Section 3:
The Microsoft Identity Management Solutions

This section will provide an overview of the various identity management services within Microsoft 365 and Azure.

This part of the book comprises the following chapters:

5

Defining Identity Principles/Concepts and the Identity Services within Azure AD

The previous chapter covered the key security and compliance principles that Microsoft adheres to for its customers and how we can access this information. This chapter will discuss the role of identity in the cloud. Once you have completed this chapter, you will have an understanding of the principles and concepts that make up identity services in the cloud and the services that Azure provides for managing identity.

In this chapter, we're going to cover the following main topics:

- Defining identity as the security perimeter
- Defining authentication and authorization
- Describing identity providers, Azure Active Directory, and federated services
- Defining common identity attacks

Defining identity as the security perimeter

In *Chapter 2, Describing Security Methodologies*, we covered the defense in depth strategy and shared responsibility within the cloud. We identified that when utilizing a cloud provider for infrastructure, we no longer are responsible for the first layer of defense in depth, the physical defenses. Therefore, identity and access become the first layer of defense that we are responsible for in a cloud architecture. This is where the *identity is the new perimeter* statement comes from.

As consumers, we are consuming cloud services every day and our identities are being used with multiple companies. It is our responsibility to protect those identities as consumers. As a company, when we make a decision to utilize a cloud provider for services such as Microsoft 365 or Azure, we also need to make sure that we are putting proper controls in place to protect the identity of our users. The following sections will define what identity and access management is and some of the services that Microsoft provides to us to protect these identities. Let's start by defining identity and access management and the principles of least privilege.

Defining identity and access management

Now that we understand the importance of protecting user identity, it is important to understand the role of **identity and access management**, or what is commonly referred to as **IAM**? Identity and access management is the process in which we assign roles to users, groups, and resources to determine what permissions they have when they verify their identity. In other words, when a user verifies their identity, they are provided a level of access. IAM is the process of reviewing and providing those access permissions.

This is where the role of **identity and access administrator** becomes important. It is the role of this group to interact with executives and department supervisors to properly plan, define, assign, and test the roles that are required for every job task within the organization and provide them with the proper levels of access necessary to perform their job duties. Without proper planning and communication, access permissions could be inadequate for users to complete work requirements or, worse, they may have elevated permissions that allow them to access information that they are not authorized to view.

The overall planning and implementation process will be covered in subsequent chapters, but it is important to understand this scope and the importance of properly planning for the access roles required within the company.

Principle of least privilege

When designing and scoping the company roles for IAM, the *principle of least privilege* should always be at the forefront of the discussion. This is the concept that any user or resource only has access to the applications, resources, and information that they require to perform their specific job duties. Anything above that poses a vulnerability and potential threat to the company in that sensitive information could be leaked to those that should not be allowed to view it.

The scope of IAM is to manage that any user, group, or resource has been properly assigned roles and access that adheres to this principle. This should be properly documented by a job title with role assignments, and the roles should be reviewed regularly with department owners to verify that the assignments are still accurate and valid. When we explore creating users and groups in a later chapter, we will discuss options for creating role assignments in a dynamic, auto-assigned manner, and how to automate the review of these roles.

As you continue through this book and when you perform your duties as an identity and access administrator, you must always be thinking about the principle of least privilege. This is the foundation of identity and access management.

Now that we understand IAM and the principle of least privilege, let's look at how these concepts pertain to authentication and authorization.

Defining authentication and authorization

Authentication and authorization are key components of IAM and how we enforce the principle of least privilege.

There are multiple aspects of the process to prepare for a Microsoft exam. These include the resources available to prepare for the exam, the ability to access a subscription for hands-on learning, and the manner in which you are going to take your exam. If this is your first Microsoft exam, understanding the format that most of these exams will follow is important.

Let's take a closer look at each of these areas:

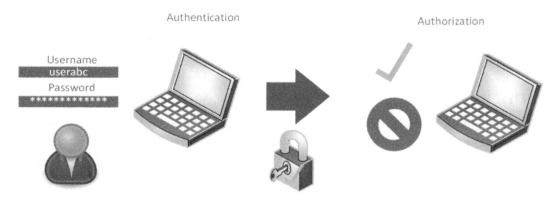

Figure 5.1 – Authentication and authorization comparison

Authentication is defined as the verification and validation of who you are. This is generally accomplished with a username and password. For additional security verification, we should use multi-factor authentication to make sure that the person entering in the username and password is who they say that they are. This aligns with the zero-trust methodology.

Once someone has authenticated to the systems that they are attempting to access, then authorization takes place. **Authorization** verifies the permissions for that user and determines what they are allowed to do when accessing the company systems. The authorization may determine that the person accessing is an administrator that has full access to view and make changes on the system or a user that can only view an application on the system. Authorization to data on systems could even hide or mask sensitive data from being viewed by users that are not authorized to view it.

In *Chapter 6, Describing the Authentication and Access Management Capabilities of Azure AD,* we will further discuss authentication and access management with Azure Active Directory to determine different user roles and privileges. The next section will discuss the role of identity providers, federated services, and Azure Active Directory.

Describing identity providers, Azure Active Directory, and federated services

As defined in the previous section, the process of authentication verifies that someone is who they say that they are; this is their identity. This section will discuss the role of the identity provider in the process of authentication, where Azure Active Directory fits within this process, and how federated services can play a role for companies to work together, even when using different identity providers.

Identity providers

The process of the validation within the authentication process is completed by the **identity provider**. The identity provider acts as the source that stores a user's identity and provides the service of validating that identity when authenticating. In traditional on-premises data center infrastructures, the identity provider is Windows Active Directory.

As we have moved to use cloud services for both our business and personal use, we interact with numerous identity providers throughout the day. Identity provider services are provided by Facebook, Twitter, LinkedIn, Salesforce, Workday, and so on. They are also provided by various cloud providers, such as Google and Microsoft. *Figure 5.2* shows how the identity provider provides this authentication to access a session:

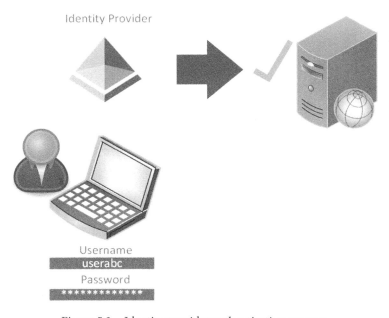

Figure 5.2 – Identity provider authentication process

Microsoft's cloud identity service is provided through **Azure Active Directory**, or Azure AD. The next section will discuss how Azure AD is used.

Azure AD

Azure AD is a cloud-based identity provider that is used for all Microsoft cloud services, including **Microsoft 365** and **Microsoft Azure**. Unlike Windows Active Directory, which utilizes Kerberos or **Lightweight Directory Access Protocol (LDAP)**, for directory services, Azure AD utilizes industry-recognized cloud protocols, **Security Assertions Markup Language (SAML)**, and WS-Federation. This allows Azure AD to be utilized as an identity provider for other cloud-native applications outside those created by Microsoft. *Figure 5.3* shows how Azure AD can be used for Microsoft and third-party application authentication as the identity provider:

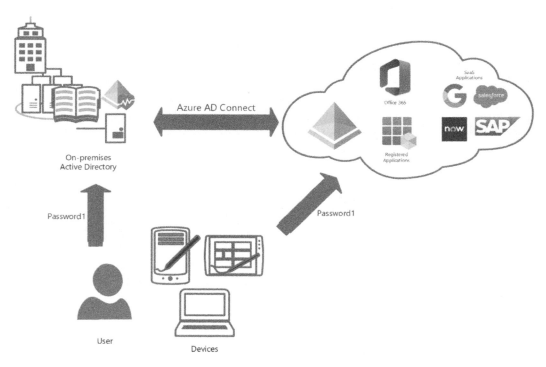

Figure 5.3 – Azure AD for Microsoft and third-party applications

Azure AD can also connect to your existing on-premises Windows Active Directory through Azure AD Connect. Azure AD Connect provides a synchronization service to allow for a hybrid identity between on-premises and cloud services for a single sign-on user experience. Azure AD Connect has three options for identity synchronization between Windows Active Directory and Azure AD. These three options are password hash synchronization, pass-through synchronization, and **Active Directory Federated Services** (**AD FS**) synchronization. Password hash and pass-through synchronizations require no additional infrastructure on-premises other than Azure AD Connect. AD FS synchronization requires an additional AD FS proxy server, as shown in *Figure 5.4*:

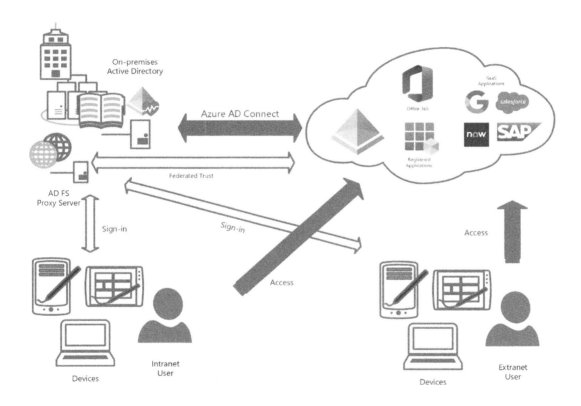

Figure 5.4 – AD FS hybrid identity infrastructure

Within the scope of this exam, only knowing these three options is necessary. AD FS is the more complex of the three options. AD FS is also an example of federated services as it relates to identity providers. The next section will define federated services further.

Federated services

Federated services is the process of utilizing one identity provider to authenticate to systems that utilize a different identity provider. In the example shown in *Figure 5.4*, the federated services are between Windows Active Directory and Azure AD within a single company. Federated services can also be accomplished between two separate companies.

At the center of federated services is a trust relationship. When connecting an on-premises Windows Active Directory of a company to Azure AD in the same company, the trust is created through Azure AD Connect and logging in with the domain administrator role on Windows Active Directory and global administrator on Azure AD. If we as a company want to allow another organization access to services or applications that we own, then we can either add the users that need access as guests and provide them with licenses, or we can create a trust relationship between the two companies.

Creating this trust relationship allows the users of the other company to utilize their current identity provider for authentication to the services of your company. *Figure 5.5* shows how access to the service provider is provided through the trust relationship created with the identity provider:

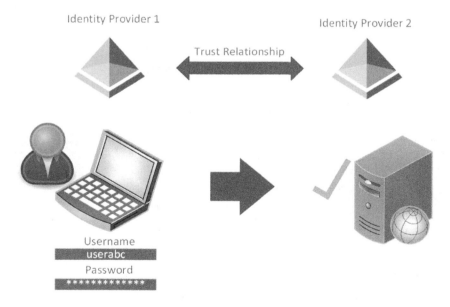

Figure 5.5 – Federated trust relationship

Federated services are commonly used in a merger and acquisition where two companies are already utilizing an identity provider within their existing systems, but they now need to access other systems for the other identity provider resources. Federated services are also used for partner and contractor relationships between companies. Utilizing federated trust services within Azure AD with another company that has Azure AD allows the company to use their existing Azure AD credentials to authenticate and also utilize their existing Microsoft 365 licensing for collaboration tools, such as Microsoft Teams and theMicrosoft Office suite.

Now that we understand how identity providers and federated services are used, let's show how these can be configured within Azure AD.

Configuring identity providers

As we have already established, Azure AD is a cloud-based authentication service that is used by Microsoft 365, Azure, and all of Microsoft's cloud services and solutions for identity and authentication management. Some companies may have another IAM solution that they are using. Azure AD allows for these companies to utilize these providers as part of the B2B authentication relationship as guests on the Azure AD tenant.

Azure AD is built on open source standards and, therefore, has the ability to support **Security Assertion Markup Language (SAML)** or **WS-Federation**. Configuring these direct federation relationships allow users to begin collaborating, utilizing their existing identity credentials from their existing *identity provider*. These relationships are configured within the Azure AD tenant to create this federated B2B relationship between companies.

The way users would then access the Azure AD tenant as a guest would be through the same portal URL that is used in the guest user invitation, but with the federated tenant ID added to the end to create a customized URL – for example, `https://myapps.microsoft.com/?tenantid=tenant id` or `https://portal.azure.com/tenant id`, with the tenant ID being created as part of the identity provider configuration, which will be discussed in the next sections. If the guest is using their own Azure AD tenant, the URL would look like this: `https://myapps.microsoft.com/guesttenantname.onmicrosoft.com`.

When using identity provider federation for these guest user B2B relationships, there are a few points to note:

- If a guest user has accepted an invitation onto the Azure AD tenant prior to the federation relationship being created, they will continue to authenticate in the same manner.

- Guest users that have been invited through direct federation as a partner company when the partner company moves to Azure AD will continue to have access, as long as the direct federation relationship between tenants exists.

- Guest users invited through direct federation between partner companies will lose access if that direct federation relationship is removed.

With direct federation, the login experience for the user is the same as if they are logging into their own company resources. This maintains a consistent and unchanged experience for these users when collaborating with partner companies.

To create a direct federation relationship, you start by navigating to **External Identities** from under the **Manage** section of the **Azure AD** portal, as shown in *Figure 5.6*:

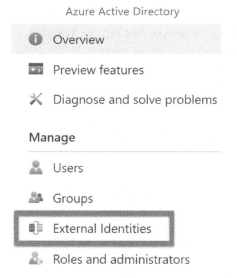

Figure 5.6 – External Identities in Azure AD

From there, you select **All identity providers**, as shown in *Figure 5.7*:

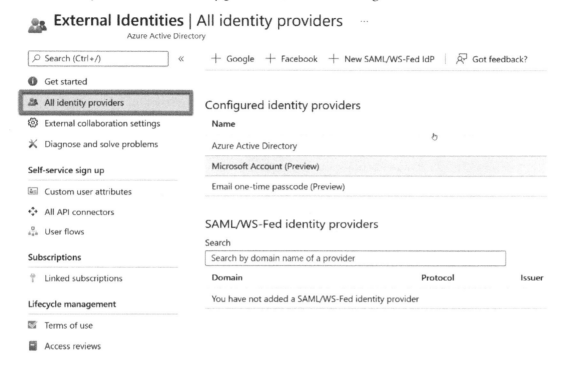

Figure 5.7 – All identity providers within the External Identities blade

For additional information and the steps for configuring direct federation, you can use this link: `https://docs.microsoft.com/azure/active-directory/external-identities/direct-federation`.

From within the **External Identities | All identity providers** blade, you will see that **Azure Active Directory**, **Microsoft Account (Preview)**, and **Email one-time passcode (Preview)** are default preconfigured identity providers. These providers require no additional steps to allow direct federation. For **Azure AD** and **Microsoft Account (Preview),** the guest user invitation process is used to collaborate. *Figure 5.8* shows what opens when selecting either of these identity provider options:

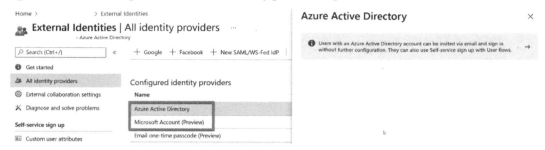

Figure 5.8 – Azure AD and Microsoft Account direct federation configuration

To allow a user to have guest access with a one-time passcode, there are multiple options that can be used for configuration. These are shown in *Figure 5.9*:

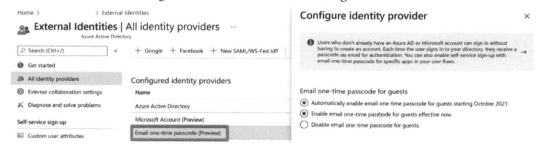

Figure 5.9 – Configuring a one-time passcode for guest user federation

The one-time passcode option is helpful when you have a single guest user that needs to be added, rather than multiple guest users from a partner company.

In addition to the default identity providers of **Azure Active Directory**, **Microsoft Account (Preview)**, and **Email one-time passcode (Preview)**, additional *SAML* and *WS-Federation* identity providers can be configured, as well as Google and Facebook. In the next sections, we will discuss how this configuration is done with these two popular identity providers.

Google configuration

Microsoft provides a direct federation for Google as an identity provider. This can be initiated by selecting **+ Google** from the **External Identities | All identity providers** blade, as shown in *Figure 5.10*:

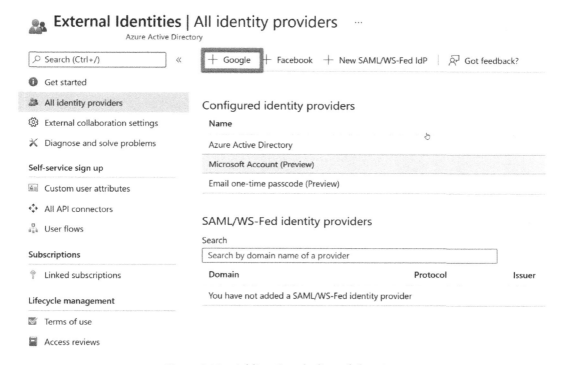

Figure 5.10 – Adding Google direct federation

After selecting **+ Google**, another blade will open with additional information that is required to configure Google as an identity provider. To obtain this information, the Microsoft Azure AD account must be configured within Google. There is a link to these directions within the blade that opens, as shown in *Figure 5.11*:

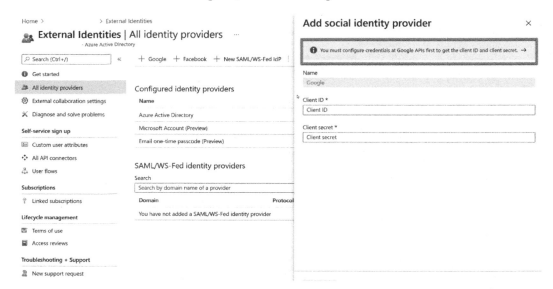

Figure 5.11 – Google identity provider configuration

The link for these directions is also provided here: `https://docs.microsoft.com/azure/active-directory/external-identities/google-federation`.

After going through the steps within Google for federation, **Client ID** and **Client secret** fields will be provided. You will copy these values into the fields in *Figure 5.11* and click **Save** to complete the direct federation.

The next section will show how to configure Facebook as a direct federation identity provider.

Facebook configuration

Microsoft provides a direct federation for Facebook as an identity provider. This can be initiated by selecting **+ Facebook** from the **External Identities | All identity providers** blade, as shown in *Figure 5.12*:

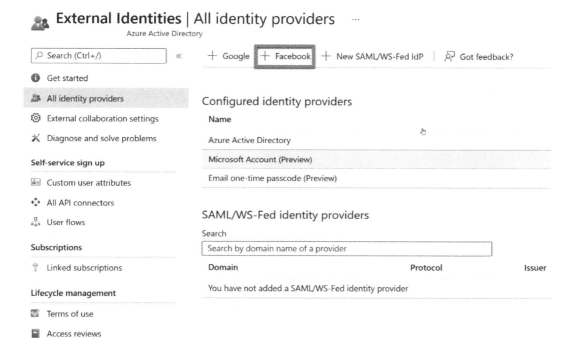

Figure 5.12 – Adding Facebook direct federation

After selecting **+ Facebook**, another blade will open with additional information that is required to configure Facebook as an identity provider. To obtain this information, the Microsoft Azure AD account must be configured within Facebook. There is a link to these directions within the blade that opens, as shown in *Figure 5.13*:

Figure 5.13 – Facebook identity provider configuration

The link for these directions is also provided here: `https://docs.microsoft.com/azure/active-directory/external-identities/facebook-federation`.

In the final section of this chapter, we will address some common identity attacks.

Defining common identity attacks

As stated in the first section of this chapter, identity and access is the security perimeter when utilizing cloud services. Therefore, many of the most common security threats to our companies are identity-based attacks. Identity attacks are focused on stealing the credentials of a user and then using these credentials to authenticate to services that that user is authorized to access.

Let's look at some of the more common types of identity attacks.

A **password-based attack** is when an attacker is attempting to guess the combination of username and password to gain access. A **password spray attack** is a password-based attack where the attacker is utilizing a list of weak passwords against a username to gain access. A **brute-force attack** is similar to a password spray attack; it attempts many passwords against multiple accounts to find a weak password on an account. In all of these attacks, when an attacker finds a match on a username and password, they have gained access to that account and the systems that user is authorized to view. *Figure 5.14* shows how an attacker carries out a password-based attack:

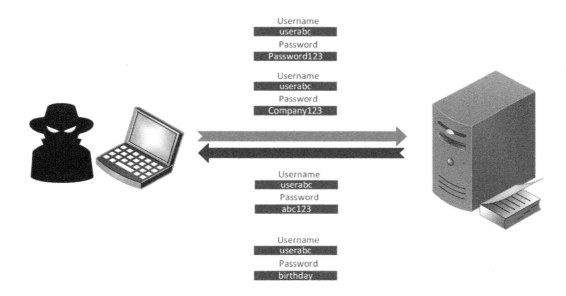

Figure 5.14 – Password-based attack

Having proper password attempt lockouts in place on user accounts can assist in protecting against these types of attacks.

Phishing attacks are extremely common, and you probably see various phishing attacks throughout the day. In a phishing attack, the attacker is attempting to get the user to either provide sensitive information, such as a username/password or personal information, or they want the user to go to a website or execute malicious files on the user device that allow them access to systems. A phishing attack is executed by taking advantage of something that you trust, such as a shopping site that you regularly use. The attacker will pretend to be from that merchant and will usually have a link that they want you to select. This link will take you to the phishing website for the attacker to gather information. This process is shown in *Figure 5.15*:

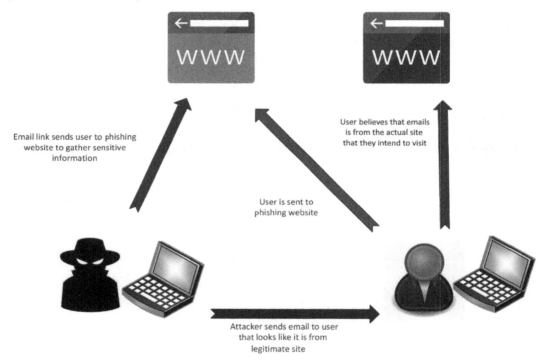

Figure 5.15 – Phishing attack

Spear-phishing attacks are similar to phishing attacks. The main difference is that these attacks focus on information that you may receive from the company in which you work. This may be spoofing human resources about merit increases or an employee survey with a prize to entice you. These attacks are focused on obtaining information to access business resources. *Figure 5.16* shows the workflow of a spear-phishing attack:

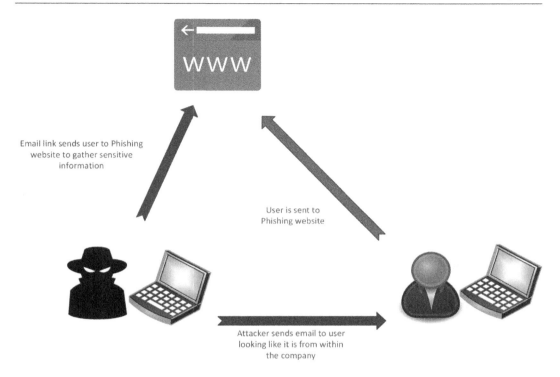

Figure 5.16 – Spear-phishing attack

The common tactics and methodology that you should put in place to protect against identity-based attacks are to adhere to a zero-trust model. This includes enforcing the use of **Multi-Factor Authentication (MFA)** for all administrators, at a minimum. The best practice would be that all users would also be required to utilize MFA. *Chapter 7, Describing the Identity Protection and Governance Capabilities of Azure AD,* of this book will discuss additional identity protection options within Azure AD.

The next section will provide a summary of what you have learned in this chapter.

Summary

In this chapter, we covered the concepts of identity. We provided information on how identity is now the first line of a defense in depth security posture. We also discussed the concept of authentication and authorization for identity and access management. We then discussed the role of the identity provider for authentication and some common threats that deal in identity theft.

The next chapter will discuss more about how identity and access management is handled within Azure AD.

6
Describing the Authentication and Access Management Capabilities of Azure AD

In the previous chapter, we covered the principles and concepts that make up identity services in the cloud and the services that Azure provides for managing identity, including an introduction to **Azure Active Directory** (**Azure AD**). In this chapter, you will gain a greater understanding of Azure AD and how it is used to manage and protect identities within the cloud and hybrid infrastructures.

In this chapter, we're going to cover the following main topics:

- Describing Azure AD
- Describing the types of identities in Azure AD
- Describing how hybrid identity works within Azure AD
- Describing how external users and groups are used in Azure AD
- Describing the different ways in which to protect identity in Azure AD

Technical requirements

In this chapter, we will begin exploring how to configure a tenant for the use of Microsoft 365 and Azure. There will be exercises that will require you to have access to Azure AD. If you have not yet created the trial licenses for Microsoft 365, please follow the directions provided in *Chapter 1, Preparing for Your Microsoft Exam.*

Describing Azure AD

Azure AD is a cloud-based identity provider that is used for all Microsoft cloud services, including **Microsoft 365** and **Microsoft Azure**. Unlike Windows Active Directory, which utilizes Kerberos or LDAP for directory services, Azure AD utilizes the industry-recognized cloud protocols, **SAML** and **WS-Federation**. This allows Azure AD to be utilized as an identity provider for other cloud-native applications outside those created by Microsoft:

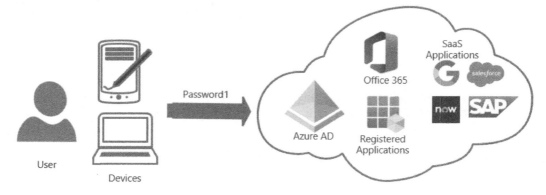

Figure 6.1 – Azure AD for cloud identity

There are four Azure AD editions that you should understand. They are as follows:

- Free Azure AD is enabled whenever a Microsoft account is created. If you have `outlook.com`, you have an Azure AD account.
- **Office 365 Apps** is created when you subscribe to **Office 365**.
- Premium P1 is used for business-level and enterprise-level Azure AD subscriptions. This is part of Microsoft 365 Business Premium and Office/Microsoft 365 E3.
- Premium P2 provides advanced security features with this license. This license is part of the Office/Microsoft 365 E5 licenses. Premium P2 can also be purchased as a standalone license.

Now that we understand Azure AD, let's look at the types of identities within Azure AD.

Describing the types of identities in Azure AD

Four identity types are found with Azure AD, making up the identity types that you will find in Azure AD. They are as follows:

- **Users**: These include the member users within the domain and any external/guest users invited to the domain.
- **Devices**: These are the registered devices to the domain. Generally, these are company-owned and managed devices on Intune.
- **Managed Identity**: This identity is specific to Azure. These identities are managed using Azure IAM/RBAC.
- **Service principals**: These are used to provide an identity to Azure resources to authenticate to access other resources.

In the next section, we will discuss the hybrid identity infrastructure and how to use Azure AD identities with identities that are part of an on-premises infrastructure.

Describing how hybrid identity works within Azure AD

In order to be able to configure hybrid identities and synchronization in Azure AD and on-premises, you will need to have the *Global Administrator* role or the *Hybrid Identity Administrator* role within the Azure AD tenant and the *Domain Enterprise Administrator* role within the on-premises Windows Active Directory tenant. In this section, we will explain, in more detail, the differences between these two directory services.

Before we discuss the implementation of *hybrid identity*, it is important to understand what it is and why it is necessary. The following sections will provide this information.

Hybrid identity

The term **hybrid identity** is meant to signify that the company has users that use on-premises resources and users that use cloud-native resources. Within this hybrid identity infrastructure, there is going to be an on-premises **Windows Active Directory** domain controller that is used to manage the on-premises users. Additionally, **Azure AD** will manage the cloud-native users, both members and guests. This infrastructure coincides with companies that use a *hybrid cloud*. Many companies have this Windows Active Directory domain controller in place today. In the next section, we will provide some understanding of what this means before we discuss how we can connect it to our Azure AD.

Azure AD

To review, Azure AD is Microsoft's cloud-based identity and access management solution. The role of Azure AD is to manage cloud identities for Microsoft and Azure resources, along with other third-party cloud applications that utilize open source identity protocols, such as *SAML* or *WS-Federation*. For users to access these cloud applications and services, their identity needs to be configured and recognized within the Azure AD tenant.

Many companies do not only utilize cloud-native applications and services. In fact, they rely on an on-premises Windows Active Directory tenant to manage access to these applications. In the next section, we will explain Windows Active Directory and its role in the hybrid identity infrastructure.

Windows Active Directory

Windows Active Directory is the software that we are referencing. Within the on-premises infrastructure, we also refer to the role of the domain controller and the overall solution of **Active Directory Domain Services (AD DS)**. AD DS is the legacy identity and access management solution for companies with an on-premises infrastructure. The focus of the exam is not to have a deep dive into Windows Active Directory and AD DS; however, it is important to understand how AD DS compares to Azure AD as it pertains to users and groups. If you would like to understand more about AD DS, please refer to https://docs.microsoft.com/en-us/windows-server/identity/ad-ds/get-started/virtual-dc/active-directory-domain-services-overview.

There are similarities and differences between AD DS and Azure AD. They both manage identities and access by assigning roles and authorizing access to users and groups. However, AD DS does this through an object-based structure. Within this object structure, there can be multiple **organizational units (OUs)** that these objects belong to. This creates a more hierarchical structure than the flat structure of Azure AD. This difference creates challenges when you want users and groups to access on-premises and cloud resources utilizing the same username and password. Additionally, creating duplicate entries in both AD DS and Azure AD will cause an issue with the management of users and groups.

To address this problem, Microsoft offers **Azure Active Directory Connect (Azure AD Connect)** as a solution to bring AD DS and Azure AD together. In the next section, we will discuss how this works.

Azure AD Connect

Since a company that is adopting the use of cloud resources has, for the most part, this on-premises identity infrastructure in place, we need to create a way to synchronize these identities to our cloud-based Azure AD. **Azure AD Connect** is a software solution that is installed within the on-premises infrastructure and configured to synchronize users and groups to Azure AD. Azure AD Connect simplifies the management of these users and groups by providing ways where an identity and access administrator can manage users in one interface and have the changes be updated in near real time.

As there are structural differences in terms of how AD DS and Azure AD are built, Azure AD Connect provides the conduit to create a consistent user and administrator experience with identity and access management.

There are some prerequisites and aspects that are beyond the scope of Azure AD Connect that you should understand. The installation prerequisites can be found at `https://docs.microsoft.com/en-us/azure/active-directory/hybrid/how-to-connect-install-prerequisites`. When planning to implement Azure AD Connect, the following information should be understood and planned accordingly:

- Azure AD Connect synchronizes users and groups, not devices or applications. There are ways in which to comanage devices and support on-premises application access within Azure AD; these will both be covered in later chapters.

- Azure AD Connect synchronizes a single AD DS forest per Azure AD tenant. If there are multiple forests, then multiple tenants will be required in Azure AD.

There are additional considerations when it comes to planning for AD DS and Azure AD synchronization with Azure AD Connect, but these will be covered within the use cases for each synchronization type.

There are three options when configuring Azure AD Connect for synchronization:

- Password hash synchronization

- Pass-through synchronization

- **Active Directory Federated Services** (**AD FS**) synchronization

The first step of a hybrid identity infrastructure is to download and install Azure AD Connect in the on-premises infrastructure. This can be done on the on-premises Active Directory domain controller server or on another member server that is joined to the domain. For more details on how to install Azure AD Connect and configure the various synchronization types, please refer to https://docs.microsoft.com/en-us/azure/active-directory/hybrid/how-to-connect-install-roadmap.

In the upcoming sections, we will discuss the use cases for each synchronization type.

Password hash synchronization

Password hash synchronization is the easiest type to configure and is the default option within the express setup. Password hash synchronization maintains both the on-premises identities and the cloud identities of users. This takes place through providing on-premises user identities to Azure AD along with an encrypted hash of their passwords. This allows users to sign into on-premises and cloud applications with the same authentication credentials.

Password hash synchronization is a good option when a company has a single on-premises domain and is quickly moving to a cloud-native infrastructure. Password hash synchronization is not for companies with complex authentication and password requirements within the on-premises Active Directory.

As mentioned earlier, password hash synchronization maintains authentication credentials on-premises and in Azure AD. Therefore, password hash synchronization can have users authenticate to cloud applications through Azure AD, while passing the authentication responsibilities of the on-premises applications to the on-premises Active Directory. Here, the benefit is that if the connection fails in Azure AD Connect between the on-premises AD DS and Azure AD, users are still able to authenticate to their cloud applications and remain partially productive. *Figure 6.8* provides a visual diagram of how this workflow is handled. Additional information can be found at https://docs.microsoft.com/en-us/azure/active-directory/hybrid/whatis-phs:

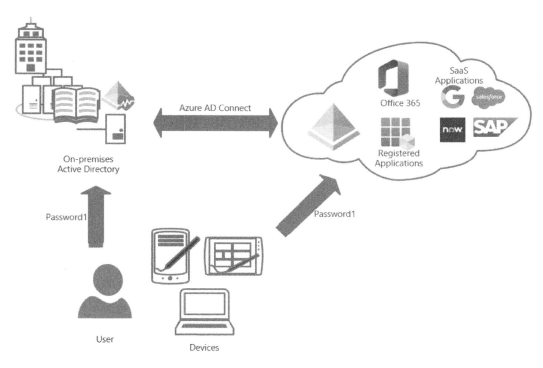

Figure 6.2 – A password hash synchronization diagram

Azure AD Connect will be configured to synchronize users from the on-premises Active Directory to Azure AD by utilizing password hash synchronization. This configuration for Azure AD Connect is the least complex of the three options. In the upcoming sections, we will provide information about pass-through synchronization and AD FS synchronization.

Pass-through synchronization

The next hybrid identity synchronization option that we will discuss is **pass-through synchronization**. Unlike password hash synchronization, which allows user identities to be authenticated in either the on-premises Active Directory or Azure AD, pass-through synchronization requires all users to authenticate to the on-premises Active Directory.

In this configuration, if the Azure AD Connect connection between Azure AD and the on-premises Active Directory were to become disconnected, no users would be able to authenticate to the on-premises resources or the cloud resources. Therefore, it is important to actively monitor this connection and build resiliency in the architecture. *Figure 6.14* shows a diagram of how pass-through synchronization functions and how you can architect resiliency with redundancy in **pass-through agents (PTAs)** alongside a backup domain controller:

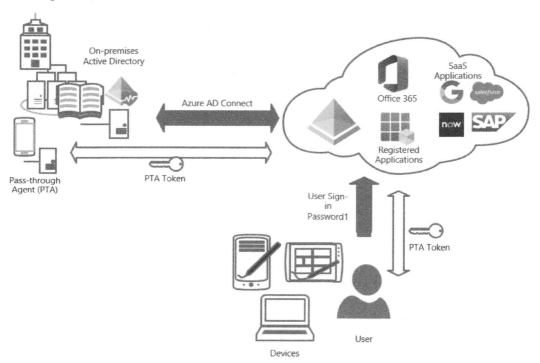

Figure 6.3 – A pass-through synchronization diagram

There are several reasons to utilize pass-through synchronization. If a company requires authentication parameters and limits that only allow users to access resources during certain times, at present, these rules can only be configured on an Active Directory domain controller. With pass-through synchronization, you can utilize modern authentication features with Azure AD, such as **multi-factor authentication (MFA)** and **self-service password reset (SSPR)**. However, for SSPR, you will need to enable the password writeback feature within Azure AD Connect. Additional information about pass-through synchronization can be found at `https://docs.microsoft.com/en-us/azure/active-directory/hybrid/how-to-connect-pta`.

> **Note**
> All of the synchronization types are available in the custom setup blade, including password hash synchronization. These custom steps would be used with password hash synchronization if only certain OUs were going to be synchronized with Azure AD.

One component that is installed on the Active Directory domain controller server is a PTA. In order to have a resilient architecture, it is recommended that at least two of these PTAs be installed on member servers in the on-premises infrastructure. For more information regarding this configuration, please refer to `https://docs.microsoft.com/en-us/azure/active-directory/hybrid/how-to-connect-pta-quick-start`.

In the next section, we will discuss the third and final synchronization type within hybrid identity infrastructures, AD FS.

AD FS synchronization

AD FS synchronization is the most complex of the three Azure AD Connect synchronization types. Unlike password hash synchronization and pass-through authentication, which, in many cases, can be installed directly on the on-premises domain controller, AD FS requires an additional infrastructure in place to support the authentication process. *Figure 6.29* shows the complexity of the necessary infrastructure and components:

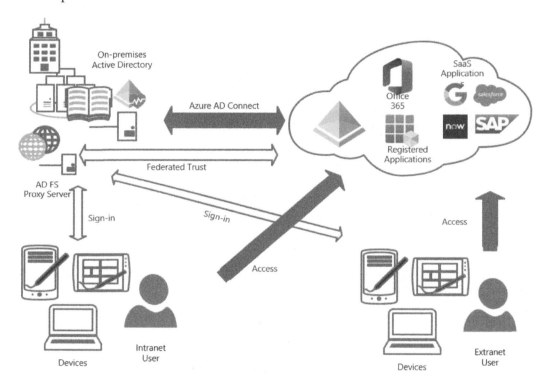

Figure 6.4 – An AD FS synchronization diagram

AD FS synchronization is utilized in complex Active Directory infrastructures where there are multiple domains, and third-party MFA solutions or smart cards are utilized. For additional information regarding the configuration of AD FS synchronization, you can navigate to https://docs.microsoft.com/en-us/azure/active-directory/hybrid/how-to-connect-fed-management.

Password hash synchronization and pass-through synchronization are the more widely discussed of the three Azure AD Connect options. It is important to understand when each should be used within a hybrid identity architecture, as we will discuss in each of the corresponding sections.

In the next section, we will discuss how external users and groups are used in Azure AD.

Describing how external users and groups are used in Azure AD

Guest users and external users are invited to the Azure AD tenant and have access to resources that they have been authorized. This is helpful when someone outside your company needs access to an application to collaborate, or a partner or subsidiary company needs to be given access to resources.

Guests are invited from within the **User** tile by selecting **+ New Guest User** and providing their external email address. Once they accept the invitation, they are now added to the Azure AD tenant and can be assigned permissions to authorize them access to resources.

In order to be able to create users in Azure AD, you will need to have the *Global Administrator* role or the *User Administrator* role. Since the best practice is to adhere to the principle of least privilege, the user administrator role assignment should be given to anyone that is required to create, configure, and manage users within Azure AD.

Once you are in Azure AD with the proper role, you have the ability to create users. In this chapter, we will focus on external users and guest users. There are different types of external users that require separate configuration settings. The primary categories are *business-to-business*, or *B2B*, and *business-to-consumer*, or *B2C*. The following sections will define each of these categories before we move on to discuss external collaboration settings.

B2B

The primary focus of the identity and access administrator exam is based on B2B collaboration and guest users. B2B guests are best described by a partnership relationship between users within two separate companies that need to collaborate together on a project. These B2B relationships might be created through business mergers and acquisitions, project needs, or support relationships.

Within these B2B relationships, the external company can bring their own **Azure AD** and **Microsoft 365** licenses for collaboration, or these licenses can be assigned if the external users do not come from an Azure AD tenant with Microsoft 365 licenses. External company collaboration settings allow these users a **single sign-on** (**SSO**) experience for both business tenants. If an external user does not use these licenses, then the username and password can be used from another identity, and that user can be assigned licenses from within the invited tenant.

B2C

The B2C relationship is an external account used for customers who are accessing applications and resources within the tenant. An example of this would be using a LinkedIn, Facebook, or Google username and password to log in and access your account on a shopping site. This provides a convenience to customers by not requiring them to create another username and password. As mentioned earlier, B2C guest users are beyond the scope of the **Identity and Access Administrator** exam. We are only mentioning this here for clarity between the types of external users and for you to understand that this capability exists. We will discuss this further within the configuring of identity providers section later. These identity provider relationships can allow for a B2C authentication relationship, but for the purposes of this book, we will discuss them as they pertain to B2B authentication.

Now that we have defined the types of external users, let's discuss how external collaboration is configured within Azure AD.

Configuring external collaboration settings

Whether the external users are B2B or B2C, there is a level of collaboration that needs to be planned for and configured within Azure AD to allow these guests to have access. These settings can be found within the Azure AD portal under **External Identities | External collaboration settings**. *Figure 6.5* shows the settings available within the external collaboration settings:

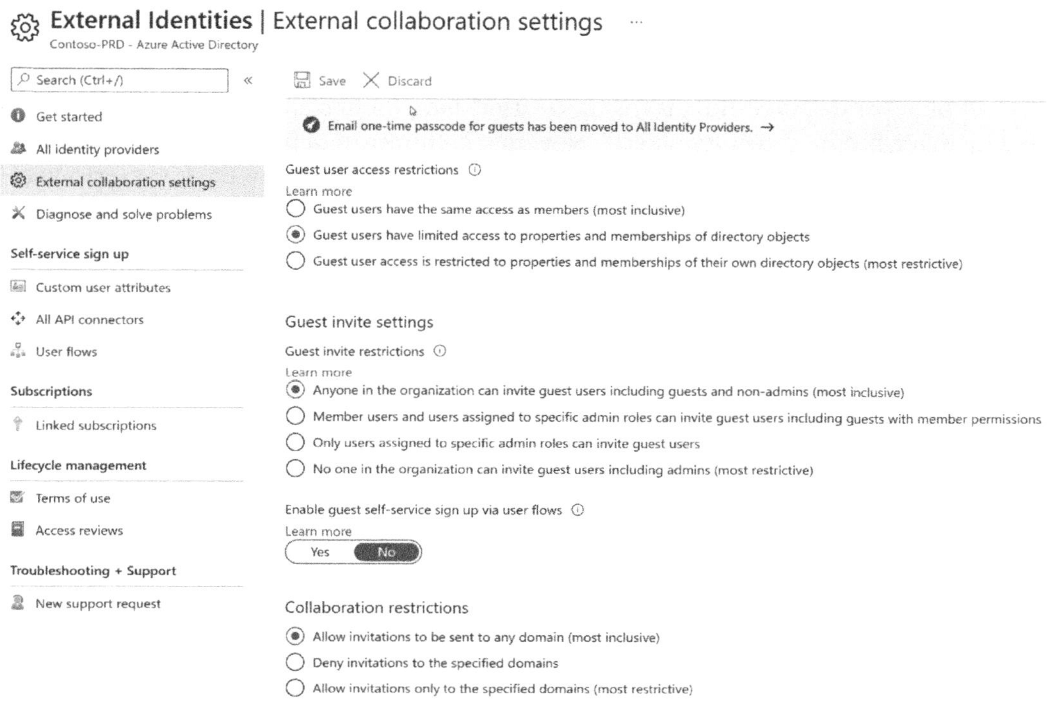

Figure 6.5 – External collaboration settings

Within the collaboration settings, you will define what guest users can access, who is allowed to invite guest users, and the restrictions regarding collaboration for the tenant. *Figure 6.5* shows the default settings for external collaboration. These settings should be discussed with stakeholders to provide a proper plan for external guest access. Let's discuss each of these sections and how they could be utilized.

Guest user access

The first section within **External collaboration settings** is the overall guest user access restrictions. The default setting is that guest users have limited access to the properties and memberships of directory objects. Note that within each of these sections, Microsoft provides a level of guidance regarding what is the most inclusive and the most restrictive within these settings. *Figure 6.6* shows these settings. More information can be found at `https://aka.ms/aadguestpermissions`:

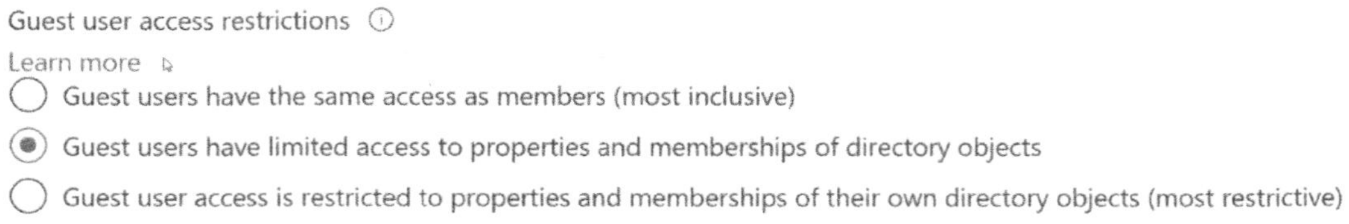

Guest user access restrictions ⓘ

Learn more ⤵
○ Guest users have the same access as members (most inclusive)

◉ Guest users have limited access to properties and memberships of directory objects

○ Guest user access is restricted to properties and memberships of their own directory objects (most restrictive)

Figure 6.6 – Guest user access restrictions

As shown in *Figure 6.6*, the default setting creates a level of inclusion and restriction in terms of how guests can interact within the tenant that might be more restrictive than a member user. Using this setting will allow administrators within the applications to determine guest user permissions specifically for those objects.

Guest invite settings

The next section within the external collaboration settings is **Guest invite settings**. Here, there are two settings: **Guest invite restrictions** and **Enable guest self-service sign up via user flows**. The default settings for these options are **Anyone in the organization can invite guest users including guests and non-admins (most inclusive)** and **No** for **Enable guest self-service sign up**.

In *Figure 6.7*, note that the **Guest invite restrictions** settings are set to be as inclusive as possible, even allowing guests and non-administrator members to invite other guest users to the tenant. Although this option takes some administrative burden off the IT department, it could also be a security risk, especially since this allows guest users from outside the company to invite other guests. Additionally, selecting the most restrictive option would completely block guest users from being invited to the tenant. If your company is highly regulated and has certain compliance requirements around guest access, then this might be a good option:

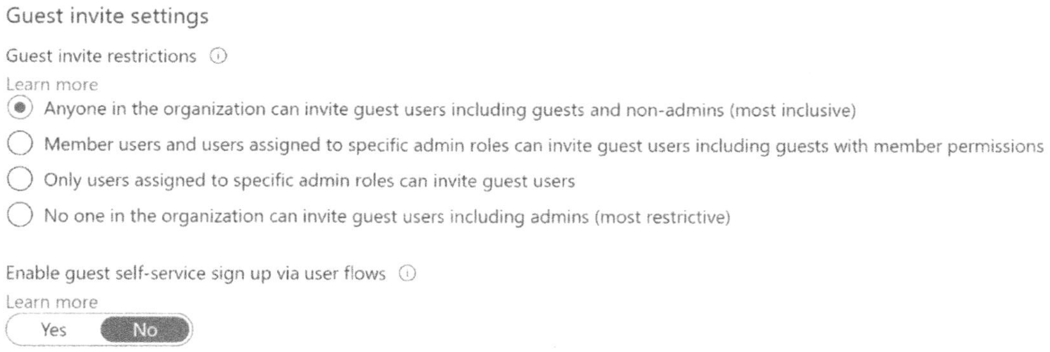

Guest invite settings

Guest invite restrictions ⓘ

Learn more

(●) Anyone in the organization can invite guest users including guests and non-admins (most inclusive)

( ) Member users and users assigned to specific admin roles can invite guest users including guests with member permissions

( ) Only users assigned to specific admin roles can invite guest users

( ) No one in the organization can invite guest users including admins (most restrictive)

Enable guest self-service sign up via user flows ⓘ

Learn more

(Yes   **No**)

Figure 6.7 – Guest invite settings

In most cases, the best practice would be to not allow guests to invite other guests and to limit the member users that can invite guest users, which is one of the middle options, as shown in *Figure 6.7*. More information regarding these settings can be found at `https://aka.ms/guestinvitesettings`.

The **Enable guest self-service sign up via user flows** setting is one that is used alongside **External identities**, such as personal Microsoft accounts, Facebook, or Google. Before allowing these identity providers to be utilized for B2B or B2C logins to the company Azure AD tenant, this setting will need to be changed to **Yes**. The default is **No**, as shown in *Figure 6.7*. More information regarding guest user flows can be found at `https://aka.ms/exidenablesssu`.

Collaboration restrictions

The final section within **External collaboration settings** is **Collaboration restrictions**. Here, you have the option to **Allow invitations to be sent to any domain (most inclusive), Deny invitations to the specified domains**, or **Allow invitations only to the specified domains (most restrictive)**. As you can see in *Figure 6.8*, allowing invitations to only specified domains is the most restrictive because you set a very narrow scope of companies that can be invited to the company tenant:

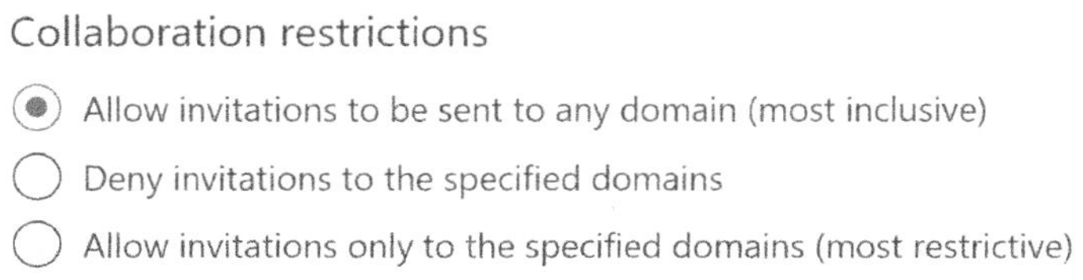

Collaboration restrictions

(●) Allow invitations to be sent to any domain (most inclusive)

( ) Deny invitations to the specified domains

( ) Allow invitations only to the specified domains (most restrictive)

Figure 6.8 – Collaboration restrictions: allowing invitations

The default setting is to allow invitations to any domain, which puts no restrictions and is the most inclusive, as shown in *Figure 6.8*.

Figure 6.9 shows that when selecting the **Deny invitations to the specified domains** option, an entry field appears to enter in those blocked domains:

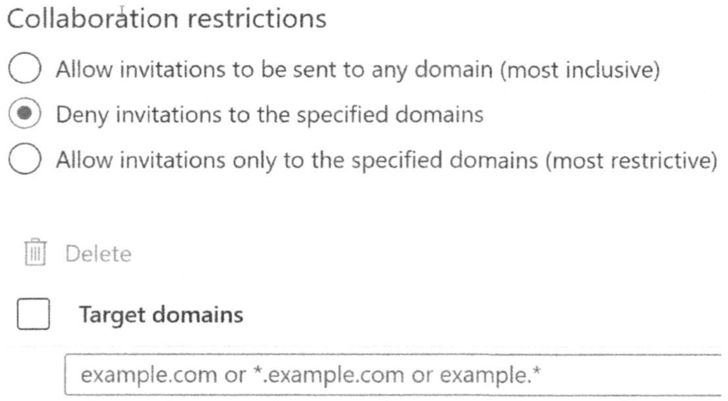

Collaboration restrictions

○ Allow invitations to be sent to any domain (most inclusive)

◉ Deny invitations to the specified domains

○ Allow invitations only to the specified domains (most restrictive)

🗑 Delete

☐ **Target domains**

example.com or *.example.com or example.*

Figure 6.9 – Collaboration restrictions – denying invitations

Target domains can be used to block competitor companies or companies that could create a conflict of interest if they were to be allowed within your company tenant.

Figure 6.10 shows that the same field appears when selecting the option to allow invitations to only the specified domains:

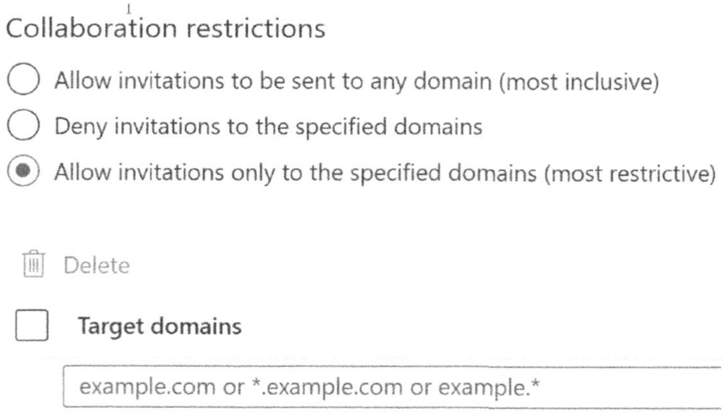

Collaboration restrictions

○ Allow invitations to be sent to any domain (most inclusive)

○ Deny invitations to the specified domains

◉ Allow invitations only to the specified domains (most restrictive)

🗑 Delete

☐ **Target domains**

example.com or *.example.com or example.*

Figure 6.10 – Collaboration restrictions – allowing invitations from specified domains

Here, the difference is that you are only specifying the domains that are allowed to be invited to the company tenant. Unless the guest user invitation has this domain as their email, they will be blocked from receiving an invitation. In a company that handles sensitive information, this high level of restricting guests might be required. As the identity and access administrator, you will be responsible for identifying what these domains are and should have a process in place for approvals before additional domains are added.

Once these collaboration settings have been planned, approved, and completed, external users can be invited to the company tenant.

In the next section, we will discuss ways in which to protect identities within Azure AD.

Describing the different ways to protect identity in Azure AD

As more companies move to cloud technologies and have identities within the cloud, the ability to protect those identities becomes paramount to avoid security breaches. Microsoft and Azure AD provide many ways in which to protect these identities and mitigate risks. Some of these solutions can be listed as follows:

- **Password complexity rules** are used to protect against users utilizing common terms and easy-to-guess passwords. Enforcing certain lengths and complexities, such as the use of alphanumeric and special characters, along with a minimum length, can deter attackers from their ability to utilize password dictionary attacks or identify dates and information from social media accounts that could be used as a password.

- **Password expiration rules** are utilized to avoid a password from remaining the same for an extended period of time. The longer a password is used by a user, the more likely it is to eventually be exposed. Having a password expire, enforcing users to change their passwords, and blocking the use of previously used passwords assist in disrupting an attacker's ability to gain access to systems through exposed passwords.

- **SSPR** allows users to perform their own password changes when they forget their password or if they feel that their password has been compromised. We will discuss this in more detail later.

- **Azure AD Identity Protection** is a solution within Azure AD that provides additional capabilities for monitoring and managing user identities and determining whether an identity has been compromised. Azure Identity Protection will be discussed in further detail in *Chapter 9, Describing Security Management and Capabilities of Azure.*

- **Azure AD Password Protection** works together with Azure AD Identity Protection to enforce password complexity rules, expiration rules, and also to block common passwords from being utilized. Azure AD Password Protection will also be discussed in *Chapter 9, Describing Security Management and Capabilities of Azure*.

- **Azure AD smart lock** is part of Azure AD Identity Protection and will be discussed further in *Chapter 9, Describing Security Management and Capabilities of Azure*.

- **Azure AD application proxy** allows Azure AD identity and access management to be utilized for enterprise applications that might remain in on-premises infrastructures in a hybrid cloud architecture. Enterprise application IAM will be discussed in further detail in *Chapter 10, Describing Threat Protection with Microsoft 365 Defender*.

- **SSO** was discussed in *Chapter 6, Describing the Authentication and Access Management Capabilities of Azure AD* when configuring hybrid identities and a user's ability to access resources in the cloud and on-premises utilizing the same username and password. SSO utilization will be extended to other cloud applications and on-premises enterprise applications in *Chapter 10, Describing Threat Protection with Microsoft 365 Defender*.

- **Azure AD Connect** provides the synchronization between on-premises Windows Active Directory and cloud Azure AD for a single identity management platform in a hybrid architecture. This allows password requirements and rules to be utilized across the hybrid architecture. Azure AD Connect was discussed in *Chapter 6, Describing the Authentication and Access Management Capabilities of Azure AD*.

These solutions assist in protecting against certain attacks, such as brute-force and password dictionary attacks by making it more difficult to guess passwords. However, passwords are still a vulnerability, and stolen passwords are the primary cause of security breaches. To protect user access to company assets and technologies, additional identity verification should be utilized. This can be accomplished by utilizing Azure AD MFA.

What is MFA?

In the previous section, we discussed some of the requirements and solutions that can be put in place to protect and manage our identities and avoid the exposure of user passwords. Unfortunately, there is nothing that can completely avoid a user password from being stolen, and the majority of security breaches are caused by passwords that have been compromised.

However, if passwords are so insecure, why do we continue to use them? The foundation of authentication and authorization has been built around the concept of usernames and passwords. This means that applications that have been developed for years and years have utilized this concept, so rewriting these applications now is not an option.

So, how can we protect our users and make sure that a user is who they say they are when authenticating? Since username and password authentication is not going away anytime soon, additional solutions should be utilized to protect identities and verify that a username and password being entered is from the person to whom it has been assigned. This can be done by utilizing MFA.

MFA addresses the potential of a password becoming compromised by requiring the user who is requesting access to provide an additional form of identification before they are authenticated and authorized access. There are three forms, or factors, of identification that are used for MFA, and MFA is configured to require any two of these three factors to verify a user's identity. The three forms are as follows:

- Something you know
- Something you have
- Something you are

Let's look at each of these in more detail by defining each of them and giving some examples of how they are used.

Something you know

Something you know is a form of identification that you provide from your memory. In many cases, this is your password. It could also be a **personal identification number (PIN)** or the answer to a security question. In most verification systems, this is usually the first factor for verification, and then the second layer of verification is one of the next two options.

Something you have

Something you have is probably the most difficult to comprehend at times. This factor requires something that is physically in your possession to verify your identity. In most cases, this is generally a cell phone that you have identified when enrolling in the MFA service. On that cell phone, you can be provided a few ways to verify your identity, such as through a code being sent via text message, a phone call to that cell phone number, a code within an authenticator app on the phone, or pushing an approval notification on the authenticator app. In addition to a cell phone being something that you have with you, some companies might provide a separate token-generating device that rotates a code every few minutes.

Something you are

Something you are is when some form of biometrics is used as the second factor for verification. Usually, the most popular use here is fingerprints or facial recognition. To use this factor, the devices being used for this factor must be equipped with the capability to provide and process this information. This is a more complex factor than the other two and might not be technically or financially feasible for a company that has older systems. However, many new systems have these capabilities built in, such as Windows 10 and Apple or Android smartphones.

Figure 6.11 shows how these three factors can work together to verify user identities for authentication:

Figure 6.11 – A diagram of MFA

Now that we understand the concept of MFA and what is required to verify a user's identity for authentication, let's discuss how MFA can be used within the Azure AD MFA solution. In the following sections, we will go through how Azure AD MFA works, how it is licensed and configured, and how it is enabled and enforced for administrators and users.

How does Azure AD MFA work?

In the previous section, we discussed the overall concept of MFA. Now, we will go through how MFA works within the embedded Azure AD MFA solution in Azure AD. Conceptually, it is the same as it requires two factors to authenticate. The important things to note within Azure AD MFA are what licenses you need for users, how it is configured and enforced, and the handling of MFA for administrators and standard users.

We will start with the licensing of Azure AD MFA before getting into the technical aspects of configuring, enabling, and enforcing MFA.

Which licenses include Azure AD MFA?

Microsoft has made many changes to Azure AD MFA over the past few years, as MFA has become more popular for use within companies. Different levels of Azure AD MFA are included with both the Free and Premium Azure AD licenses.

Azure AD Free is standard with any Azure account or standalone Microsoft 365 account. This allows anyone to utilize Azure AD MFA for their personal accounts or users on Azure at no cost. This allows the protection of cloud identities and cloud resources on Azure using MFA. The limitations of the Azure AD Free license are that it does not have the advanced identity protection features regarding conditional access and user risk that are part of the Azure AD Premium license.

Azure AD Premium licenses are recommended for company use. The Premium licenses provide advanced identity and access management security solutions that allow the protection of identities. In addition, Premium licenses are required to utilize Azure AD for hybrid identity. When subscribing to an Azure AD Premium P1 or P2 license, Azure AD MFA is a fully licensed feature and can be used with conditional access policies. Azure AD Premium P2 licenses are required for Azure AD Identity Protection and Privileged Identity Management. Conditional Access policies, Azure AD Identity Protection, and Privileged Identity Management will be discussed, in more detail, in *Chapter 7, Describing the Identity Protection and Governance Capabilities of Azure AD*.

Azure AD MFA is available with any Azure subscription to enable, assign, and enforce global administrators. Enforcing Azure AD MFA for all global administrators should always be the first step of how to utilize MFA within your company.

Now, let's discuss the authentication methods that will be used for Azure AD MFA.

Azure authentication methods

As a company, you have the option to determine which authentication methods will be utilized within Azure AD as the factors for MFA. The first factor of a password does not change. The additional Azure authentication method is the second factor that will be used for Azure AD MFA verification.

As an administrator, you need to determine the methods that are going to be used for the second factor. The options are shown in *Figure 6.12* and can be found in the MFA service settings. In the next section, we will go through these steps in further detail:

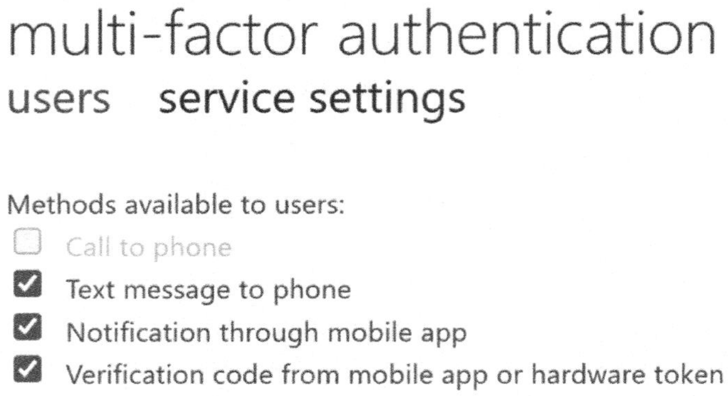

multi-factor authentication
users   service settings

Methods available to users:

☐ Call to phone
☑ Text message to phone
☑ Notification through mobile app
☑ Verification code from mobile app or hardware token

Figure 6.12 – Azure AD MFA authentication methods

The call to phone feature is only enabled if the company administrator has populated a phone number in the global directory for users. Otherwise, this option is not available as an option, as indicated in *Figure 6.12*. The other options of sending a text message to a phone, receiving a notification through a mobile app, and sending a verification code from a mobile app or hardware token are still available to select. Selecting all of these options will allow users to choose which option they would like as their preferred second factor for Azure AD MFA when they enroll. We will discuss this, in further detail, in the section on implementing and managing MFA settings.

In the next section, we will go through an exercise of how to configure Azure AD MFA and the user enrollment process.

Configuring Azure AD MFA

So far, we have been discussing the ways that Azure AD MFA can be used for identity verification and protection. This section will step through the configuration of Azure AD MFA. Before implementing and utilizing MFA within your company, it is important to let the users know how the process of authentication will change. Microsoft has provided templates that can be used as a communication plan at `https://www.microsoft.com/en-us/download/details.aspx?id=57600&WT.mc_id=rss_alldownloads_all`.

Configuring for Azure AD MFA is a two-step process. The first step is for the IT administrator to configure and enable users for MFA, and the second step is for the users to complete the enrollment process to enforce Azure AD MFA. Let's go through the steps that administrators will complete to enable users for Azure AD MFA.

Enabling users for Azure AD MFA

After the IT department has communicated with users that MFA is going to be utilized to protect and verify user identities, users need to be configured and enabled to enroll in Azure AD MFA. This starts within Azure AD, in the list of users:

1. Navigate to **Azure Active Directory** and select **Users** to display all users, as shown in *Figure 6.13*:

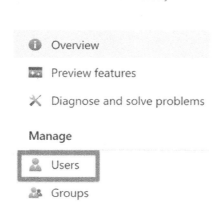

Figure 6.13 – The Azure AD manage all users option

2. Next, select **Per-user MFA**, as shown in *Figure 6.14*:

Figure 6.14 – Selecting Per-user MFA

3. The Azure AD MFA portal opens. Here, you can select all users to be enabled for Azure AD MFA or specific users only. *Figure 6.15* shows the list of users and an option to select all users to be enabled for Azure AD MFA. If there are already users that are utilizing or have MFA enabled, you will need to select **Manage user settings**:

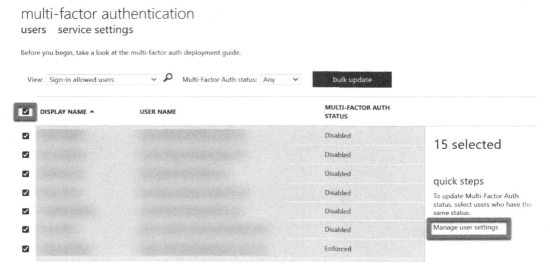

Figure 6.15 – Selecting all users in Azure AD

4. When selecting **Manage user settings**, a new tile opens where you can require current MFA users to re-enter their information for additional verification. *Figure 6.16* shows the options for selecting users to provide their contact methods again and restoring MFA on all remembered devices. Select **save** to continue:

Manage user settings

☑ Require selected users to provide contact methods again

☐ Delete all existing app passwords generated by the selected users

☑ Restore multi-factor authentication on all remembered devices

Figure 6.16 – Manage user settings

5. If Azure AD MFA currently does not have any users enrolled, navigating back and selecting all users or only a single user allows us to immediately **Enable** Azure AD MFA for those users, as shown in *Figure 6.17*:

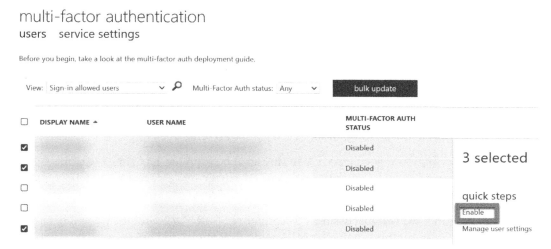

Figure 6.17 – Enabling Azure AD MFA

6. Selecting **Enable** will open up a tile that will provide you with a link to the deployment guide if you have not already reviewed it. This also provides the communication template links, as discussed earlier. Once you are ready, select **enable multi-factor auth** to enable the selected users, as shown in *Figure 6.18*:

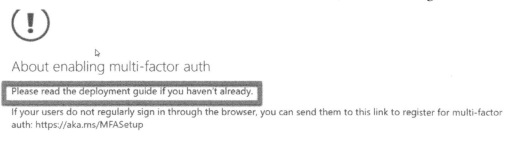

Figure 6.18 – Enabling MFA

As an administrator, you have completed the steps for enabling and enforcing Azure AD MFA. In the next section, we will add user enrollment requirements to complete the process.

User enrollment in Azure AD MFA

Once the company administrators have enabled or enforced MFA for users, the next step is for the process to be completed by the users. This is where the communication plan is very important. The company needs the users in the company to understand the importance of completing these steps to protect their identities, their personal information, and the assets of the company. The process that a user is going to experience whether they were set to enabled or enforced is no different.

Additional information regarding MFA settings can be found at `https://docs.microsoft.com/en-us/azure/active-directory/authentication/howto-mfa-mfasettings#remember-multi-factor-authentication`.

In the next section, we will discuss how to configure SSPR. Additionally, we will discuss how the verification methods between MFA and SSPR show similarities and differences.

Configuring and deploying SSPR

SSPR is helpful for both the user and the administrators. SSPR saves time because passwords can be reset without a phone call to a support team. There is the convenience of a user being able to change their password when they forget them. It also helps you from a security perspective if a user believes that their password has been compromised.

With this convenience, there is also a level of risk. With SSPR enabled, it allows someone that has obtained user credentials to potentially change a user password and lock them out of their account. Therefore, it is important that the configuration and deployment of SSPR protect you from this taking place. This section is going to go through the steps and best practices for configuring SSPR.

To access the SSPR configuration, navigate to **Azure AD | Users**. Within the **Users** tile, select **Password reset**, as shown in *Figure 6.19*:

Figure 6.19 – Password reset

The following steps will go through the configuration settings of SSPR:

1. Once you navigate to **Password reset**, you will determine whether to assign to all users or selected users only. We will choose all users and select **Save**, as shown in *Figure 6.20*:

Figure 6.20 – SSPR enabled for all users

2. The next step is to configure the **Authentication methods** setting. The best practice is to request more than one method to reset the user password. These include the configuration and selection of security questions to use for resetting passwords. The options are shown in *Figure 6.21*. Configure these options, and select **Save**:

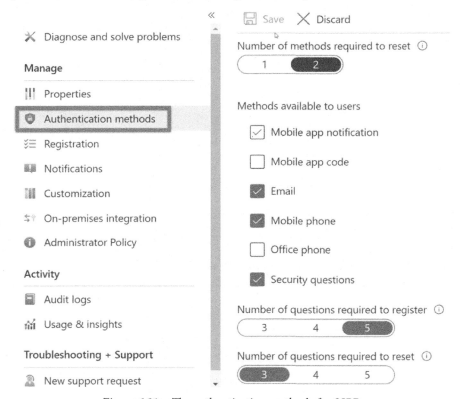

Figure 6.21 – The authentication methods for SSPR

SSPR is now configured for all users. In the same manner as enrolling in Azure AD MFA, users will be required to provide and enter the information required for SSPR before they are able to use this service.

It is important to note that there is similar information that is used for both MFA and SSPR. Both utilize text codes, phone calls, and can utilize the mobile authenticator app. Security questions are only used for SSPR and not for MFA. Email verification codes are used for SSPR and can only be used for MFA in circumstances where security policies prohibit mobile phones within a facility.

Now we have gained an understanding of the process of configuring users for Azure AD MFA and SSPR. The next section will discuss how MFA is used to protect identities within modern authentication methods.

Modern authentication

The goal of a company should be to move further away from the traditional authentication methods of just using passwords and adopt the modern authentication techniques as they move toward an optimal identity and access management infrastructure. For many companies, implementing MFA, SSO, and SSPR are the first steps. Microsoft's Azure AD security defaults provide the best practices in modern authentication implementation to get you started:

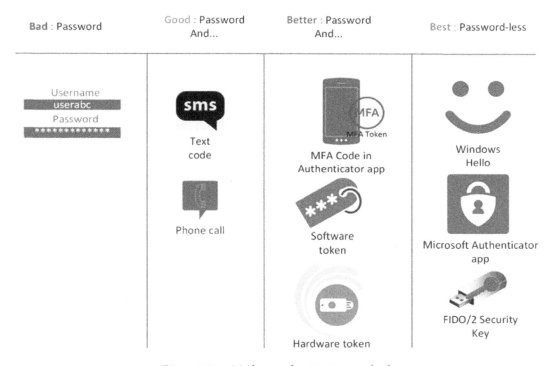

Figure 6.22 – Modern authentication methods

The goal of modern authentication is to decrease the amount that a company relies on passwords as its primary source of authentication.

Windows Hello

Windows Hello for Business is popular with Windows 10 users. Windows Hello is a biometric authentication technique that utilizes facial recognition with the camera of your Windows 10 device. Windows Hello can be enabled on Windows 10 devices for this form of authentication. Windows Hello for Business can be used by a company to create groups of users, where this type of authentication will be enforced on joined Windows 10 devices in Azure AD:

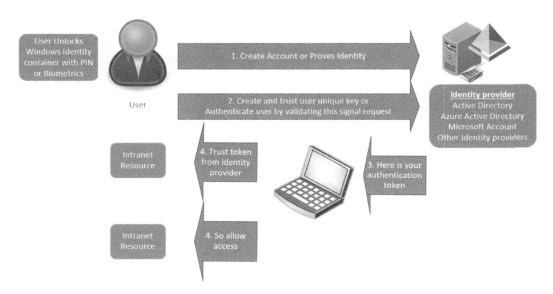

Figure 6.23 – The Window Hello workflow

Windows Hello is considered a password-less authentication method that utilizes MFA. Although you are only using facial recognition as the user to log in to your device, when you register your device for Windows Hello, you are required to enter a PIN. This PIN is encrypted in the **trusted platform module** (**TPM**) within the device as part of the overall BitLocker encryption. When a user authenticates with the device camera, it calls that encrypted PIN to verify that it matches the user that registered that device for Windows Hello. Azure AD then authorizes access to the device. *Figure 8.2* shows the steps of this process. These steps are transparent to the user when accessing their Windows 10 devices.

Deploying and managing password protection

Azure AD Password Protection is used to configure certain parameters to avoid brute-force or dictionary attacks on user identities. These attacks are accomplished by an attacker sending multiple requests with a username and multiple passwords to attempt to find the password being used and gain access. Setting up a threshold of how many attempts before being locked out followed by the lockout duration will stop these attacks. In addition, administrators can identify passwords that are not allowed to be used within the Azure AD tenant. Microsoft also has a list of passwords that they might block when attempting to use them.

Once Azure AD password protection has been configured, it can be set to be enforced across the company or simply set up as an initial audit to gauge its effectiveness. *Figure 6.24* shows the Azure AD **Password protection** tile and the fields that can be configured. This can be accessed in the Azure portal by searching for Azure AD password protection:

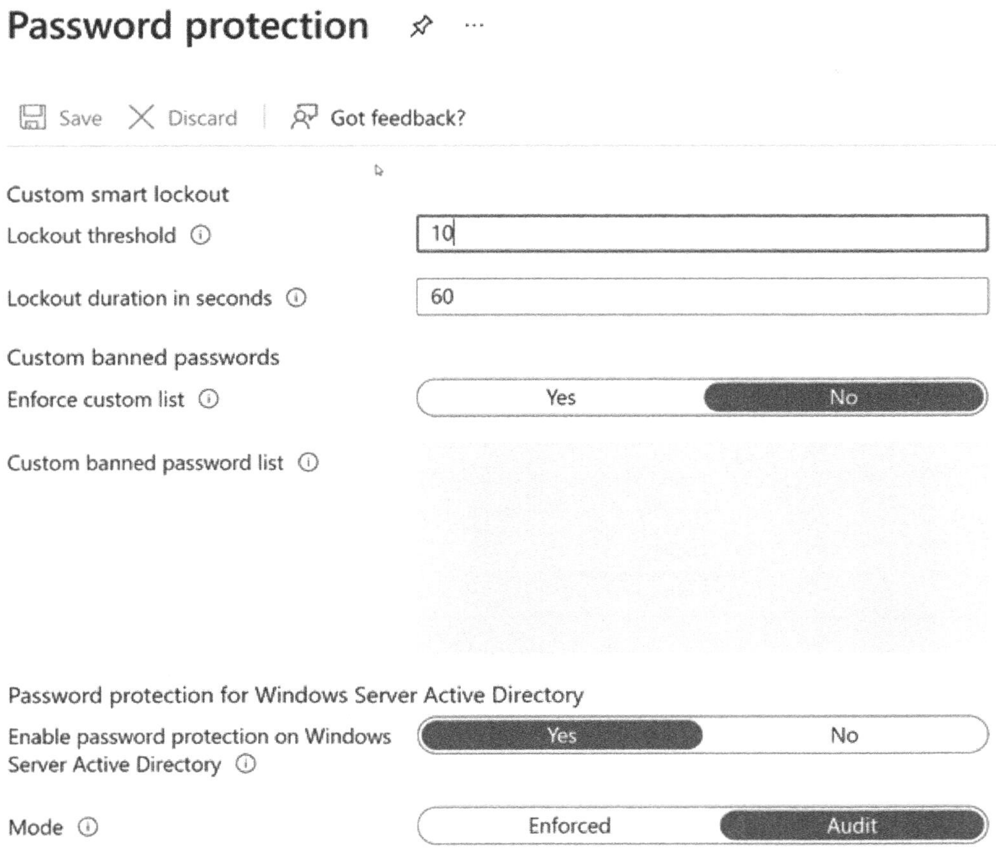

Figure 6.24 – The Azure AD Password protection settings

As stated earlier, enforcing Azure AD password protection can protect user identities from brute-force and dictionary attacks. The final section of this chapter will explore the use of security defaults.

Planning and implementing security defaults

Microsoft provides security defaults within Azure AD to assist companies that are new to Azure AD and Microsoft's cloud in protecting identities. In new tenants, security defaults are already turned on and in place, so there isn't any planning or implementation required. However, there are situations where security defaults will need to be turned off as more advanced identity protection solutions are enabled, such as Conditional Access policies. To access the security defaults, navigate to Azure AD and scroll down under **Manage** in the left-hand menu to **Properties**. Then, scroll down in the **Properties** tile to **Manage Security defaults**, as shown in *Figure 6.25*:

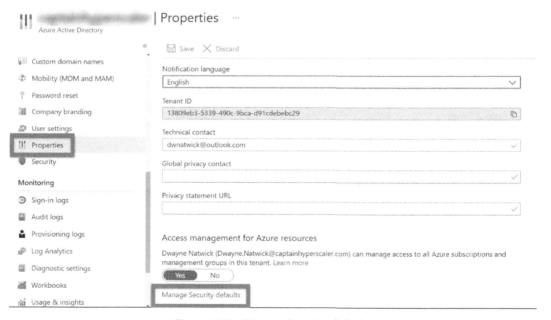

Figure 6.25 – Manage Security defaults

Security defaults provide basic identity security settings to the entire tenant and are very helpful to protect a company. These settings include the following:

- Requiring all users to register for Azure AD MFA
- Requiring administrators to perform MFA
- Blocking legacy authentication protocols
- Requiring users to perform MFA when necessary
- Protecting privileged activities such as access to the Azure portal

Additional information regarding security defaults can be found at `https://docs.microsoft.com/en-us/azure/active-directory/fundamentals/concept-fundamentals-security-defaults`.

The next section will provide a summary of what you have learned in this chapter.

Summary

In this chapter, we covered details about how Azure AD can be used for identity and access management. We discussed the synchronization of identities through a hybrid infrastructure with Azure AD Connect. Additionally, we discussed how to protect identities using the modern authentication concepts of MFA, SSPR, Windows Hello, Azure password protection, and security defaults.

In the next chapter, we will further discuss identity and access protection and governance in Azure AD with Conditional Access policies, Azure Identity Protection, Entitlement Management, and Privileged Identity Management.

7
Describing the Identity Protection and Governance Capabilities of Azure AD

The previous chapter covered **Azure Active Directory** (**Azure AD**) and how it is used to manage and protect identities in cloud and hybrid infrastructures. In this chapter, you will gain more understanding about identity and access protection and governance in Azure AD with Conditional Access policies, Azure Identity Protection, entitlement management, and Privileged Identity Management.

In this chapter, we're going to cover the following main topics:

- Describing Identity Governance
- Describing entitlement and access reviews
- Describing the capabilities of **Privileged Identity Management (PIM)**
- Describing Azure AD Identity Protection and Conditional Access policies

Technical requirements

In this chapter, we will begin to explore configuring a tenant for use with Microsoft 365 and Azure. There will be exercises that require access to Azure AD. If you have not yet created the trial licenses for Microsoft 365, please follow the directions provided within *Chapter 1*, *Preparing for Your Microsoft Exam*.

Describing Identity Governance

Identity Governance is the full lifecycle monitoring and management of users in the company directory. This includes when they are first created or invited to Azure AD, their various roles within the company, and when they leave the company and no longer require access. *Figure 7.1* outlines this lifecycle:

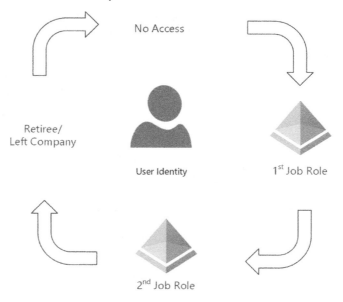

Figure 7.1 – Identity Governance lifecycle

There are four levels to the Identity Governance lifecycle and the user identity:

- No access
- 1st job role
- 2nd job role (and subsequent job roles)
- Retiree/Left company

The next section will discuss how entitlements can be used for managing the Identity Governance lifecycle.

Describing entitlement and access reviews

Entitlement management provides this governance through the creation of catalogs and access packages, which you can build for groups of users. Entitlement management is found under **Identity Governance** within Azure AD. *Figure 7.2* shows the **Getting started** tile of this service and where **Entitlement management** is found in the menu:

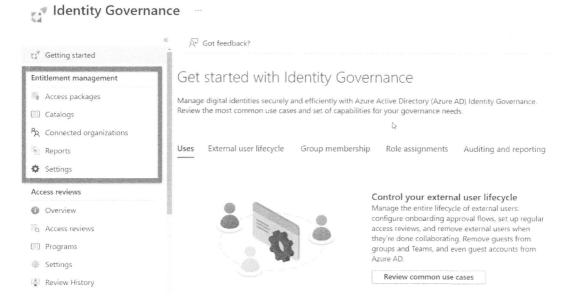

Figure 7.2 – Identity Governance services

Let's discuss how catalogs and access packages work to provide this governance.

Catalogs

The first step in entitlement management is to create catalogs. These catalogs can be created within the Identity Governance services in Azure AD under the **Entitlement management** menu, as shown in *Figure 7.3*:

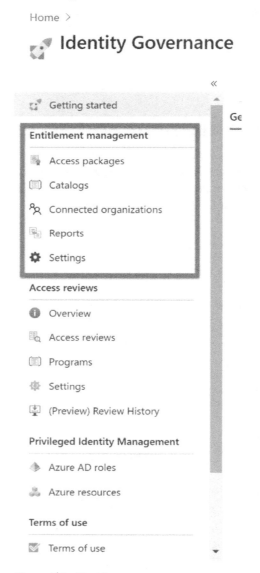

Figure 7.3 – Entitlement management menu

Catalogs are a collection of users and groups, applications, and SharePoint sites. To create these catalogs, you must be assigned the Identity Governance Administrator or Global Administrator role. Previously, the User Administrator role was authorized to create these catalogs, but that is currently being phased out. In the planning, implementing, and managing entitlements sections, we will go through the steps to create catalogs. Let's define each of the areas that make up this catalog:

- **Users and groups** are assigned to the catalogs in order to access the applications and sites that are within the catalog. These users and groups can include internal members and external users. The ability to create catalogs with internal and external users allows us to use entitlements for project-based access or other applications, such as branch offices and departmental assignments.

- **Applications** are the enterprise and cloud applications that are registered through the steps that were completed in *Chapter 10, Describing Threat Protection with Microsoft 365 Defender*. The applications that are added to the catalog provide the users and groups assigned with authorization to use these applications.

- **SharePoint sites** can be added to the catalog. These sites can be a project-based created internal SharePoint site, a file share site on SharePoint, or any SharePoint URL that you determine should be assigned to the catalog. Multiple sites can be added to a single catalog.

Once these three areas are configured, we have our catalog prepared and ready to be assigned. We will go through the configuration process in the *implementing entitlements* section of this chapter.

The next section will discuss the next step of entitlement management, which is the access package.

Access packages

As discussed in the previous section, the catalogs define the groups and teams, applications, and SharePoint sites within Identity Governance. Creating a catalog does not establish access to these catalogs. You must go through the creation of access packages to approve and allow access to these catalogs.

When creating an access package, at a minimum, you define the catalog that the access package governs, how requests are handled, and the lifecycle of the access package, as shown in *Figure 7.4*:

Figure 7.4 – MCAS Cloud Discovery dashboard

Access reviews

Access reviews can manage the access lifecycle. Azure AD Identity Governance provides an overview dashboard showing the status of access reviews, as shown in *Figure 7.5*:

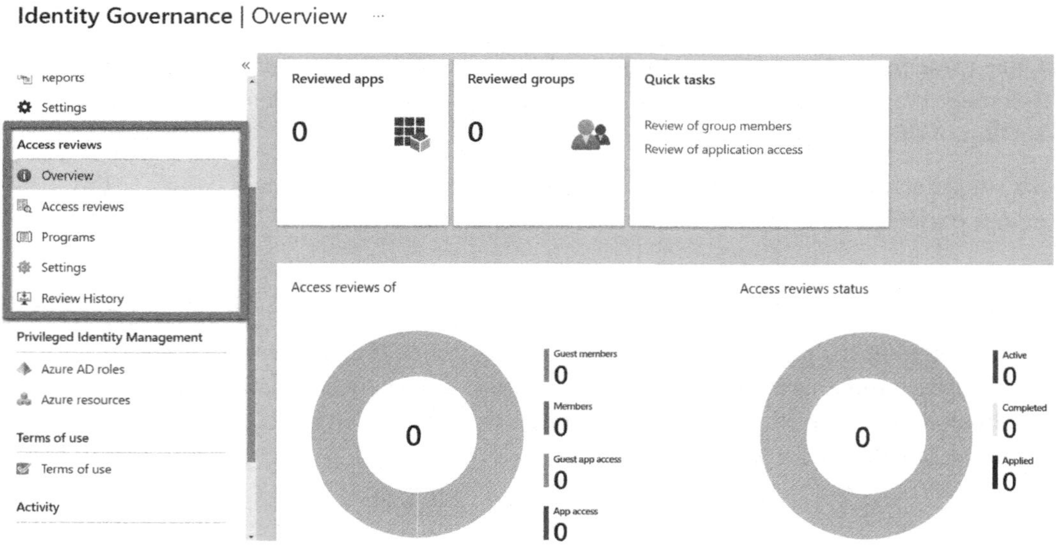

Figure 7.5 – Access review overview

Under the **Access reviews** menu, you can select **Access reviews** to configure an access review for guest users. You select **+ New access review** to create your guest user access review. The tile will open to configure the access review for guest users. *Figure 7.6* shows this tile and how to configure the access review for guest users:

Home > Identity Governance >

New access review   ...

| Review type | Reviews | Settings | Review + Create |

Schedule an access review to ensure the right people have the right access to access packages, groups, apps, and privileged roles.
Learn more

Select what to review *   Teams + Groups ⌄

Select review scope *   ● All Microsoft 365 groups with guest users
                                ○ Select Teams + groups

Group   + Select group(s) to exclude

Select user scope *   ● Guest users only
                                ○ All users ⓘ

Next: Reviews

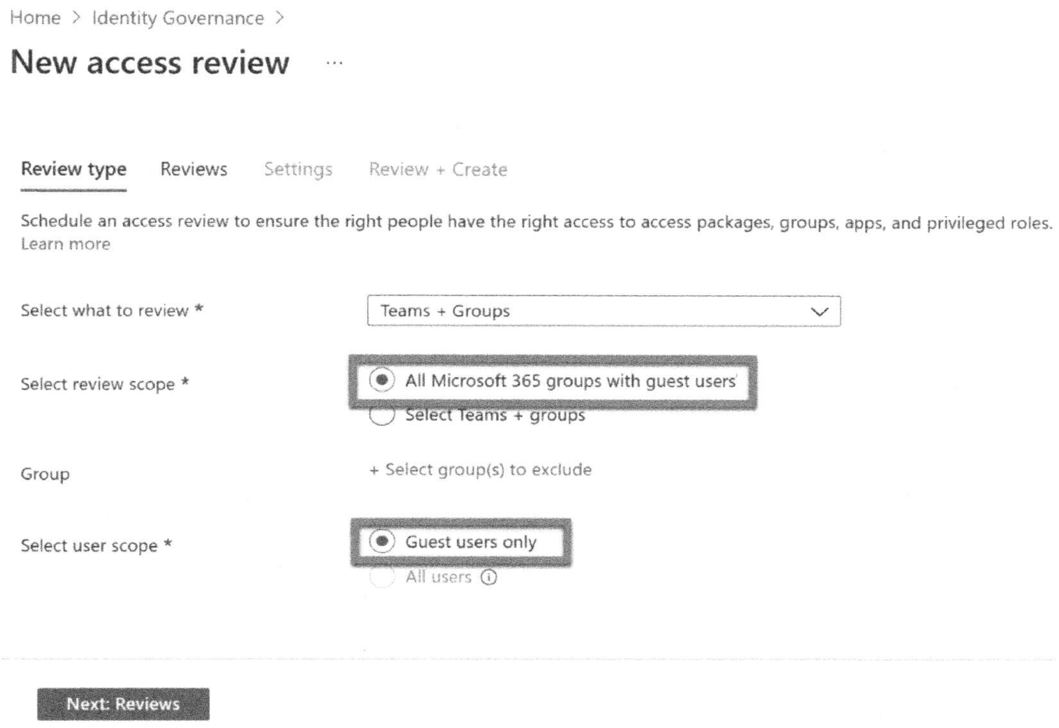

Figure 7.6 – Guest user access review

The next tile is where you configure who reviews and approves access, how often access will be reviewed, and when access will expire. This is shown in *Figure 7.7*:

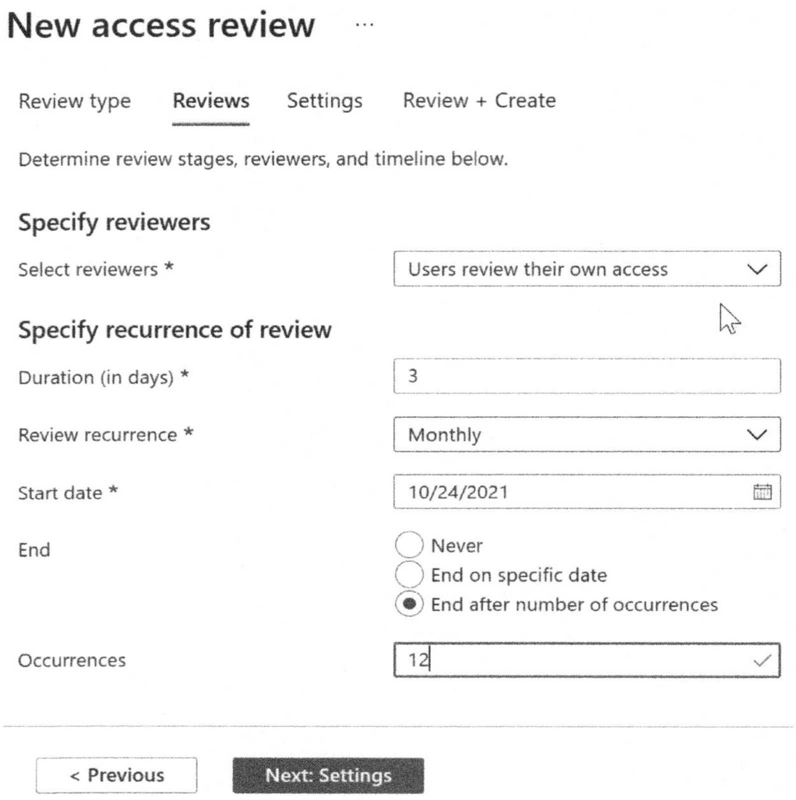

Figure 7.7 – Review settings

Finally, you will configure the settings for how the review will take place and what happens when the guest user responds or does not respond. This is shown in *Figure 7.8*:

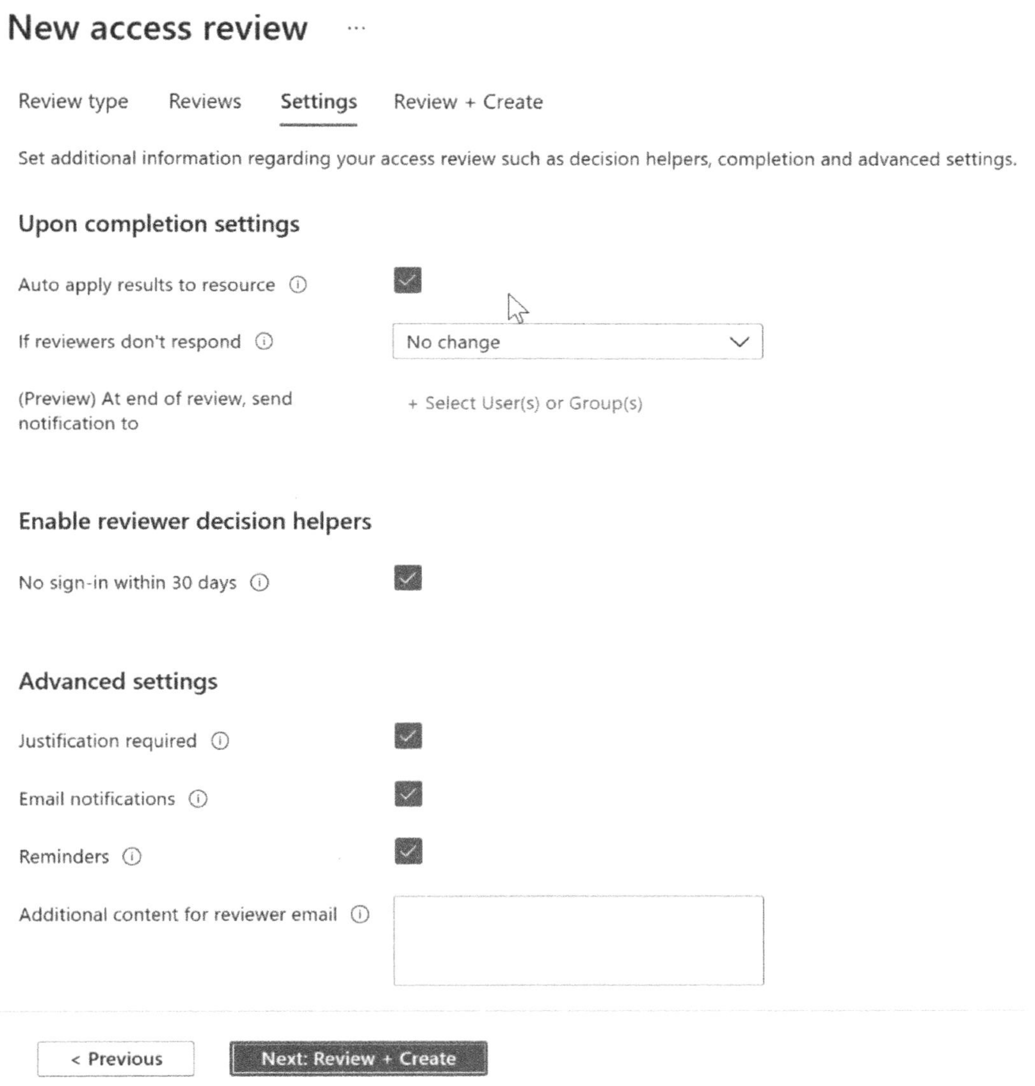

New access review   ⋯

Review type   Reviews   **Settings**   Review + Create

Set additional information regarding your access review such as decision helpers, completion and advanced settings.

Upon completion settings

Auto apply results to resource ⓘ   ☑

If reviewers don't respond ⓘ | No change   ⌄ |

(Preview) At end of review, send   + Select User(s) or Group(s)
notification to

Enable reviewer decision helpers

No sign-in within 30 days ⓘ   ☑

Advanced settings

Justification required ⓘ   ☑

Email notifications ⓘ   ☑

Reminders ⓘ   ☑

Additional content for reviewer email ⓘ   [   ]

[< Previous]   [Next: Review + Create]

Figure 7.8 – Settings for the access review

Once you review and create the access review, this will show as an access review in the list. It will also show within the access review overview dashboard as a guest member's review.

The next section will discuss how to manage Identity Governance for administrators with PIM.

Describing the capabilities of PIM

In the previous sections, we discussed Identity Governance as it pertains to user access packages for applications and SharePoint sites. A major area of Identity Governance that we need to manage is privileged access based on administrative user accounts. In this book, we have identified administrator roles necessary to manage services within Azure AD. As we continue to add and activate these administrative roles within our tenant, we begin to increase the attack surface that someone that gains unauthorized access to a compromised account may have elevated privileges.

As identity and access administrators, it is our duty to protect and defend this layer through utilizing the concepts of zero-trust and the principle of least privilege to assign and manage these administrator accounts. You should have a clear strategy with defined job tasks for every administrator user account to plan for the proper assignment of these roles. This strategy should include meeting with stakeholders and discussing the roles that each department member requires to complete their job tasks. In addition, you should be monitoring the activity of these accounts and verifying the continued requirement for users to have these privileged access roles.

To enforce the concepts of zero-trust, you have the capability to assign Conditional Access policies to these accounts. This will be discussed in the *Describing Azure AD Identity Protection and Conditional Access policies* section of this chapter. To address and protect privileged assignments, Azure AD provides PIM within the Identity Governance solutions.

PIM provides just-in-time privileged access to users. Since users are only provided active administrator roles for a short window of time, this reduces the attack surface and potential for these user accounts to cause-exposure to privileged access from an attack. PIM provides an approval and justification process for activating privileged role assignments, which includes notifications when a role is activated and an audit trail of these activations.

PIM requires an Azure AD Premium P2 license. To assign PIM to member accounts, each user must have this license. However, for guest users that require privileged access with PIM, five guests can be assigned PIM roles for every one Azure AD Premium P2 license that you have in your tenant.

PIM can be accessed directly by searching for `Privileged Identity Management` or can be found in the Azure AD Identity Governance tile, as shown in *Figure 7.9*:

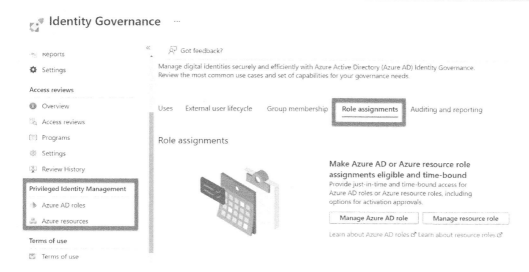

Figure 7.9 – PIM within Identity Governance services

Let's discuss how to configure PIM and assign roles to users.

Configuring PIM for Azure AD roles and Azure resources

In the previous section, we discussed planning role assignments and defined PIM. In this section, we will discuss how to configure PIM for Azure AD roles and resources:

1. Navigate in the search bar to **Privileged Identity Management**. Under the **Quick start** menu, select **Manage**, as shown in *Figure 7.10*:

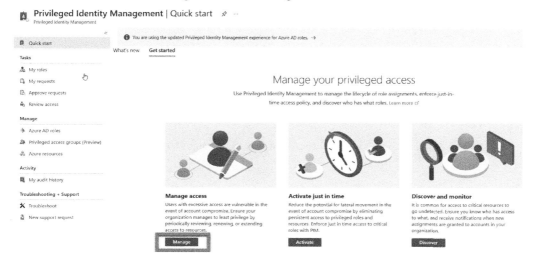

Figure 7.10 – Manage PIM access

2.　Select **Roles** under **Manage** in the menu bar and then select **+ Add assignments** to create a new PIM role assignment:

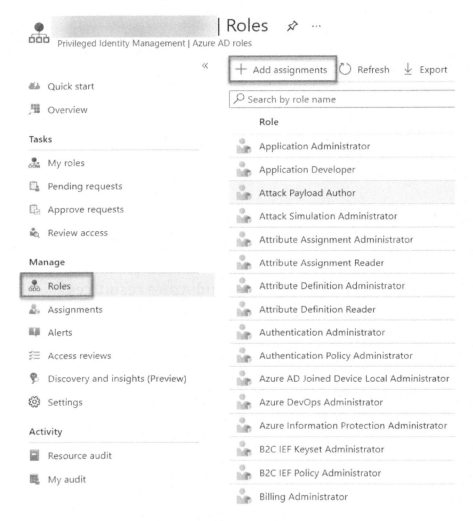

Figure 7.11 – Add a new PIM assignment

3. In the **Add assignments** tile, choose the **Select role** dropdown and find **Privileged Role Administrator**:

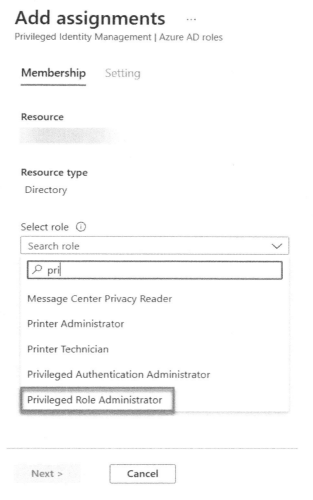

Figure 7.12 – Select the Privileged Role Administrator role

4.   Select **No members selected** under **Select members** and choose a user or group to assign this role:

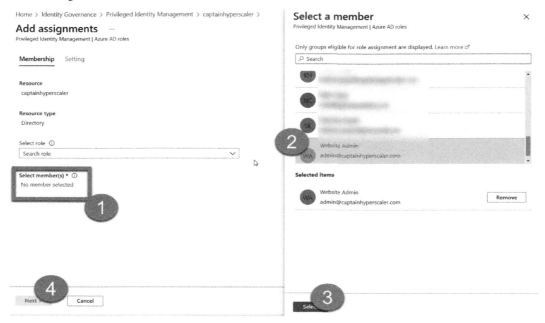

Figure 7.13 – Select members for role assignment

5. Select **Next** to navigate to the next step in the configuration process:

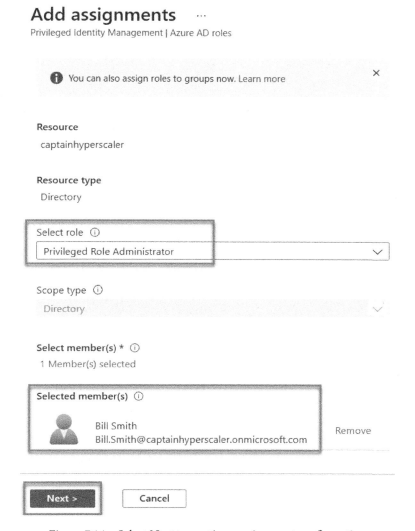

Figure 7.14 – Select Next to continue assignment configuration

6. On the next tile, verify that **Eligible** is set as **Assignment type** and deselect the **Permanently eligible** checkbox. Leave the assignment start and end dates as the default values, as shown in *Figure 7.15*. Select **Assign**:

Figure 7.15 – Role assignment settings

7. The new role assignment will appear in the **Assignments** tile under the **Eligible assignments** tab. To change this eligible assignment to active, choose **Update**, as the arrow shows in *Figure 7.16*:

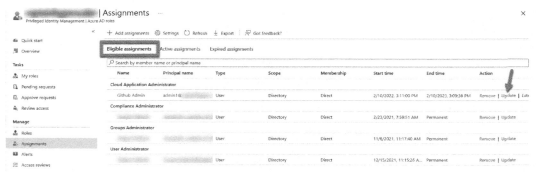

Figure 7.16 – Update role assignment

8. In the **Membership** settings, change the **Assignment type** dropdown to **Active**, deselect **Permanently assigned**, set an assignment end date, and provide a justification. Click **Save** to save the changes:

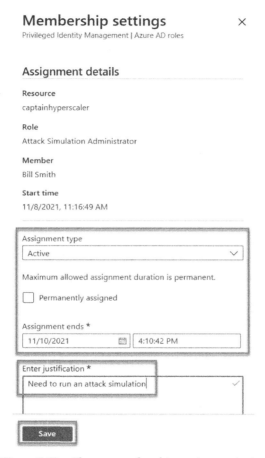

Figure 7.17 – Change membership settings to Active

9. On the **Assignments** tile, navigate to the **Active assignments** tab and you will see the now active role assignment for your user with the end date that you set:

Figure 7.18 – Active assignments

10. You have now created a **Privileged Role** assignment and activated it within PIM.

As we continue to secure our identities with security and governance features, such as multi-factor authentication, Conditional Access policies, Identity Governance, and PIM solutions, it is important to make sure that we do not mistakenly get locked out of Azure AD. To protect against potential lockout, and to make sure that access is still available in a potential emergency situation, you should configure at least two emergency access or *break-glass* accounts. These accounts are accounts of high privilege with access at the level of a Global Administrator. These accounts are not protected with multi-factor authentication so that they can gain access quickly to resources when other administrator accounts cannot gain access. The use of these accounts should be limited to this scenario and the credentials should be locked away until the time that they are absolutely needed.

Break-glass accounts are member accounts that are tied directly to the Azure AD tenant. Therefore, they can be utilized in situations where federated identity providers are being utilized for authentication and there is an outage to that identity provider. Other use cases would be that the Global Administrator has lost access to their MFA device to verify their identity, a Global Administrator has left the company and it is needed to delete that account, and a storm has taken down cellular services and you cannot verify with MFA.

Additional information on emergency access or *break-glass* accounts can be found at this link: `https://docs.microsoft.com/en-us/azure/active-directory/roles/security-emergency-access`.

In the next section, we will discuss how to enforce zero-trust to identity and access management with Conditional Access policies and Azure AD Identity Protection.

Describing Azure AD Identity Protection and Conditional Access policies

Conditional Access policies enforce additional verification actions based on a signal that a user or device may be potentially compromised. The foundation of Conditional Access policies is the zero-trust methodology. So, before we discuss planning and implementing Conditional Access, let's discuss the main points of zero-trust.

Zero-trust methodology

As we have moved as companies to using cloud providers, such as Microsoft, the responsibility for securing the physical infrastructure for cloud services is provided by these cloud providers. If we are adhering to a defense in depth security posture, Microsoft is responsible for the physical first layer of defense, making the first layer that we are responsible for as a company the identity and access layer. Therefore, the statements *identity is the new perimeter* and *identity is the new control plane* have become extremely important in securing a cloud infrastructure. So, the concept of the zero-trust methodology becomes the core concept that a company should adhere to when securing identity and access.

The **zero-trust methodology** is a process of continuously requiring someone on the network to verify that they are who they say they are. The concept seems to be straightforward and simple, but if you were to constantly ask users to enter their username and password, they would get frustrated. To avoid this frustration, zero-trust implementation utilizes various signals that alert potential anomalous behavior, leaked credentials, or insecure devices that trigger the need for a user to re-verify their identity. These signals lead to a decision on what is needed to provide access to applications, files, or websites. This workflow is shown in *Figure 7.19*:

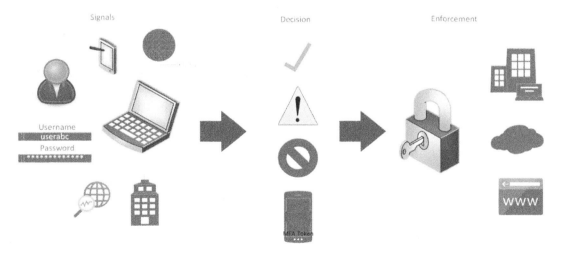

Figure 7.19 – Diagram of the Zero-Trust model workflow

In the next sections, we will describe each of these components of the workflow in more detail.

Signal

As stated in the previous section, the **signal** is the state that the user or device is in that triggers a potential need for a user to re-verify their identity. This state could be that the user has been identified to be at risk of having a compromised password, that they are at an IP address that has been flagged as vulnerable, or that their device is not compliant with current security patches. These are only a few examples of the signals that may be reviewed to trigger a decision to invoke the need for more information. Microsoft utilizes several tools within Azure and Microsoft 365 to identify the vulnerabilities and risks of users and devices that create these signals. Once a signal has been identified to require more information to verify a user's identity, then a decision is made as to what happens next.

Decision

As stated in the previous section, when a signal is triggered, a **decision** is made on what we are going to require or allow to provide access to the resources requested. There are several options here and this is where a company creates policies on how zero-trust is going to be handled depending on the resource requesting access. This could include a user re-verifying that they have not been compromised by requiring MFA before they are given access. The policies may limit or block access to that application entirely until the user or device changes the status or location that they are requesting access to. The least likely policy decision is to allow access if a user or device is seen to have an at-risk status. The allow access decision is generally used in a policy that identifies a user or device as being in a trusted location. Once the decision is made within the policy, the policy then enforces the workflow.

Enforcement

The **enforcement** is the action of the decision based on the user or device signal as defined by the company policy. As stated in the previous section, there are multiple enforcements that could take place. The level of access and enforcement of zero-trust is usually dependent on the application and information being accessed. If the application contains highly sensitive information that the company cannot have exposed, the level of zero-trust enforcement should be at the highest level, by either blocking access, limiting the level of access, or requiring additional verification from the user, such as MFA and/or a password reset. The ability of a company to identify the risks and vulnerabilities of the users and determine a plan for protecting access to their applications is a critical factor to the success of implementing a zero-trust model for identity and access management.

As stated previously, the principles of zero-trust are an important aspect of protecting access to applications within a cloud and hybrid infrastructure. The decreased access and ability to protect physical access and the increased access to applications from various locations across public internet connections require a company to do their due diligence in identifying the various scenarios that users may request access to company resources and the numerous devices that they may use to access. Policies that identify the potential vulnerabilities and threats that can make a correct decision on how to enforce zero-trust will protect the company while maintaining a positive user experience.

Conditional Access policies

The solution within Microsoft that enforces the zero-trust methodology is **Conditional Access**. As you will notice in *Figure 7.20*, the flow from signal to decision to enforcement is the same. The policies that we determine for our company are what then enforce these Conditional Access requirements:

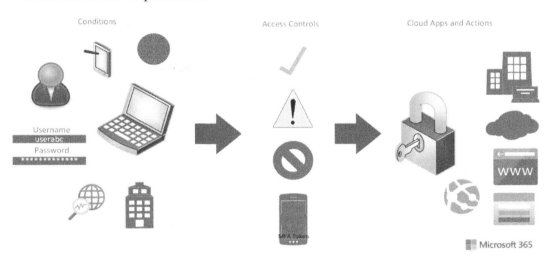

Figure 7.20 – Conditional Access workflow

A key aspect of putting Conditional Access policies in place is to properly plan and understand how they could potentially affect the user experience. There is a balance that a company should attempt to maintain between the enforcement of policies to secure and protect data, and the ability of a user to have access to the applications and data that they need to be effective at their required tasks. In the next sections, we will go through the steps to plan, test, and implement Conditional Access policies in your company.

Preparation and planning

Before we can create a Conditional Access policy, we need to make sure that we can. There are a couple of areas that we need to address for implementing this solution: licensing and security defaults. For licensing, Conditional Access policy features are available with an Azure AD Premium P1 level license. This level of Azure AD licensing is included with Microsoft 365 Business Premium, Office 365 E3/A3, Microsoft 365 E3/A3, Office 365 E5/A5, and Microsoft 365 E5/A5. These licenses must be assigned to the users that we are attempting to enforce Conditional Access policies for. The full list of licensing requirements can be found at this link: `https://docs.microsoft.com/azure/active-directory/conditional-access/overview`.

In addition to having the proper licenses, we will be required to turn off the Azure AD security defaults. Security defaults are turned on when we create our Azure AD tenant that provides a baseline level of protection to require, for example, users to enroll in MFA, enforce MFA for administrators, and block the use of legacy authentication for applications. Security defaults were discussed in *Chapter 6, Describing the Authentication and Access Management Capabilities of Azure AD*. In that chapter, we were verifying that they were enabled. To be able to implement Conditional Access, navigate back to security defaults and turn them off. When you do this, there will be reasons that appear, and you will see the selection for using Conditional Access policies.

Once we have proper licensing assigned and security defaults turned off, we can begin our planning for Conditional Access policies. Some commonly used Conditional Access policies can be found in the Microsoft documentation at this link: `https://docs.microsoft.com/azure/active-directory/conditional-access/plan-conditional-access`. The key to planning for Conditional Access is to understand the groups of users that are accessing company applications and data, the devices that they are using to access those applications and data, the locations that they may be accessing those applications and data from, and the applications being used to access the company data.

Azure AD Identity Protection

Azure AD Identity Protection provides additional capabilities within Azure AD to monitor user activity and recognize, through Microsoft's machine learning capabilities, anomalous and suspicious activity on user accounts. *Figure 7.21* shows how to search and access Azure AD Identity Protection within the Azure portal:

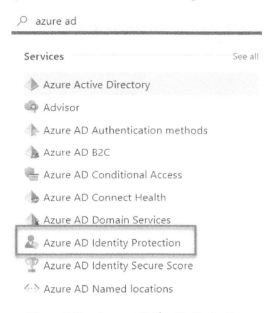

Figure 7.21 – Azure AD Identity Protection

Azure AD Identity Protection provides feedback in two areas: user risk and sign-in risk. Both are related to user behavior, but it is important to understand the differences between them:

- User risk is an activity that pertains directly to a user. This is primarily seen in the form of potentially leaked credentials, or something identified through threat intelligence attack patterns being targeted on a particular user.

- Sign-in risk identifies that a request for authentication might not be requested by the authorized identity owner. Some examples of a sign-in risk would include login attempts from anonymous IP addresses, atypical travel, suspicious browsers, and IP addresses linked with malware, among others.

- Additional information and examples can be found at this link: `https://docs.microsoft.com/en-us/azure/active-directory/identity-protection/concept-identity-protection-risks`. It is important to identify the difference between user risk and sign-in risk for the exam.

- *Figure 7.22* shows the **Protect** and **Report** menus of Azure AD Identity Protection. We will discuss reports in the next section. To protect against attackers gaining access to resources, policies can be put in place to block access or require additional verification when a user or sign-in is flagged at a certain risk level, low, medium, or high:

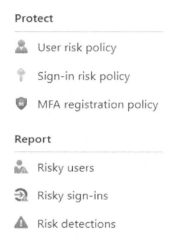

Figure 7.22 – Protect and Report in Azure AD Identity Protection

- These policies work in the same way as the Conditional Access policies that we discussed previously in this chapter. User and sign-in risk policies can be stand-alone policies within Azure AD Identity Protection or integrated into Conditional Access policies.

Once we have our protections in place, we also want to understand the level of risk for our users and sign-ins. In the final section of our chapter, we will look at how Azure AD Identity Protection can be used to monitor, investigate, and remediate risky users.

Monitoring, investigating, and remediating elevated risky users

If you are utilizing resources that are touching the internet, then someone is scanning and attempting to gain access to it. There is an abundance of bad actors that have automated tools to scan usernames and attempt to authenticate with common passwords. Azure AD Identity Protection utilizes the Microsoft Threat Intelligence database and machine learning tools to look for these threats, identify the users affected, and identify the type of threat that exists. This information feeds into the **Identity Protection | Overview** dashboard shown in *Figure 7.23*:

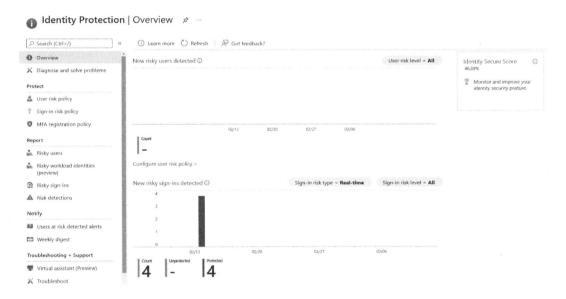

Figure 7.23 – Identity Protection dashboard

The **Report** section of the **Identity Protection** menu provides additional information on the users who are at risk, what their risk level is, and allows you to drill down and investigate the potential attacks that have taken place on those user accounts. *Figure 7.24* shows how you can view this information and select the user for more information:

Figure 7.24 – Risky user information

Once you open the details, you can view the basic information that provides the level of administrative roles that the user has, the status and level of risk, and when the last event took place. This information is shown in *Figure 7.25*:

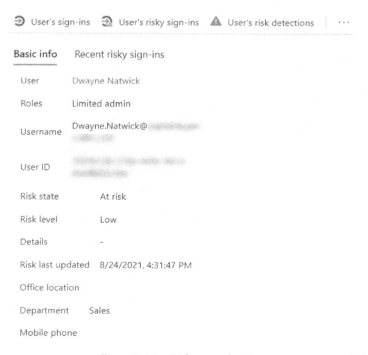

Figure 7.25 – Risky user details

Moving on to **Recent risky sign-ins**, this provides a deeper level of detailed information about the risk activity that took place. In *Figure 7.25*, you can see that although there was risk activity that took place, that attack failed. This explains why **Risk level** was set to **Low** for this user, even though they were attacked. This view also shows the IP address that was identified as the source of the attack, and scrolling to the right also shows the location that the IP address is associated with. If there was a Conditional Access policy applied to this user that was triggered by this event, that would also be reflected here. *Figure 7.26* shows the details of the application, status, date, and IP address for each of the risky user events:

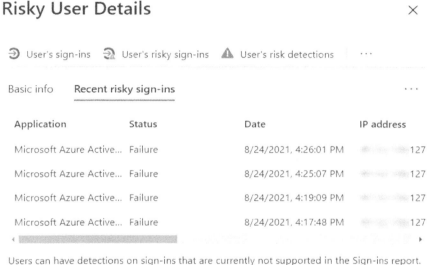

Figure 7.26 – Risky user sign-in details

Scrolling to the right provides additional details about the risk state, risk level, and whether Conditional Access policies apply to the event, as shown in *Figure 7.27*:

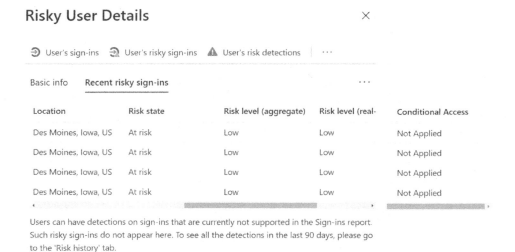

Figure 7.27 – Risky user sign-in risk level details

The final area to discuss is what we need to do to protect the user and our company once we have identified the user at risk. *Figure 7.28* shows the selection menu for actionable items for remediating this user. This includes resetting their password, confirming or dismissing that the user was compromised, blocking the user entirely, or taking additional steps to investigate in Azure Defender:

Figure 7.28 – Menu of remediation steps

Taking these steps will protect our Azure AD users, and also our company, from compromised identities.

In the next section, we will provide a summary of what you have learned in this chapter.

Summary

In this chapter, we covered details on identity and access protection and governance in Azure AD with Conditional Access policies, Azure Identity Protection, entitlement management, and PIM. We discussed the various Azure AD solutions that can govern and monitor identity and access for users and guests that require access to applications and sites, and administrator roles to manage services. In the next chapter, we will discuss the various security services and management capabilities within Azure.

Section 4: The Microsoft Security Solutions for Microsoft 365 and Azure

This section will focus on the security solutions that are available within Azure and Microsoft 365.

This part of the book comprises the following chapters:

8
Describing Basic Security Services and Management Capabilities in Azure

The previous chapter covered understanding about identity and access protection and governance in Azure AD with Conditional Access policies, Azure Identity Protection, entitlement management, and Privileged Identity Management. In this chapter, we will describe the various security services within Azure for network, compute, and data protection. This will include perimeter and application security services.

In this chapter, we're going to cover the following main topics:

- Describe network segmentation
- Describe Azure Network Security Groups
- Describe Azure DDoS protection
- Describe Azure Firewall and Web Application Firewall

- Describe secure remote management of virtual machines
- Describe Azure data encryption

Technical requirements

In this chapter, we will begin to explore configuring a tenant for use of solutions within Azure. There will be exercises that will require access to Azure. If you have not yet created the trial licenses for Microsoft 365 and a free trial of Azure, please follow the directions provided within *Chapter 1, Preparing for Your Microsoft Exam*.

Network segmentation

Chapter 2, Describing Security Methodologies, discussed the layers of a defense-in-depth security strategy. The physical layer is Microsoft's responsibility as the cloud provider. *Chapter 7, Describing the Identity Protection and Governance Capabilities of Azure AD*, described how to protect the identity and access layer. This chapter will discuss Azure solutions that will protect the perimeter, network, compute, application, and data layers.

Network segmentation provides a secure boundary between resources by placing these resources within separated network segments. As you begin to explore Azure security capabilities, it is important to understand components that are the foundation of networking in Azure. Those components are **Virtual Networks** (**VNets**), subnets, and virtual network interfaces. Though defining these components is not currently within the scope of this exam, it is important to understand each as we move through this chapter.

VNets are the foundational network component within Azure. VNets provide the boundary for our resources and allow us to segment our networks with different IP address schema by geography, applications, solutions, and so on. Resources that connect to a VNet are within the same region as the VNet. VNets can be interconnected through peering to make use of the Azure backbone, but they have to be on IP address ranges that do not overlap.

Subnets are a component of VNets used to segment a VNet. Subnets are created using a subset of the IP address ranges of the VNet, and they are generally used to separate applications, data, and management layers for security purposes.

Virtual network interfaces are used to provide connectivity to the VNet for Azure resources, such as virtual machines. These interfaces assign the IP addresses to the resources to allow them to connect to the VNet and subnet to communicate on the network. In a physical network and server infrastructure, the network interface would be where you would plug a network cable into a server or workstation.

In the next section, we will describe how **Network Security Groups (NSGs)** protect our network segments.

Describe Azure Network Security Groups

Now that you understand the network segmentation and the components that make up your network, we can discuss the security features to protect the network. The first of these is the NSG. An NSG is a security solution within Azure that is associated with a subnet or network interface within the VNet to enforce a list of inbound and outbound rules. The NSG provides protection at the network security layer.

Figure 8.1 shows the architecture for an NSG when used to enforce rules across the entire subnet. The NSG is associated with the subnet and therefore has allow or deny rules that can protect resources within that subnet. In *Figure 8.1*, this is illustrated with a Linux and a Windows virtual machine to protect management ports 22 and 3389 respectively on the left side of the diagram. On the right, these ports are open to the internet and are exposed to potential attacks:

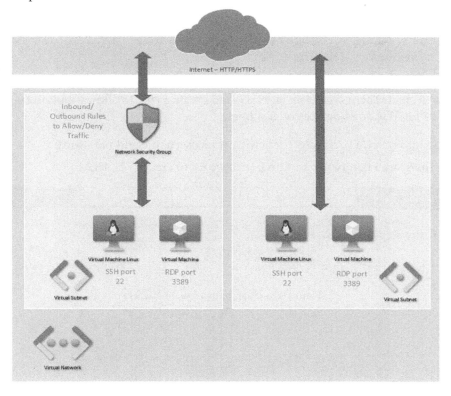

Figure 8.1 – NSG architecture

There are three default inbound and outbound rules for all NSGs when they are created. The default inbound rules are, in order of priority, the following:

- Allow VNet to VNet communication for any source and any destination.
- Allow inbound internet traffic from any source to a load balancer.
- Deny all traffic from any source and any destination.

The default outbound rules are, in order of priority, the following:

- Allow VNet to VNet communication for any source and any destination.
- Allow outbound traffic from any source to the internet.
- Deny all traffic from any source and any destination.

These default rules provide the basis for allowing and denying traffic to either the subnet or the network interface that the NSG is associated with. These default rules start at a 65000 priority number. To allow or deny traffic with a higher priority than the default rules, create a new NSG inbound or outbound rule with a priority lower than 65000, with the highest priority being 100. Additional information on NSGs can be found here: `https://docs.microsoft.com/en-us/azure/virtual-network/network-security-groups-overview`.

Now that you know about VNets, subnets, network interfaces, and NSGs, let's go through the steps to create them, associate an NSG, and create a rule to allow inbound traffic to port `3389` for Windows devices on a subnet:

1. Log into `portal.azure.com` with your username and password.
2. In the search bar, type `virtual network` to create a VNet:

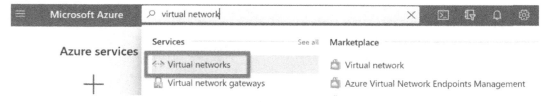

Figure 8.2 – Search for virtual networks

3. Select **+ Create** on the **Virtual networks** tile to create a new VNet:

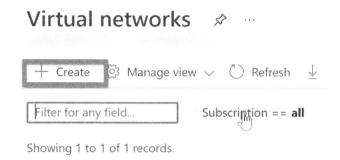

Figure 8.3 – Create a new VNet

4. Create a VNet named SC-900-VNET1 with a new **Resource** group named SC-900-RG in a region close to you. Make note of the region. Select **Next : IP Addresses**:

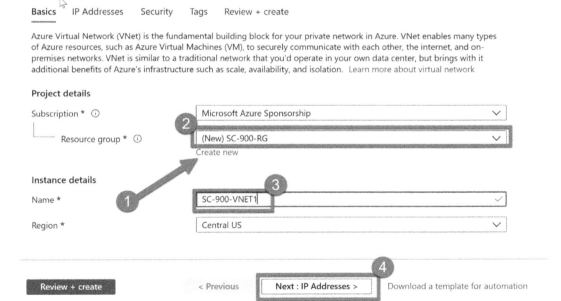

Figure 8.4 – Basic VNet information

5. On the **IP Addresses** tile, use the default subnet name and IP address schema. This is typically a `10.x.x.x/16` address and the subnet name is a default `10.x.x.x/24` address. Select **Next : Security**:

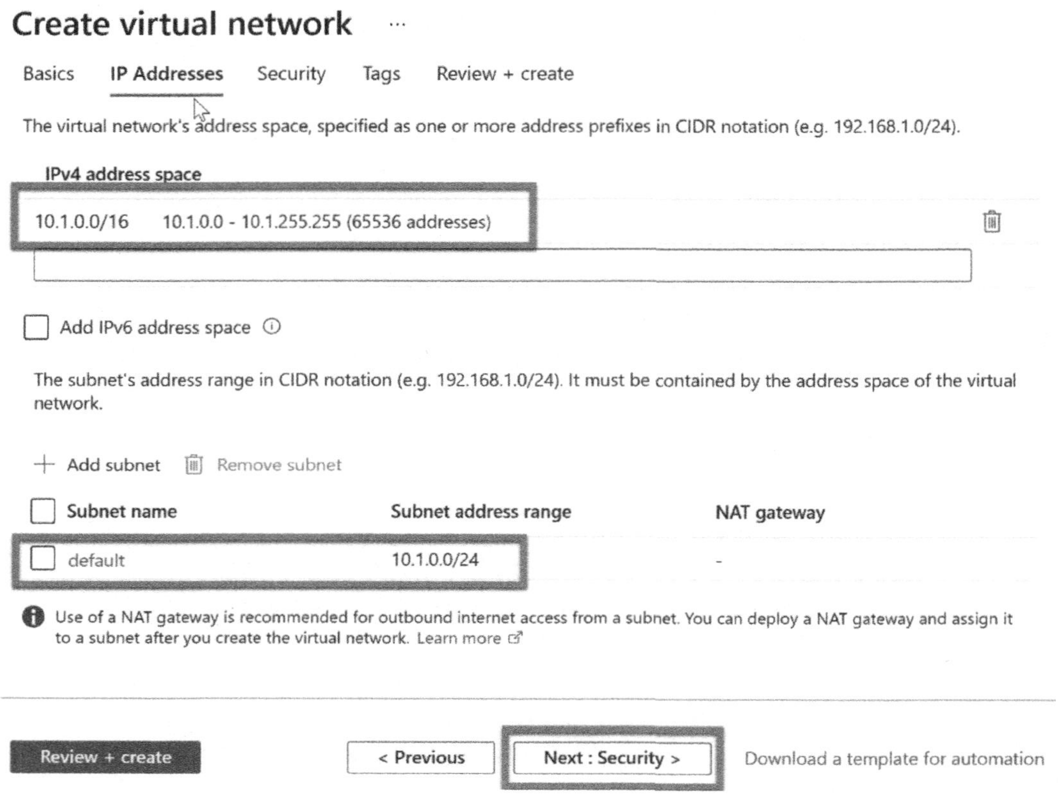

Create virtual network ···

Basics   **IP Addresses**   Security   Tags   Review + create

The virtual network's address space, specified as one or more address prefixes in CIDR notation (e.g. 192.168.1.0/24).

IPv4 address space

10.1.0.0/16   10.1.0.0 - 10.1.255.255 (65536 addresses)   🗑

☐ Add IPv6 address space ⓘ

The subnet's address range in CIDR notation (e.g. 192.168.1.0/24). It must be contained by the address space of the virtual network.

➕ Add subnet   🗑 Remove subnet

☐	Subnet name	Subnet address range	NAT gateway
☐	default	10.1.0.0/24	-

ℹ Use of a NAT gateway is recommended for outbound internet access from a subnet. You can deploy a NAT gateway and assign it to a subnet after you create the virtual network. Learn more ☐

| Review + create | | < Previous | Next : Security > | Download a template for automation |

Figure 8.5 – IP addresses and the subnet

6. Leave the options on the **Security** tile disabled by default. Note that this tile provides options for creating an Azure Bastion and Azure Firewall and enabling DDoS Protection Standard – all solutions that we will discuss later in this chapter. Select **Review + create** to create the VNet:

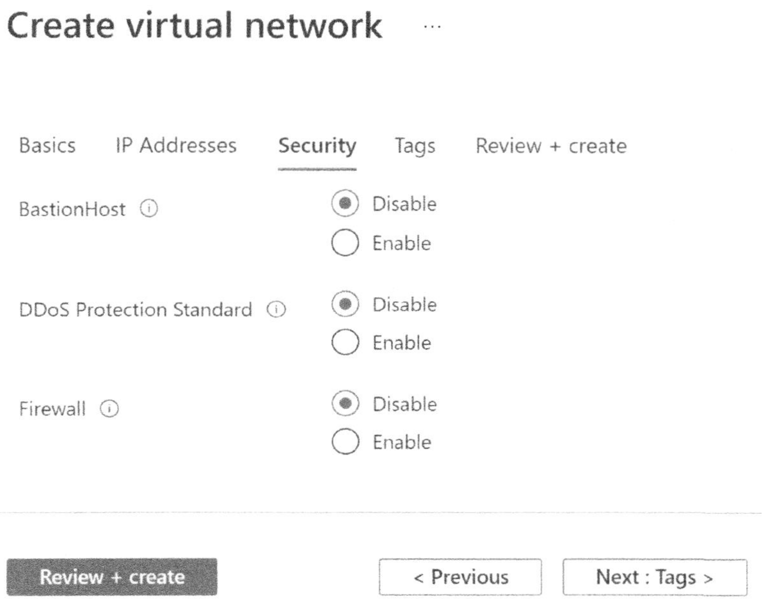

Create virtual network ⋯

Basics   IP Addresses   **Security**   Tags   Review + create

BastionHost ⓘ
  ● Disable
  ○ Enable

DDoS Protection Standard ⓘ
  ● Disable
  ○ Enable

Firewall ⓘ
  ● Disable
  ○ Enable

[Review + create]   [< Previous]   [Next : Tags >]

Figure 8.6 – Security options for creating a VNet

7.   Once validation has passed, click **Create** to create the VNet:

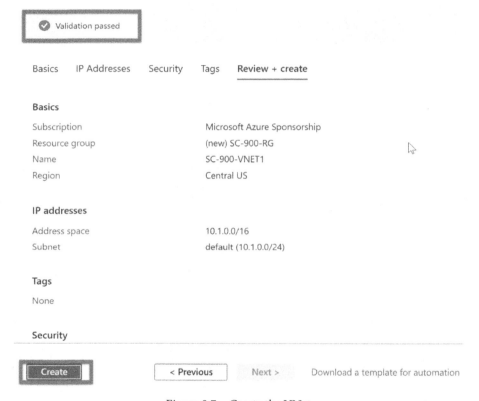

Figure 8.7 – Create the VNet

8.   After the VNet is created, go to the resource:

Figure 8.8 – Go to the VNet

9. You will be taken to the VNet overview tile, as shown in *Figure 8.9*. Navigate
    through the menu options to review the various solutions available:

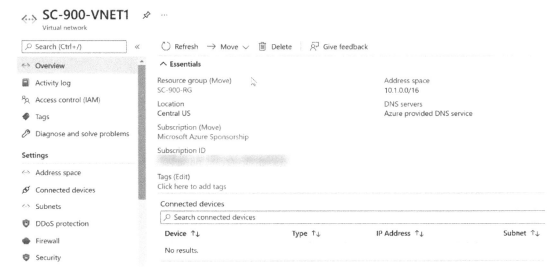

Figure 8.9 – A VNet overview

10. Next, you will create the NSG and associate it to the default subnet of SC-900-
    VNET1. In the search bar, type network security groups and select the
    relevant result:

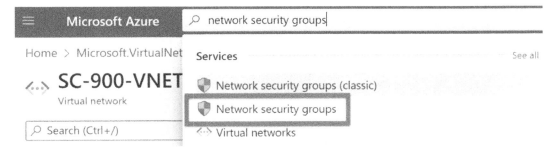

Figure 8.10 – Search for network security groups

11. In the **Network security groups** tile, click **+ Create** to create the NSG:

Network security groups
+ Create
Manage view
Refresh
Filter for any field...
Subscription == all

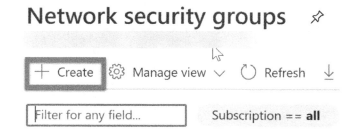

Figure 8.11 – Create a new NSG

12. On the NSG creation **Basics** tile, use the dropdown to select the resource group that was created previously. Name your NSG, and select the region that is the same as the VNet that you created previously. *Figure 8.12* shows what your configuration should look like. Select **Review + create** to create the NSG:

Create network security group
Basics
Tags
Review + create
Project details
Subscription *
Microsoft Azure Sponsorship
Resource group *
SC-900-RG
Instance details
Name *
SC-900-NSG1
Region *
Central US
Review + create
< Previous
Next : Tags >
Download a template for automation

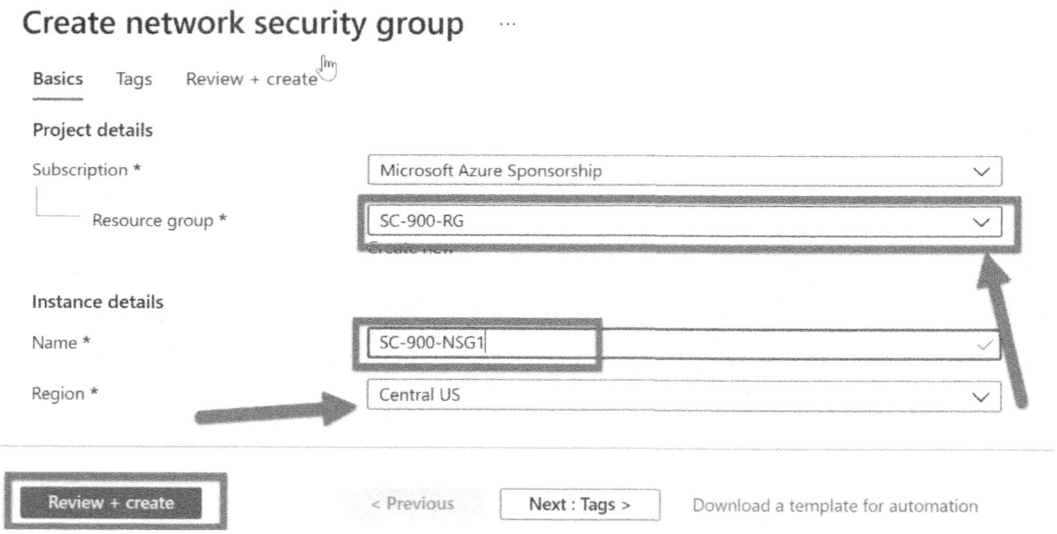

Figure 8.12 – Configure the NSG

13. After validation has passed, click **Create**:

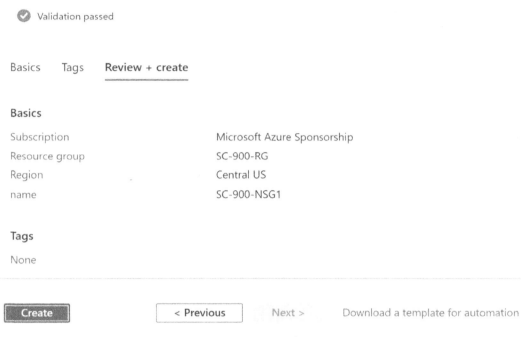

Create network security group   ...

Validation passed

Basics   Tags   **Review + create**

Basics

Subscription   Microsoft Azure Sponsorship
Resource group   SC-900-RG
Region   Central US
name   SC-900-NSG1

Tags

None

Create   < Previous   Next >   Download a template for automation

Figure 8.13 – Create the NSG

14. After the NSG resource completes the deployment, click **Go to resource**:

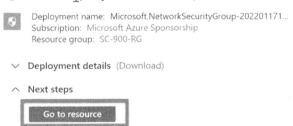

Your deployment is complete

Deployment name: Microsoft.NetworkSecurityGroup-202201171...
Subscription: Microsoft Azure Sponsorship
Resource group: SC-900-RG

˅ **Deployment details** (Download)

˄ **Next steps**

Go to resource

Figure 8.14 – Go to the NSG resource

15. In the NSG overview, you will see the default inbound and outbound rules that were discussed earlier in this section. Under the **Settings** menu, you will see **Network interfaces** and **Subnets** listed, which are highlighted in *Figure 8.15*. The **Network interfaces** and **Subnets** options under the **Settings** menu are where you will associate this NSG. Select **Subnets** in the menu:

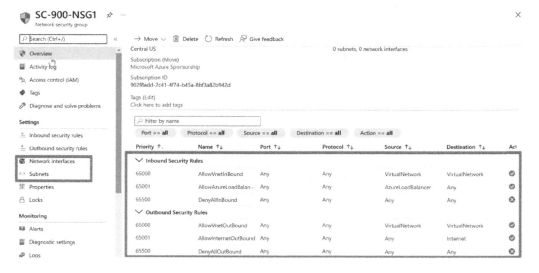

Figure 8.15 – An NSG overview and the default rules

16. In the **Subnets** tile, you will now associate this NSG with SC-900-VNET1. *Figure 8.16* shows the steps in order. Select **Subnets**, **+ Associate**, and then select the dropdown to find the VNet that you want to associate:

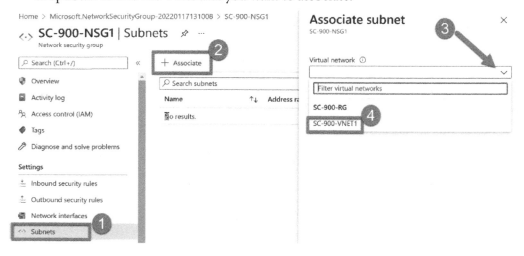

Figure 8.16 – Associate the NSG with the VNet

17. Next, select the **Subnet** dropdown to select the subnet to associate. Select **OK** to associate the subnet:

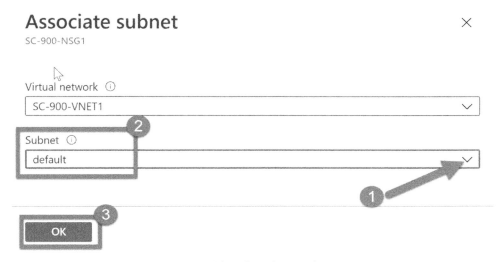

Figure 8.17 – Select the subnet and associate

18. *Figure 8.18* shows the associated subnet. Now, create a new inbound rule. Select **Inbound security rules** under the **Settings** menu:

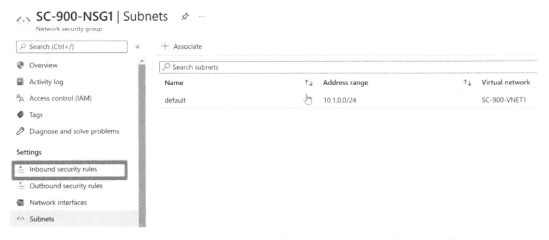

Figure 8.18 – The associated subnet and selecting the inbound security rules

19. Go through the steps shown in *Figure 8.19* to configure the new inbound security rule. Select **Inbound security rules** and **+ Add**. In the **Add inbound security rule** tile, leave the source and destination as **Any**, change **Destination port ranges** to 3389, rename the rule Allow_Port_3389, and click **Add**:

Figure 8.19 – Create a new inbound security rule

20. The new inbound security rule has been created and is now at the top of the list of rules with the highest priority. Note that we have created a rule that Microsoft views as a security vulnerability, which is outside recommended best practices. This is flagged by **!** within an orange triangle, as shown in *Figure 8.20*:

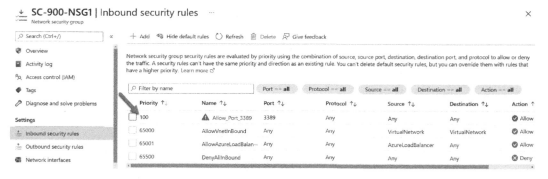

Figure 8.20 – A new inbound security rule with a warning flag

A better option for this inbound security rule is to set a specific source IP address range for the user, or users, that need to access this subnet for management purposes.

You now know how to create an NSG and associate it with a VNet subnet. The next section will discuss Azure's **Distributed Denial of Service (DDoS)** protection.

Describe Azure DDoS protection

In *Chapter 3, Understanding Key Security Concepts*, you learned about common threats, including DDoS attacks. To review, DDoS attacks are created by an attacker deploying a bot to flood your **Internet Service Provider (ISP)** with requests to your resources, such as your web applications. The flood of requests overloads the ability to process requests, and legitimate users receive responses that the site is unavailable. This attack doesn't steal from the company but can have an impact on revenue from an e-commerce site not being available.

Microsoft provides basic DDoS protection at no cost to all Azure subscriptions and protects the perimeter layer within defense in depth. This is a win-win for Microsoft and its customers. If you think about how a DDoS attack works, a successful attack on a customer that is using Microsoft Azure will also affect other customers that are using the same ISP as the customer under attack. Therefore, it is in Microsoft's best interest to identify and block these attacks on ISPs that are servicing customers within its data centers. DDoS Protection Basic is automatically turned on for all Azure subscriptions. Customers do not have any options or reporting capabilities with DDoS Protection Basic.

If a company requires the ability to access DDoS protection reports or make configuration adjustments for certain solutions, then the company is required to upgrade to DDoS Protection Standard. DDoS Protection Standard is a paid solution that adds to the monthly recurring charges. Companies with a DDoS Protection Standard plan can also connect this reporting to Microsoft Sentinel. Microsoft Sentinel will be discussed further in *Chapter 9, Describing Security Management and Capabilities of Azure. Figure 8.21* shows how Azure DDoS protection identifies legitimate user traffic for routing to company VNets:

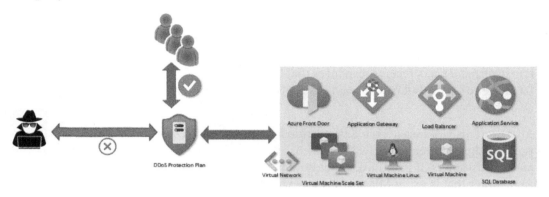

Figure 8.21 – Azure DDoS protection

Additional information on DDoS Protection Standard can be found at this link: `https://docs.microsoft.com/en-us/azure/ddos-protection/ddos-protection-overview`.

The next section will discuss Azure Firewall and Web Application Firewall.

Describe Azure Firewall and Web Application Firewall

The solutions that will be discussed in this section can be thought of as protecting at multiple layers of the Defense in Depth strategy. Azure Firewall has security capabilities that can be viewed on both the perimeter and network security layers. In addition to these layers, Web Application Firewall can also be viewed as a security solution at the application layer.

Let's discuss the Azure Firewall solution and how it is used.

Describe Azure Firewall

Azure Firewall is a stateful firewall as a service within Azure. Azure Firewall provides a highly available and unrestricted scalable firewall solution. *Figure 8.22* shows the architecture of Azure Firewall in an Azure network. Azure Firewall is placed in a separate subnet to isolate traffic from resources on other subnets. Firewalls provide packet inspection for malicious activity as well as inbound and outbound rules, similar to an NSG. The difference between the rules for a firewall and an NSG is that firewall rules use **Network Address Translation (NAT)**, which can route traffic to different resources and subnets. Information on Azure Firewall can be found here: `https://docs.microsoft.com/en-us/azure/firewall/overview`:

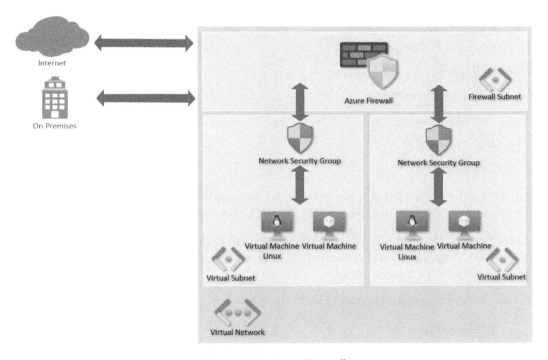

Figure 8.22 – Azure Firewall

Azure Firewall is available as a Standard or Premium version. Azure Firewall Standard and Azure Firewall Premium include the following features:

- Built-in high availability
- Availability Zones
- Unrestricted cloud scalability
- Application FQDN filtering rules

- Network traffic filtering rules
- FQDN tags
- Service tags
- Threat intelligence
- DNS proxy
- Custom DNS
- FQDN in network rules
- Deployment without public IP address in Forced Tunnel Mode
- Outbound SNAT support
- Inbound DNAT support
- Multiple public IP addresses
- Azure Monitor logging
- Forced tunneling
- Web categories
- Certifications

Additional detail on each of these features can be found at this link: `https://docs.microsoft.com/en-us/azure/firewall/features`.

Azure Firewall Premium has additional features and higher bandwidth throughput capabilities. Azure Firewall Premium also has a **Service Level Agreement (SLA)** of 99.99% and is PCI DSS-compliant.

Azure Firewall Premium features include the following:

- TLS inspection
- An **Intrusion Detection and Prevention System (IDPS)**
- URL filtering
- Web categories

Additional detail on these features can be found at this link: `https://docs.microsoft.com/en-us/azure/firewall/premium-features`.

Using Azure Firewall rather than a virtual firewall appliance in Azure provides high availability and a highly scalable firewall solution to your network perimeter security.

Let's discuss a web application firewall within Azure and how it works with the various traffic management solutions for applications.

Describe Web Application Firewall

In the previous section, we discussed Azure Firewall and how it can provide perimeter protection at the network layer. Azure's **Web Application Firewall** (**WAF**) provides perimeter protection at the application layer. WAF works with other Azure traffic management services such as Azure Application Gateway or Azure Front Door to inspect the traffic for common application layer threats, such as SQL injections, cross-site scripting, and other attacks listed in the OWASP Top 10 (`owasp.org`).

Figure 8.23 shows how WAF is used within Azure Application Gateway or Azure Front Door to recognize and block these threats while allowing legitimate users to access resources. WAF can protect Azure resources, such as databases and virtual machines, along with on-premises applications:

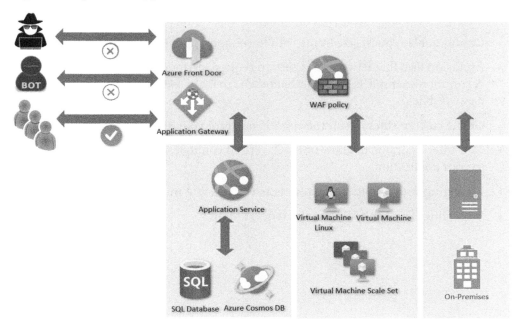

Figure 8.23 – Azure WAF

Like Azure Firewall, WAF can be configured with rules to allow and block traffic from flowing in and out of the network. There is also a log option that allows the traffic but logs it for later review.

The key features of WAF are as follows:

- SQL-injection protection.

- Cross-site scripting protection.

- Protection against other common web attacks, such as command injection, HTTP request smuggling, HTTP response splitting, and remote file inclusion.

- Protection against HTTP protocol violations.

- Protection against HTTP protocol anomalies, such as missing host user-agent and accept headers.

- Protection against crawlers and scanners.

- Detection of common application misconfigurations (for example, Apache and IIS).

- Configurable request size limits with lower and upper bounds.

- Exclusion lists that let you omit certain request attributes from a WAF evaluation. A common example is AD-inserted tokens that are used for authentication or password fields.

- Create custom rules to suit the specific needs of your applications.

- Geo-filtering traffic to allow or block certain countries/regions from gaining access to your applications.

- Protecting your applications from bots with the bot mitigation ruleset.

- Inspecting JSON and XML in the request body.

Additional information on WAF can be found at this link: `https://docs.microsoft.com/en-us/azure/web-application-firewall/ag/ag-overview`.

The next section will discuss how to securely access virtual machines for remote management.

Describe secure remote management of virtual machines

The previous sections have discussed how to segment and protect traffic that is inbound and outbound on your Azure network. Since you are now using resources on Azure and not on-premises, you need to consider how to manage your virtual machines securely without leaving them open to attacks. Typically, you are managing either a Linux virtual machine on SSH port 22 or a Windows virtual machine on RDP port 3389. Attackers know this and are known to run programs that check IP addresses to see if these ports are open. They can then leverage this for a brute-force attack on your resources. Therefore, it is important that you do not leave these ports open to the internet.

Azure provides options to avoid having these ports open to the internet, while still making them available to you to remotely manage at the operating system level. The two that will be discussed are Just-in-Time Virtual Machine access and Azure Bastion. Let's talk first about Just-in-Time Virtual Machine access.

Describe Just-in-time Virtual Machine access

Just-in-Time (**JIT**) **VM** access provides you with a specific amount of time to access your virtual machine through ports 22 or 3389. When a JIT VM access request is made, a temporary rule is created in the NSG for that VM network interface that allows the inbound traffic through for the port requested. *Figure 8.24* shows how this works, with the NSG providing an inbound rule for a limited access time:

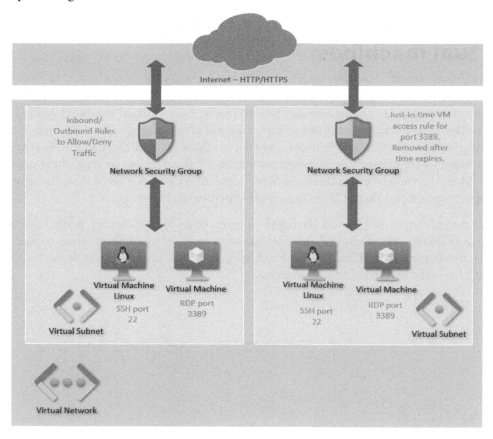

Figure 8.24 – The NSG with the JIT VM access inbound rule

The maximum amount of time allowed within JIT VM access is set by an administrator within Microsoft Defender for Cloud when JIT VM access is activated. Additional information on JIT VM access can be found at this link: `https://docs.microsoft.com/en-us/azure/defender-for-cloud/just-in-time-access-usage?tabs=jit-config-asc%2Cjit-request-asc`.

JIT VM access is just one way to provide secure remote management to VMs. Next, we will describe secure remote management for VMs using Azure Bastion.

Describe Azure Bastion

Azure Bastion works differently from JIT VM access in remotely managing VMs. JIT VM access utilizes the NSG that is associated with the subnet or network interface to create a temporary inbound allow rule for one of the management ports. Azure Bastion provides additional protection and isolation through the Azure portal and a Bastion subnet to avoid inbound access to these management ports from the internet entirely.

Azure Bastion leverages the ability to access VMs through the Azure portal and then opens port 22 or 3389 through a secure connection within the portal. The concept of Azure Bastion is similar to that of a jump box, where an isolated device is used with a different username and password than the destination device for remote management. An attacker would need to obtain two sets of usernames and passwords to carry out their attack. This workflow is shown in *Figure 8.25*:

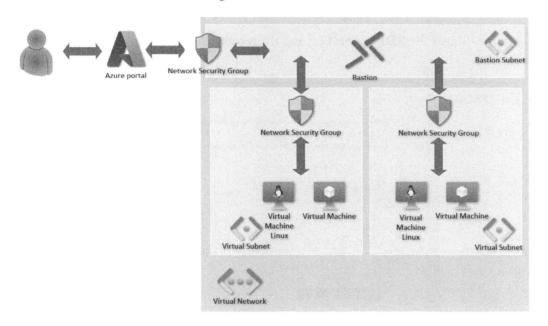

Figure 8.25 – Azure Bastion

When using Azure Bastion for secure remote management, the Azure portal is necessary to connect to the VMs. Therefore, users need to perform these management tasks will need to have the Virtual Machine Contributor role assigned to them for access to the Azure portal and the VMs. Additional information about Azure Bastion can be found at this link: https://docs.microsoft.com/en-us/azure/bastion/bastion-overview.

Figure 8.26, *Figure 8.27*, and *Figure 8.28* show VM connections within Azure. *Figure 8.26* shows the **Connect** dropdown with the **RDP**, **SSH**, or **Bastion** options:

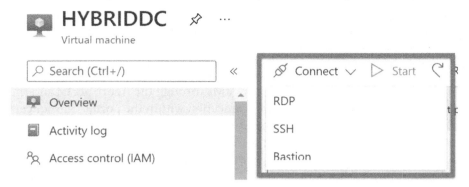

Figure 8.26 – The VM Connect options

Figure 8.27 shows the **RDP** connection and the recommended option to enable JIT VM access:

Figure 8.27 – RDP with the option to enable JIT VM access

Figure 8.28 shows the start of enabling and using Azure Bastion:

Figure 8.28 – Use Azure Bastion to connect

Since Azure Bastion provides secure access of SSH port 22 and RDP port 3389 to VMs through the Azure portal, it is considered more secure than using JIT VM Access. These options for secure remote management can be used together within Azure for secure remote management. The best practice is that VMs that can be managed through Azure Bastion should not have external IP addresses. VMs that require an external IP address should not have ports 22 or 3389 open to the internet.

The next sections will describe Azure data encryption, including Azure Key Vault.

Describe Azure data encryption

This section will discuss the protection of data through the different encryption options within Azure for encrypting data at rest. This will include encryption key management and other features that are included with Azure Key Vault. There are three types of encryption services within Azure; they are **Storage Service Encryption** (**SSE**), **Azure Disk Encryption** (**ADE**), and **Transparent Data Encryption** (**TDE**). The following sections will describe the use of each of these.

Describe Storage Service encryption

Storage Service Encryption (**SSE**) is the encryption service within Azure storage accounts for encrypting data at rest. SSE is turned on by default for all objects and files that are saved within a storage account container or file share. When creating a storage account within Azure, SSE with Microsoft-managed keys is turned on and encryption keys are created for the storage account. These storage account encryption keys can be located and viewed on the **Storage account** menu in the **Security + networking** section as **Access keys**. *Figure 8.29* shows this menu section:

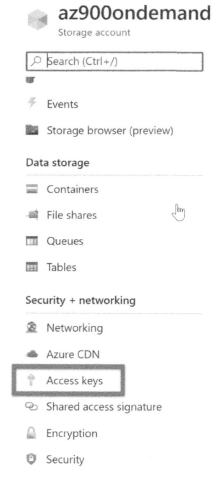

Figure 8.29 – Storage account access keys

Within the **Access keys** tile, you can rotate the primary and secondary keys if they have become compromised or are suspected to have been compromised. The **Encryption** tile is where you can change from Microsoft-managed keys to customer-managed keys with Azure Key Vault. We will describe Azure Key Vault later in this section.

For more information on SSE, please visit this link: `https://docs.microsoft.com/en-us/azure/storage/common/storage-service-encryption`.

Next, we will describe Azure disk encryption for VMs.

Describe Azure Disk encryption

Azure Disk Encryption (**ADE**) is used to encrypt VMs and their attached disks. ADE can be used to encrypt VMs with Windows and Linux operating systems, and ADE can also be used to encrypt VM scale sets. ADE for Windows VMs utilizes BitLocker for encrypting the VM and attached disks. DM-Crypt is used for Linux VMs and attached disks.

For more information on ADE, please visit this link: `https://docs.microsoft.com/en-us/azure/security/fundamentals/azure-disk-encryption-vms-vmss`.

Describe Transparent data encryption

The final type of encryption at rest that will be described is **Transparent Data Encryption** (**TDE**). TDE is encryption at rest for data that is stored within Azure SQL Database, Azure SQL Managed Instance, and Azure Synapse Analytics. These are all platform services within Azure built on Microsoft SQL. TDE is enabled by default on all new SQL databases and SQL managed instances but is manually configured on Azure Synapse Analytics.

For more information on TDE, please visit this link: `https://docs.microsoft.com/en-us/azure/azure-sql/database/transparent-data-encryption-tde-overview?tabs=azure-portal`.

Each of these encryption services has keys managed by Microsoft as the default configuration. Let's discuss how to use Azure Key Vault to separate key management duties.

Describe Azure Key Vault

If your company has a requirement, company or legal, to manage their own keys, Azure provides the ability to separate these duties with Azure Key Vault. This can be used as a centralized location to protect and manage encryption keys, secrets, and certificates.

Figure 8.30 shows where to configure customer-managed keys within an Azure storage account:

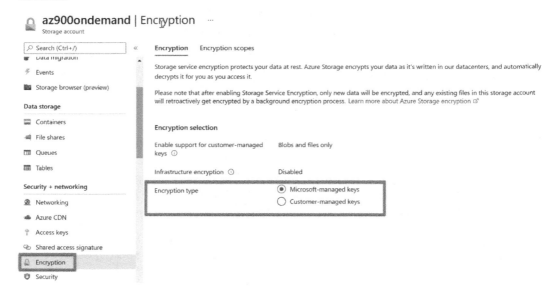

Figure 8.30 – Configure customer-managed keys with Azure Key Vault

The features of security management are as follows:

- **Secrets Management**: Securely store and control access to tokens, passwords, certificates, API keys, and other secrets.

- **Key Management**: Azure Key Vault makes it easy to create and control the encryption keys used to encrypt your data.

- **Certificate Management**: Provision, manage, and deploy public and private **Transport Layer Security/Secure Sockets Layer (TLS/SSL)** certificates for use with Azure and your internal connected resources. Azure Key Vault can also be configured to automatically renew these certificates before they expire, maintaining secure availability to websites.

There are two tiers of Azure Key Vault, Standard and Premium. With Premium, you can use Azure Key Vault to synchronize on-premises **Hardware Security Module (HSM)** keys and secrets.

For more information on Azure Key Vault, please visit this link: https://docs.microsoft.com/en-us/azure/key-vault/general/overview.

The next section will provide a summary of what you have learned in this chapter.

Summary

In this chapter, we discussed the various security services and management capabilities within Azure. This included perimeter and network security with network segmentation, NSGs, DDoS protection, Azure Firewall, and WAF. We also discussed how to securely remote manage VMs with JIT VM access and Azure Bastion. We ended the chapter describing how to use encryption to protect data, and managing keys, secrets, and certificates with Azure Key Vault. The next chapter will describe the security management capabilities within Azure.

9

Describing Security Management and Capabilities of Azure

The previous chapter covered the various security services within Azure for network, compute, and data protection. This included network segmentation, NSGs, DDoS protection, firewalls, remote virtual machine management, and encryption. In this chapter, we will describe how to manage the protection of resources within Azure through **Cloud Security Posture Management** within **Microsoft Defender for Cloud**. We will also describe how to use security baselines within Azure to set up best practice protection for your compute, application, and data resources.

In this chapter, we're going to cover the following main topics:

- Describing **Cloud Security Posture Management (CSPM)**
- Describing the enhanced security features of Microsoft Defender for Cloud
- Describing security baselines for Azure

Technical requirements

In this chapter, we will begin to explore configuring a tenant for use of solutions within Azure. There will be exercises that will require access to Azure. If you have not yet created the trial licenses for Microsoft 365 and a free trial of Azure, please follow the directions provided within *Chapter 1, Preparing for Your Microsoft Exam*.

Describing Cloud Security Posture Management (CSPM)

Chapter 2, Describing Security Methodologies, discussed the layers of a defense-in-depth security strategy. *Chapter 8, Describing Basic Security Services and Management Capabilities in Azure*, described some of the Azure solutions that can be used to protect these layers of defense. Simply enabling and deploying these solutions into your infrastructure is not enough. You should also have a strategy for how you are going to monitor and manage these layers of defense within your infrastructure.

CSPM is the method for monitoring and managing these defenses to audit, assess, and identify potential vulnerabilities and threats that may be within your infrastructure. This constant process allows you to address the possibility of potential attacks before they take place and be diligent and proactive in the changing threat landscape and evolving cloud infrastructure.

A strong CSPM solution evaluates and provides the following features and characteristics:

- **Zero-trust based access control**: This considers the active threat level during access control decisions.

- **Threat and vulnerability management**: Providing a holistic view of an organization's attack surface and risk and integrating it into decision-making.

- **Technical policy**: The application of guardrails to audit and enforce an organization's standards and policies for technical systems.

- **Real-time risk scoring**: This will provide visibility of the top risks.

- **Discover sharing risks**: To understand the data exposure of enterprise intellectual property on sanctioned and unsanctioned cloud services.

- **Threat modeling systems and architectures**: Used alongside other specific applications.

Within Microsoft Azure, Microsoft Defender for Cloud (formerly Azure Security Center) provides CSPM for Azure and hybrid infrastructure resources.

In the next section, we will describe how Microsoft Defender for Cloud is used for CSPM.

Describing the enhanced security features for Microsoft Defender for Cloud

Microsoft Defender for Cloud is Microsoft's CSPM solution. It offers two options for security posture management within your Azure subscription – enhanced security off, which is a free service, or enhanced security on, which is a pay-as-you-go service based on the resources that you are monitoring.

The free subscription to Microsoft Defender for Cloud is turned on by default when you create your Azure tenant. Defender for Cloud will then provide the following CSPM features for your Azure subscription:

- Continuous assessment and security recommendations
- Secure score

The continuous assessment of Azure resources is used to provide the secure score. It is made of the following components:

- **Current score**: Each control contributes to the total score.
- **Max score**: Points that you gain by implementing all recommendations for control.
- **Potential increase**: The score increases if you remediate all recommendations.
- **Improvement actions**: Recommendations for controls that can increase your secure score. Quick Fix applies these immediately.

These features are helpful to review your Azure infrastructure and determine actions that you can apply to better protect your subscription against vulnerabilities and threats. For increased CSPM, you should review enabling the enhanced security features of Microsoft Defender for Cloud.

These features include the features provided with the free service, plus the following features:

- **Just-in-time VM access**: *Chapter 8, Describing Basic Security Services and Management Capabilities in Azure*, discussed this capability within the *Describe secure remote management of virtual machines* section. Just-in-time VM access provides a time-bound NSG rule to open port 3389 or 22 for remote virtual machine management, decreasing the time that an attack surface is left open.

- **Adaptive application controls and network hardening**: These controls help to protect against malware and provide machine learning-powered recommendations on how to protect your workloads.

- **Regulatory compliance dashboard and reports**: For companies that have regulatory compliance requirements, these dashboards will audit and assess your current controls and infrastructure against these requirements and help you to prepare for a compliance audit.

- **Threat protection for Azure VMs and non-Azure servers (including Server Endpoint Detection and Response (EDR))**: Using hybrid infrastructure tools such as Azure Arc and Microsoft Defender for Endpoint, you can monitor and manage Azure and non-Azure servers. Non-Azure servers include on-premises, **Amazon Web Services** (**AWS**), and **Google Cloud Platform** (**GCP**).

- **Threat protection for supported PaaS services**: Enhanced security services also provide threat protection for app services, containers (Azure containers and Azure Kubernetes Service), container registries, Azure DNS, Azure Key Vault, SQL databases, and Azure storage accounts.

Figure 9.1 shows how the Azure and non-Azure infrastructure can be monitored and managed with enhanced security features turned on:

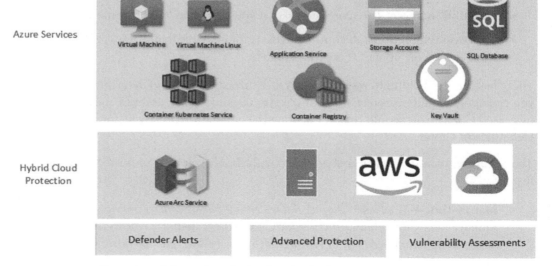

Figure 9.1 – Microsoft Defender for Cloud enhanced security features

More information on these enhanced security features can be found at this link: `https://docs.microsoft.com/en-us/azure/defender-for-cloud/enhanced-security-features-overview?WT.mc_id=Portal-Microsoft_Azure_Security`.

The next section will discuss how using the security baselines for Azure can assist in the CSPM of your infrastructure.

Describing security baselines for Azure

Microsoft Defender for Cloud provides you with in-depth features for a CSPM for your Azure, hybrid, and multi-cloud infrastructure. You may be wondering how Microsoft determines and provides the information to your subscription for recommendations for improvement within the secure score. This is accomplished through the security baselines for Azure. When your Azure and Microsoft Defender for Cloud subscription is created, the security baseline for Azure is enabled through the Azure Security Benchmark. This is used to assess your infrastructure against Microsoft and its partners' best practices.

The Azure Security Benchmark has the following components and features:

- **Azure ID**: The Azure Security Benchmark ID that corresponds to the recommendation.

- **Guidance**: The rationale for the recommendation and links to guidance on how to implement it.

- **Microsoft Defender for Cloud monitoring**: Does Microsoft Defender for Cloud monitor the control?

- **Recommendation**: The recommendation provides a high-level description of the control.

- **Responsibility**: Who is responsible for implementing the control? The possible scenarios are customer responsibility, Microsoft responsibility, or shared responsibility.

Additional information on the security baselines for Azure can be found at this link: `https://docs.microsoft.com/en-us/azure/defender-for-cloud/apply-security-baseline`.

To better understand Microsoft Defender for Cloud, we will go through an exercise that will walk you through accessing Microsoft Defender for Cloud, turning on the enhanced security features, and reviewing the secure score with improvement recommendations that are provided with the security baselines for Azure from the Azure Security Benchmark:

1. Log in to `portal.azure.com`.

2. In the search bar, enter `Microsoft defender for cloud`. Select **Microsoft Defender for Cloud**:

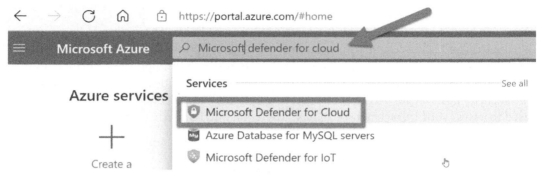

Figure 9.2 – Microsoft Defender for Cloud search and selection

3. **Microsoft Defender for Cloud** opens with the **Overview** tile. To upgrade your subscription to the enhanced security features, you can select either **Getting started** or **Environment settings** within the menu. For this exercise, select **Environment settings**, highlighted by the red box in *Figure 9.3*:

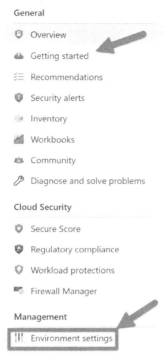

Figure 9.3 – Select Environment settings

4. Within **Environment settings**, your subscription should be shown. This is because Microsoft Defender for Cloud's free service is turned on by default. If you do not see your subscription, you can select it using the **+ Add environment** dropdown, as shown in *Figure 9.4*. If your subscription is shown, select it to go to the next tile for **Settings**:

Figure 9.4 – Select your Azure subscription

5. The **Settings | Defender plans** tile will open, and here is where you will upgrade to the enhanced security features. Select the box for the enhanced security features, as shown in *Figure 9.5*:

Figure 9.5 – Select the enhanced security features

6. Scroll down to view the resources that you can turn on for the enhanced security plans within Microsoft Defender for Cloud. For transparency, Microsoft shows the cost for each of these plans. They can be turned on or off to meet your requirements, as shown in *Figure 9.6*. After selecting the plans that you require, select **Save**, as shown in *Figure 9.5*, to save the Microsoft Defender for Cloud plans settings:

A new 'Containers' plan is available! This plan will replace the existing 'Container registries' and 'Kubernetes' plans. Click here to learn more about the benefits and and additional protection it provides

Microsoft Defender for	Resources	Pricing	Configuration	Plan
Servers	2 servers	$15/Server/Month		On Off
App Service	0 instances	$15/Instance/Month		On Off
Azure SQL Databases	0 servers	$15/Server/Month		On Off
SQL servers on machines	0 servers	$15/Server/Month $0.015/Core/Hour		On Off
Open-source relational databases	0 servers	$15/Server/Month		On Off
Storage	4 storage accounts	$0.02/10k transactions		On Off
Containers	0 container registries; 0 ku...	$7/VM core/Month		On Off
Kubernetes (deprecated)	0 kubernetes cores	$2/VM core/Month	Update available	On Off
Container registries (deprecated)	0 container registries	$0.29/Image	Update available	On Off

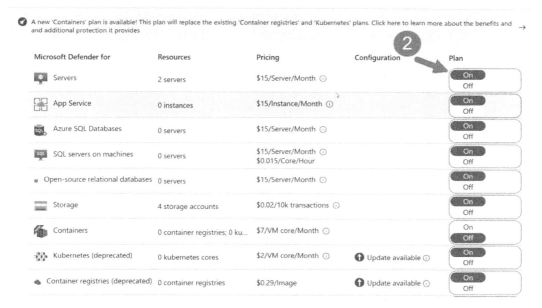

Figure 9.6 – Microsoft Defender for Cloud plans for resources

7. Note that when you scroll down to the bottom of this page, there is a statement that you will get the first 30 days of this plan for free, as shown in *Figure 9.7*. This allows you to review and test the features for threat management, alerts, hybrid management, and compliance reviews without initial charges being applied:

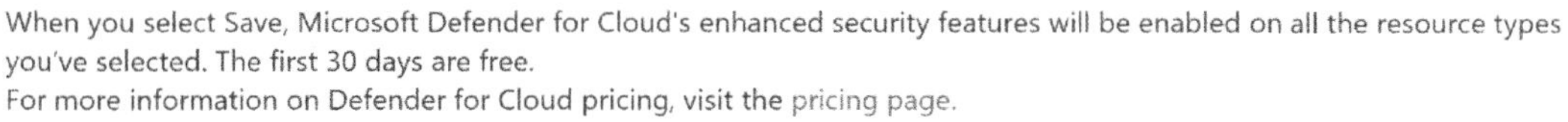

When you select Save, Microsoft Defender for Cloud's enhanced security features will be enabled on all the resource types you've selected. The first 30 days are free.
For more information on Defender for Cloud pricing, visit the pricing page.

Figure 9.7 – Enhanced security, free for 30 days

8. Explore the other menu items of the **Settings** tile. Select **Auto provisioning**, and you can select to set up virtual machines to have the Log Analytics agents necessary for Microsoft Defender for Cloud provisioned when they are deployed. You can also enable **Vulnerability assessment for machines**, as shown in *Figure 9.8*:

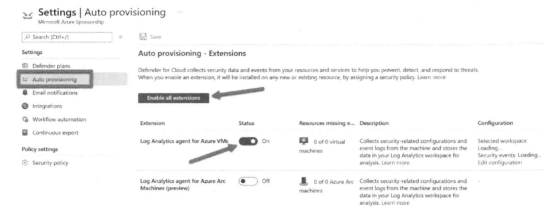

Figure 9.8 – Auto provisioning settings

9. *Figure 9.9* shows the **Continuous export** features to configure reports to be exported on recommendations, secure score, security alerts, and regulatory compliance:

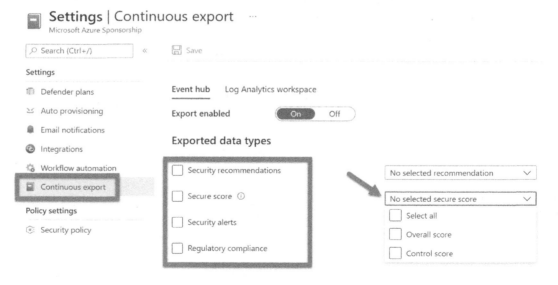

Figure 9.9 – The Continuous export settings

10. Select **Microsoft Defender for Cloud** in the navigation path to return to the main menu, as shown in *Figure 9.10*:

Figure 9.10 – Select Microsoft Defender for Cloud

11. Select **Overview** in the menu to see the dashboard of the entire CSPM environment that is Microsoft Defender for Cloud:

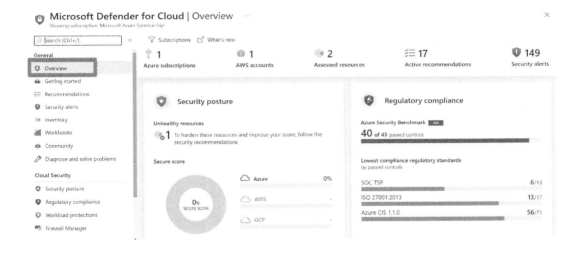

Figure 9.11 – Microsoft Defender for Cloud – Overview

12. Within the **Overview** dashboard, you can select the various tiles to go into the related sections; you can also select these from the menu. *Figure 9.12* shows the **Security alerts** list in your environment:

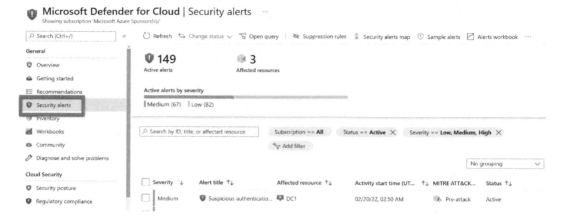

Figure 9.12 – Security alerts

13. *Figure 9.13* shows the **Secure Score** tile:

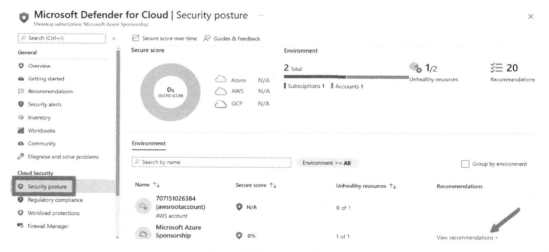

Figure 9.13 – Secure Score

14. *Figure 9.14* shows the **Regulatory compliance** dashboard:

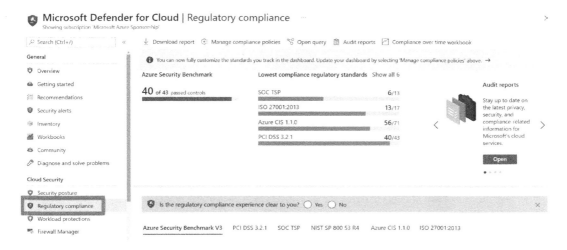

Figure 9.14 – Regulatory compliance

15. *Figure 9.15* shows the various **Microsoft Defender for Cloud** workload protections that are being protected with the enhanced security features:

Figure 9.15 – Workload protections

16. *Figure 9.16* shows **Recommendations** that can increase your secure score and create a better security posture for your infrastructure:

Figure 9.16 – Recommendations

There are many additional dashboards and features within Microsoft Defender for Cloud to explore. The exam does not cover all of these capabilities, but if you are going to be in a security operations role, these additional capabilities should be further explored.

The next section will provide a summary of what you have learned in this chapter.

Summary

In this chapter, we discussed the security management capabilities within Azure. This included describing the concept of CSPM. You also learned about Microsoft Defender for Cloud and how it is used with CSPM for Azure, hybrid, and multi-cloud infrastructures. This includes the enhanced security features of Microsoft Defender for Cloud and how the security baseline for Azure provides the foundation for CSPM within Defender for Cloud. In the next chapter, we will describe the threat protection features of the Microsoft 365 Defender suite of solutions.

10
Describing Threat Protection with Microsoft 365 Defender

In the previous chapter, we covered how to manage the protection of resources within Azure through **Cloud Security Posture Management (CSPM)** within **Microsoft Defender for Cloud**. This included how to use security baselines within Azure to set up the best practice protection for your compute, application, and data resources. In this chapter, we will describe how to manage the protection of Microsoft 365 resources through the **extended detection and response (XDR)** capabilities of Microsoft 365 Defender.

In this chapter, we're going to cover the following main topics:

- Describing the XDR and Microsoft 365 Defender services
- Describing Microsoft Defender for Office 365
- Describing Microsoft Defender for Cloud Apps
- Describing Microsoft Defender for Identity
- Describing Microsoft Defender for Endpoint

Technical requirements

In this chapter, we will continue to explore how to configure a tenant for the use of solutions within Azure. There will be exercises that will require access to Azure. If you have not yet created the trial licenses for Microsoft 365 and a free trial of Azure, please follow the directions provided within *Chapter 1, Preparing for Your Microsoft Exam*.

Describing the XDR and Microsoft 365 Defender services

Chapter 9, Describing Security Management and Capabilities of Azure, discussed the CSPM capabilities within Microsoft Defender for Cloud, along with the enhanced security capabilities that provide threat protection to Azure resources. Microsoft 365 Defender provides enhanced threat detection and protection capabilities for Microsoft 365 using a suite of Microsoft Defender products. The combination of Microsoft Defender for Cloud and Microsoft 365 Defender solutions creates the Microsoft XDR solution.

XDR refers to the approach of designing and architecting the protection of your resources to deliver automated, intelligent, and integrated security services across all domains and infrastructures. This approach helps security operations and administrators to defend against attacks by connecting all of the events and alerts from various systems into one dashboard. This provides more efficient and effective notifications and responses to threats. Additionally, it allows your operations to stay ahead of potential attacks.

XDR solutions, combined with **Security Incident and Event Management (SIEM)** and **Security Operations and Automated Response (SOAR)** solutions, provide a complete security operations solution. *Figure 10.1* shows a diagram that brings together the **Defender suite of solutions and Microsoft Sentinel for SIEM and SOAR**. We will discuss Microsoft Sentinel in *Chapter 11, Describing Security Capabilities of Microsoft Sentinel*:

Figure 10.1 – Microsoft XDR and Microsoft Sentinel

Now that you understand the concept of XDR, in the next section, we will describe Microsoft 365 Defender and each of the Microsoft Defender solutions.

The components of Microsoft 365 Defender

Microsoft 365 Defender refers to the Defender services that can be found within the Microsoft 365 suite of products. The Microsoft 365 Defender suite has the following solutions:

- **Microsoft Defender for Office 365**: This offers protection for collaboration services across Exchange Online, SharePoint, OneDrive, and Teams to avoid damaging links and attachments.

- **Microsoft Defender for Cloud Apps**: This protects against shadow IT with cloud and enterprise application monitoring and management. It is used to manage the compliance of cloud applications.

- **Microsoft Defender for Identity**: This is similar to Azure AD Identity Protection. It provides protection for hybrid identity infrastructures with on-premises Windows Active Directory.

- **Microsoft Defender for Endpoint**: This protects and decreases the attack surface of Windows 10/11 devices.

Additional information about these services can be found at `https://docs.microsoft.com/en-us/microsoft-365/security/defender/microsoft-365-defender?view=o365-worldwide`.

Microsoft provides a dashboard for Microsoft 365 Defender. The Microsoft 365 Defender portal can be accessed through the Microsoft 365 admin portal, `admin.microsoft.com`, as shown in *Figure 10.2*. If you don't see **Security** listed in the menu, select **All Admin centers**, and **Security** will become visible:

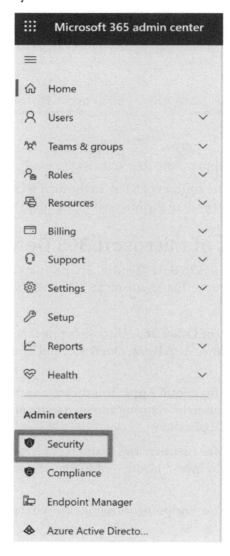

Figure 10.2 – The Microsoft 365 admin portal

Additionally, you can access it directly by navigating to `security.microsoft.com`, as shown in *Figure 10.3*:

Figure 10.3 – The Microsoft 365 Defender portal

Additional information regarding the Microsoft 365 Defender portal can be found at `https://docs.microsoft.com/en-us/microsoft-365/security/defender/microsoft-365-defender?view=o365-worldwide`.

Figure 10.4 shows how the suite of Microsoft 365 Defender solutions protects users and data against attacks:

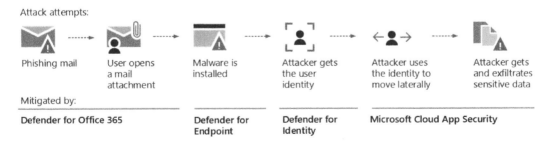

Figure 10.4 – Microsoft 365 Defender protecting against attacks

For additional information regarding how to configure and evaluate Microsoft 365 Defender solutions, please refer to https://docs.microsoft.com/en-us/ microsoft-365/security/defender/eval-overview?view=o365-worldwide.

Figure 10.5 illustrates how Microsoft 365 Defender integrates with other Microsoft cloud solutions, such as **Exchange Online Protection**, **Azure AD**, and hybrid infrastructures including devices and app traffic. Microsoft 365 Defender combines the signals from these sources, including the Microsoft Defender solutions, for full XDR across all company domains and resources:

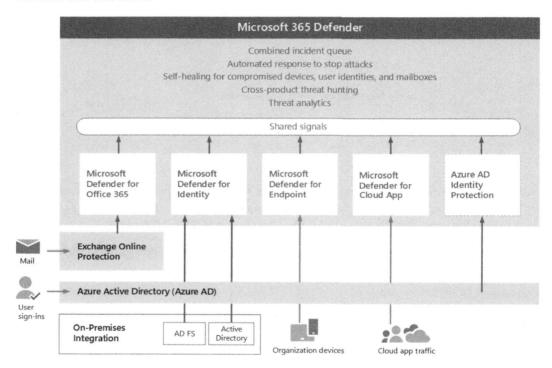

Figure 10.5 – The Microsoft 365 Defender shared signals XDR

Microsoft 365 Defender combines the signals from all of the Defender components to provide XDR across domains. This includes unified incident queues, automated responses to stop attacks, self-healing (for compromised devices, user identities, and mailboxes), cross-threat hunting, and threat analytics.

The Microsoft 365 Defender portal provides the features of Secure Score, as shown in *Figure 10.6*:

Figure 10.6 – Microsoft 365 Defender Secure Score

Microsoft Secure Score provides the following information and features to better your overall security posture:

- It allows you to view the security health of the company.

- It enables you to act to configure devices, users, and applications.

- It gets alerts regarding suspicious activity.

- Microsoft 365 Secure Score: A representation of the company's security posture.

- It provides recommendations and improvement actions for Microsoft 365, Azure AD, Microsoft Defender for Endpoint, Identity, and Cloud Apps.

- It increases security posture by enabling improvement actions to increase the secure score.

In the following sections, we will describe each of the Microsoft 365 Defender services, starting with Microsoft Defender for Office 365.

Describing Microsoft Defender for Office 365

Each of the Microsoft 365 Defender solutions has a specific focus regarding what the solution is going to protect within your Microsoft 365 infrastructure. Microsoft Defender for Office 365 focuses on the collaboration tools that are used within Microsoft 365 to avoid threats within email messages in Exchange Online, online file shares (SharePoint Online and OneDrive for Business), and Microsoft Teams collaborations. These threats include malware links (URLs) and file attachments.

The features of Microsoft Defender for Office 365 are listed as follows:

- Threat protection policies for attachments, links, and anti-phishing
- Threat investigation and response capabilities
- Reports and training with attack simulations
- Automated investigation and response capabilities

Additional information regarding Microsoft Defender for Office 365 can be found at `https://docs.microsoft.com/en-us/microsoft-365/security/office-365-security/overview?view=o365-worldwide`.

The features of Microsoft Defender for Office 365 can be accessed by navigating to `security.microsoft.com` and finding the **Email & collaboration** section from the left-hand menu, as shown in *Figure 10.7*:

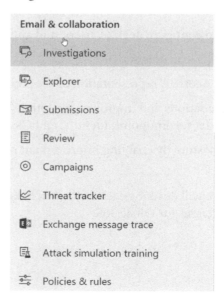

Figure 10.7 – Email & collaboration in the Microsoft 365 Defender portal menu

In the next section, we will discuss Microsoft Defender for Cloud Apps.

Describing Microsoft Defender for Cloud Apps

Microsoft Defender for Cloud Apps is a cloud service within Microsoft 365 that provides cloud access security broker services. A cloud access security broker is used as a policy enforcement point between the consumers and the providers so that applications adhere to the baseline security requirements of the company. Microsoft Defender for Cloud Apps provides these capabilities for Microsoft applications, third-party cloud applications, and registered on-premises applications.

The features of Microsoft Defender for Cloud Apps are listed as follows:

- To discover and control the use of shadow IT
- To protect sensitive information from anywhere in the cloud
- To protect against cyber threats and detect anomalies
- To assess compliance for cloud applications

Microsoft Defender for Cloud Apps is a helpful solution to aid in the discovery of applications that are being used within your company to control shadow IT within the company. Shadow IT refers to the use of applications that are not approved by the company within the company network or on devices that also access company data. Microsoft Defender for Cloud Apps will identify all applications that are being accessed through managed users and devices. These applications are then reported in the discovery dashboard. Knowing the applications that are being used and accessed allows us to plan for authorized applications and to block unauthorized applications.

For companies that have users in office locations with a firewall or a device that can log network traffic, Microsoft Defender for Cloud Apps' discovery capabilities allow you to connect these logs. Additionally, Microsoft Defender for Cloud Apps will create a discovery report that lists the applications that are being accessed. The workflow and architecture of Microsoft Defender for Cloud Apps is shown in *Figure 10.8*:

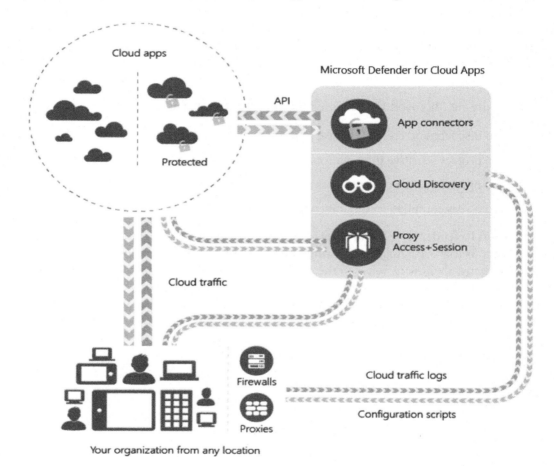

Figure 10.8 – The Microsoft Defender for Cloud Apps architecture

Additional information regarding Microsoft Defender for Cloud Apps can be found at `https://docs.microsoft.com/en-us/cloud-app-security/what-is-cloud-app-security`.

The next sections will discuss the use of Cloud Discovery for identifying application use and the next steps to take with those applications.

Cloud Discovery

As stated in the previous section, Microsoft Defender for Cloud Apps utilizes logs from network traffic to identify the applications that users are accessing. Traffic logs from on-premises firewalls will provide a snapshot report of the most common applications alongside the users that are accessing those apps. Traffic from managed devices with Intune will be fed into the Microsoft Defender for Cloud Apps discovery overview dashboard, as shown in *Figure 10.9*:

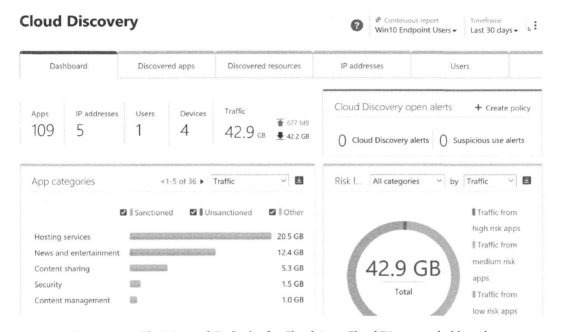

Figure 10.9 – The Microsoft Defender for Cloud Apps Cloud Discovery dashboard

This information is the basis for planning and monitoring your application's use within the organization. You can build documentation regarding user usage and habits, and then evaluate the legitimate need for various applications to be used on company resources. In the section, using Microsoft Defender for Cloud Apps to manage application access, we will discuss, in more detail, how to evaluate the app score to determine whether to sanction or un-sanction apps.

Once we have determined the applications that we are going to allow as a company, we can create a plan and enforce policies utilizing Microsoft Defender for Cloud Apps. *Figure 10.10* shows the architecture for monitoring applications within Azure AD. This architecture simplifies the management and monitoring of applications through Microsoft Defender for Cloud Apps:

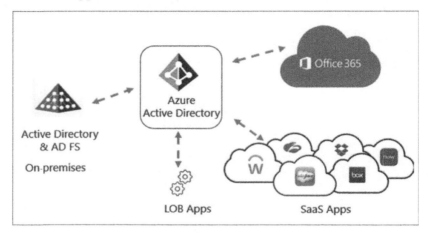

Figure 10.10 – Active Directory and cloud apps managed by Microsoft Defender for Cloud Apps

When this architecture is utilized, the company can utilize the various security, compliance, and governance tools available within Azure AD, Microsoft 365, and Azure for cloud and on-premises line-of-business applications, such as Microsoft Defender for Cloud Apps, Conditional Access policies, and Azure AD Identity Protection.

In the next section, we will describe the types of security policies for cloud apps within Microsoft Defender for Cloud Apps.

Types of Microsoft Defender for Cloud Apps app policies

When you navigate to the policy tile within Microsoft Defender for Cloud Apps, there are several different policies and templates that you can utilize. Each of these policies is categorized by the area of protection that the policy governs and the type of policy that will be implemented. The following list shows the various types of policies that are available. For more information, please refer to https://docs.microsoft.com/en-us/cloud-app-security/control-cloud-apps-with-policies:

- **Access policy** is located in the conditional access category. These policies work in the same way as Azure AD's Conditional Access policies. They monitor the users and devices that have access to applications in Microsoft Defender for Cloud Apps.

- **Activity policy** is located in the threat detection category. These policies monitor particular activities that take place across different apps and resources. These policies require the configuration of monitoring APIs to be connected to Microsoft Defender for Cloud Apps.

- **App discovery policy** is a shadow IT policy. Shadow IT refers to those applications that might not be on the list of allowed applications within the company policy. App discovery policies can monitor applications being accessed outside of these policies and send reports, through alerts and notifications, when unsanctioned apps are being accessed by users and devices.

- **Cloud Discovery anomaly detection policy** is another shadow IT policy. These policies look for unusual activity on discovered apps. These could be on sanctioned and unsanctioned apps. One example would be a large amount of data being downloaded suddenly.

- **File policy** is an information protection policy. These policies allow you to scan files within the policy scope and to verify that proper data protection is in place for potentially sensitive information within those files.

- **OAuth app policy** is a threat protection policy. These policies investigate permissions and whether they are enabled on the app. The policy can then approve or revoke that permission. These policies are built-in.

- **Session policy** is a conditional access policy. These policies monitor the activity of apps in real time and control the activity of those apps, as allowed through the policy.

Now that we understand the different policy types and their categories, let's look at the policy alert and response dashboard in Microsoft Defender for Cloud Apps.

Policy alerts and responses in Microsoft Defender for Cloud Apps

Once you have created policies to govern your cloud and enterprise apps, you need to make sure that you are monitoring and responding to these alerts. The Microsoft Defender for Cloud Apps policy dashboard provides access to this information for policy alerts and responses. *Figure 10.11* shows this dashboard and the built-in policies that are in place, along with the alerts for those policies:

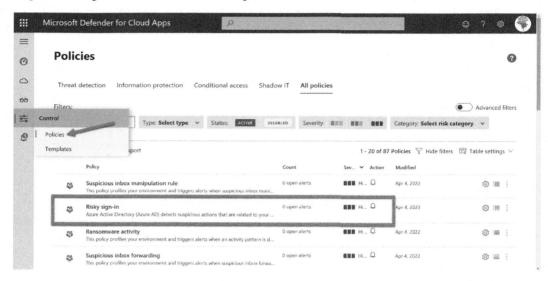

Figure 10.11 – Built-in policies and open alerts

If you look at the left-hand menu, there is a bell icon that will note whether there are any active alert notifications that you need to review. *Figure 10.12* shows the active alerts and where to see this notification:

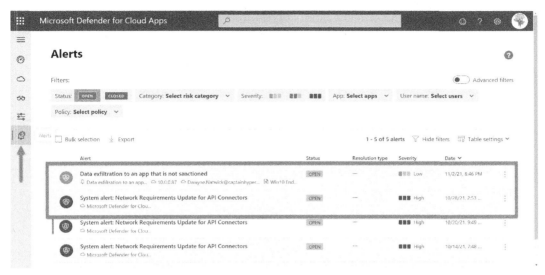

Figure 10.12 – Alert notifications and active alerts

From this dashboard, you can review and respond to these alerts.

In the next section, we will discuss cloud application scoring within Microsoft Defender for Cloud Apps.

Discovered app scoring

As a company, you have a responsibility to protect against the sharing of personally identifiable information or company data by users. This includes the potential exposure of this data through unsanctioned cloud applications that are being accessed by devices. Microsoft Defender for Cloud Apps provides an easy-to-follow scoring system for cloud applications. The level of protection of each app provides a score based on security, compliance, legal, and general criteria. *Figure 10.13* shows the scoring for **Microsoft Office Online**:

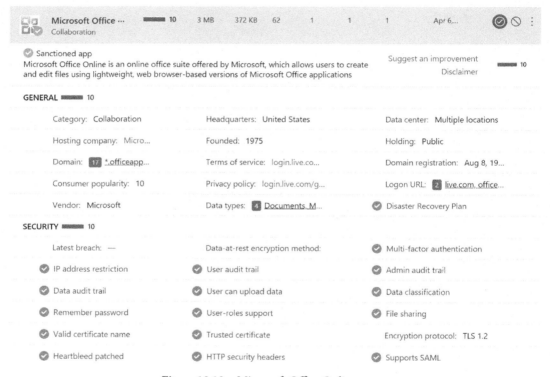

Figure 10.13 – Microsoft Office Online score

This scoring allows us to determine the applications that we can allow within our company for users and devices. The next section will describe how to allow and deny applications.

Sanctioning and un-sanctioning apps

Once you have evaluated the applications that are being accessed by your company's users and devices, you can review their scores and determine whether they will be sanctioned or unsanctioned for use. Sanctioned apps will continue to allow use by users and devices. Unsanctioned apps will be blocked on registered devices or devices that registered users are logged into. This includes apps that are installed locally, have been accessed on a web browser, or have been accessed during a private browser session. *Figure 10.14* shows the sanctioned and unsanctioned selection areas of an app:

Figure 10.14 – Sanctioned and unsanctioned apps

When un-sanctioning an app in Microsoft Defender for Cloud Apps, the access to the application is blocked on devices that are registered to Azure AD and/or users that are logged into Azure AD on those devices. This includes blocking those applications from being installed on these devices or being accessed through web browsers, in both public and private sessions.

In the next section, we will describe Microsoft Defender for Identity.

Describing Microsoft Defender for Identity

Microsoft Defender for Identity is used within a hybrid identity infrastructure. Microsoft Defender for Identity connects to the on-premises **Active Directory Domain Services (AD DS)** servers and **Active Directory Federated Services (AD FS)** servers to gather signals and events from the on-premises infrastructure and protect against threats to identity. Microsoft Defender for Identity provides similar reporting regarding the risky users and sign-ins that are provided within Azure AD Identity Protection in Azure Active Directory. We discussed Azure AD Identity Protection in *Chapter 7, Describing the Identity Protection and Governance Capabilities of Azure AD*.

The features of Microsoft Defender for Identity are listed as follows:

- It monitors and profiles user behavior and activities.

- It protects user identities and reduces the attack surface.

- It identifies suspicious activities across the cyber-attack kill chain.

- It investigates alerts and user activities.

For additional information about Microsoft Defender for Identity, please visit `https://docs.microsoft.com/en-us/defender-for-identity/what-is`.

To access Microsoft Defender for Identity and connect to on-premises AD DS, you need to create a Microsoft Defender for Identity instance by navigating to `https://portal.atp.azure.com/`. *Figure 10.15* shows what this will look like:

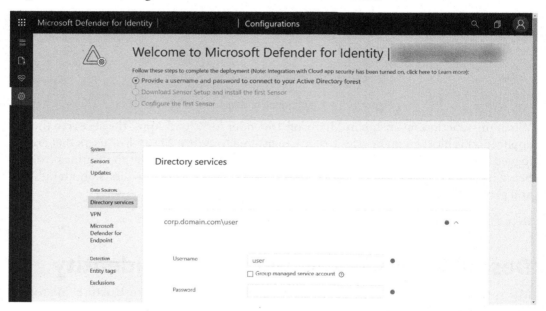

Figure 10.15 – The Microsoft Defender for Identity portal

When you select **Create**, the portal will step you through the process of downloading the Microsoft Defender for Identity agent on your on-premises AD DS server and authenticating with the Microsoft Defender for Identity portal.

Next, we will discuss Microsoft Defender for Endpoint.

Describing Microsoft Defender for Endpoint

Microsoft Defender for Endpoint protects devices that are used by the company by gathering the potential signals of threats on these devices. Microsoft Defender for Endpoint provides the ability to detect potential threats and perform automated investigations for a recommended response to these threats across our company's endpoint devices.

The features of Microsoft Defender for Endpoint can be listed as follows:

- Threat and vulnerability management
- Attack surface reduction
- Next-generation protection
- Endpoint detection and response
- Automated investigation and remediation
- Microsoft Threat Experts

For additional information about Microsoft Defender for Endpoint, please visit `https://docs.microsoft.com/en-us/microsoft-365/security/defender-endpoint/microsoft-defender-endpoint?view=o365-worldwide`.

To access the features of Microsoft Defender for Endpoint, navigate to `security.microsoft.com` and go to the **Endpoints** section of the menu. This is shown in *Figure 10.16*:

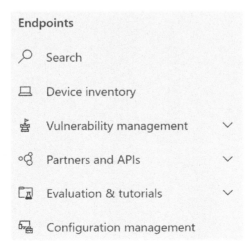

Figure 10.16 – The Defender for Endpoint menu

Microsoft Defender for Endpoint is not Microsoft Endpoint Manager or Intune. Microsoft Defender for Endpoint's features can be added to the configuration and management policies within Microsoft Endpoint Manager. Microsoft Endpoint Manager and Intune will be described further in *Chapter 12, Describing Security Management and Endpoint Security Capabilities of Microsoft 365*.

In the next section, we will provide a summary of what you have learned in this chapter.

Summary

In this chapter, we described the threat protection and XDR capabilities of Microsoft 365 Defender. This included Microsoft Defender for Office 365, Microsoft Defender for Cloud Apps, Microsoft Defender for Identity, and Microsoft Defender for Endpoint. The combination of these Microsoft 365 Defender solutions and Microsoft Defender for Cloud provides full XDR capabilities within Microsoft. In the next chapter, we will describe the security capabilities of Microsoft Sentinel and how these Microsoft Defender solutions further assist in protecting our company against threats and attacks through fully integrated security operations.

11

Describing the Security Capabilities of Microsoft Sentinel

The previous chapter covered how to manage the protection of Microsoft 365 resources through the **Extended Detection and Response (XDR)** capabilities of Microsoft 365 Defender. In this chapter, we will describe the security capabilities of Microsoft Sentinel for SIEM and SOAR, and the creation of a modern **Security Operations Center (SOC)**.

In this chapter, we're going to cover the following main topics:

- Describing the concepts of SIEM, SOAR, and XDR.
- Describing how Microsoft Sentinel provides integrated threat management.
- Describing Microsoft Sentinel in a modern SOC.

Technical requirements

In this chapter, we continue to explore configuring a tenant for use of solutions within Azure. There will be exercises that will require access to Azure. If you have not yet created the trial licenses for Microsoft 365 and a free trial of Azure, please follow the directions provided within *Chapter 1, Preparing for Your Microsoft Exam.*

Define the concepts of SIEM, SOAR, and XDR

Let's start by explaining Microsoft Sentinel and what **Security Information Event Management (SIEM)** and **Security Orchestration Automated Response (SOAR)** solutions are.

SIEM is a solution within a security operations center that gathers logs and events from various appliances and software within an information technology infrastructure. These SIEM solutions then review the logs and events for potential threats by searching for behavior that is not typical of best practices or may be seen as anomalous or atypical. The benefit of having and utilizing SIEM is that without it, security operations personnel would need to review each of these log and event files manually. Since there are thousands of log and event files within companies, this option has the potential for mistakes, as fatigue becomes an issue when scrolling through these files. SIEM picks out the logs and events that could be a threat, and security personnel can then investigate these potential threats, decreasing the time to recognize a threat or vulnerability and allowing the security operations team to be more efficient and effective in their investigations.

A SOAR solution is a complementary solution to SIEM. SOAR solutions can add automation to the response of potential events identified as threats in the log files by initiating a workflow. An example of this would be an activity log from a device that has been accessed from a location that has been flagged as a threat. The SOAR can initiate a workflow to take that device offline and send an alert to the security operations response team to investigate.

In *Chapter 10, Describing Threat Protection with Microsoft 365 Defender*, you learned about how the Microsoft Defender solutions, Microsoft 365 Defender and Microsoft Defender for Cloud, provide XDR for threat detection and response to attacks. These XDR solutions are used to provide data to Microsoft Sentinel for coordinated security operations.

Figure 11.1 shows how Microsoft Sentinel combines XDR solutions within Microsoft 365 and Azure, and data sources from multi-cloud connections and third-party security solutions, for a fully integrated and comprehensive SIEM and SOAR solution for your company:

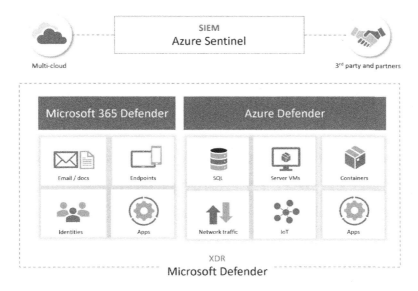

Figure 11.1 – Microsoft Sentinel with XDR and hybrid connections

The Microsoft 365 Defender portal provides a dashboard and tools to alert and respond to incidents for Microsoft 365 Defender solutions. Microsoft provides integration of this information through data connectors into Microsoft Sentinel. Since Microsoft is already gathering these events and logs within your current Microsoft 365 Defender licensing, there is no additional charge to add these data connectors to Microsoft Sentinel. *Figure 11. 2* is a diagram that illustrates the flow of log and event data through Microsoft 365 Defender as it feeds into Microsoft Sentinel for a single source of security operations and incident management:

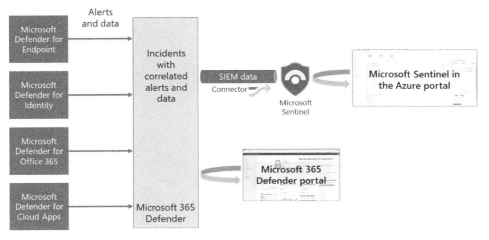

Figure 11.2 – Microsoft Sentinel integration with Microsoft Defender solutions

For additional information on Microsoft Defender integration with Microsoft Sentinel, please see this link: `https://docs.microsoft.com/en-us/microsoft-365/security/defender/microsoft-365-defender-integration-with-azure-sentinel?view=o365-worldwide`.

In the next section, you will learn how Microsoft Sentinel provides integrated threat management.

Describe how Microsoft Sentinel provides integrated threat management

Microsoft Sentinel is a scalable, cloud-native SIEM and SOAR solution. Microsoft Sentinel provides the full view across the company to recognize increasingly sophisticated attacks, increasing volumes of alerts, and long resolution time frames, making your company more efficient in responding to and eliminating threats.

Microsoft Sentinel is made up of the following workflow:

- Collect data at cloud scale across all users, devices, applications, and infrastructure in Azure, Microsoft 365, on-premises, and in multiple clouds.

- Detect previously undetected threats and minimize false positives using Microsoft's analytics and global threat intelligence.

- Investigate threats with machine learning and artificial intelligence, and hunt for suspicious activities at a global scale, utilizing the intelligence gathered through the cybersecurity work at Microsoft.

- Respond to incidents rapidly with built-in orchestration and automation of common tasks:

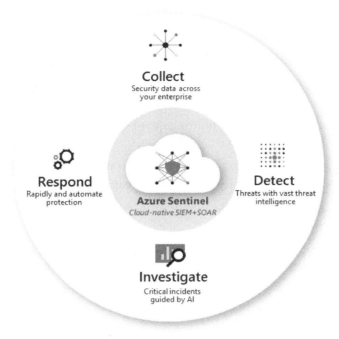

Figure 11.3 – The Microsoft Sentinel processes

There are some requirements for licensing and administrative roles before you can start using Microsoft Sentinel. These are as follows:

- All Azure AD licenses (free/O365/P1/P2) support the ability to ingest sign-in logs into Microsoft Sentinel. Microsoft Sentinel's pricing is based on per-gigabyte charges for the logs and data connector points that are ingested into Log Analytics and Microsoft Sentinel. For companies with a large amount of logs on a daily basis, there are tiered discounts that can be applied.

- The Azure Sentinel Contributor role on the workspace must be assigned to your user account.

- The Global Administrator or Security Administrator roles must be assigned to your user account on the tenant that you will be streaming the logs. Adhering to the principles of least privilege by assigning the Security Administrator role should be preferred.

- Read and write permissions to the Azure AD diagnostic settings must be assigned to the user account to be able to see the connection status.

- A Log Analytics workspace is also required to be configured to and associated with Microsoft Sentinel. This configuration will be discussed in the step-by-step exercise.

Microsoft Sentinel provides tools for managing your security operations through the use of the following:

- Workbooks to monitor collected data from data sources.

- Analytics that provide the ability to query data that has been collected from data sources.

- Incident management when a hunting query is triggered to assign, investigate, and respond to a potential threat.

- Security automation and orchestration through the use of Azure Logic Apps to create a workflow to promptly respond to threats.

- Playbook automation is a collection of procedures that can be used for your automated responses.

- Investigation provides tools that can be used to evaluate the affected resources within your environment to find the root source of an incident.

- Hunting provides queries to run and threat modeling based on the MITRE ATT&CK framework to identify the potential for an attack before it becomes a threat to your company.

- Integrated threat protection works with the XDR tools within Microsoft to identify threats based on the data collected through Microsoft Defender solutions and Microsoft's global threat intelligence.

Additional information on Microsoft Sentinel can be found at this link: `https://docs.microsoft.com/en-us/azure/sentinel/overview`.

Next, you will complete an exercise to set up Microsoft Sentinel and connect data sources in your Azure tenant.

Setting up Microsoft Sentinel and connecting log data

Now that we understand Microsoft Sentinel and what the requirements are from a licensing and role perspective, we will go through the step-by-step configuration of Microsoft Sentinel for **Azure Active Directory** (**Azure AD**) sign-in activity logs and audit logs:

1. Navigate to `portal.azure.com` and search for `Microsoft Sentinel`:

Figure 11.4 – Navigate to Microsoft Sentinel

2. Select **Create Microsoft Sentinel**:

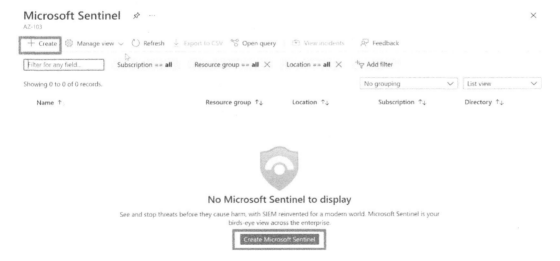

Figure 11.5 – Create a new Microsoft Sentinel service

3. The first step in the setup process of Microsoft Sentinel is to connect a Log Analytics workspace. In this exercise, select **Create a new workspace**:

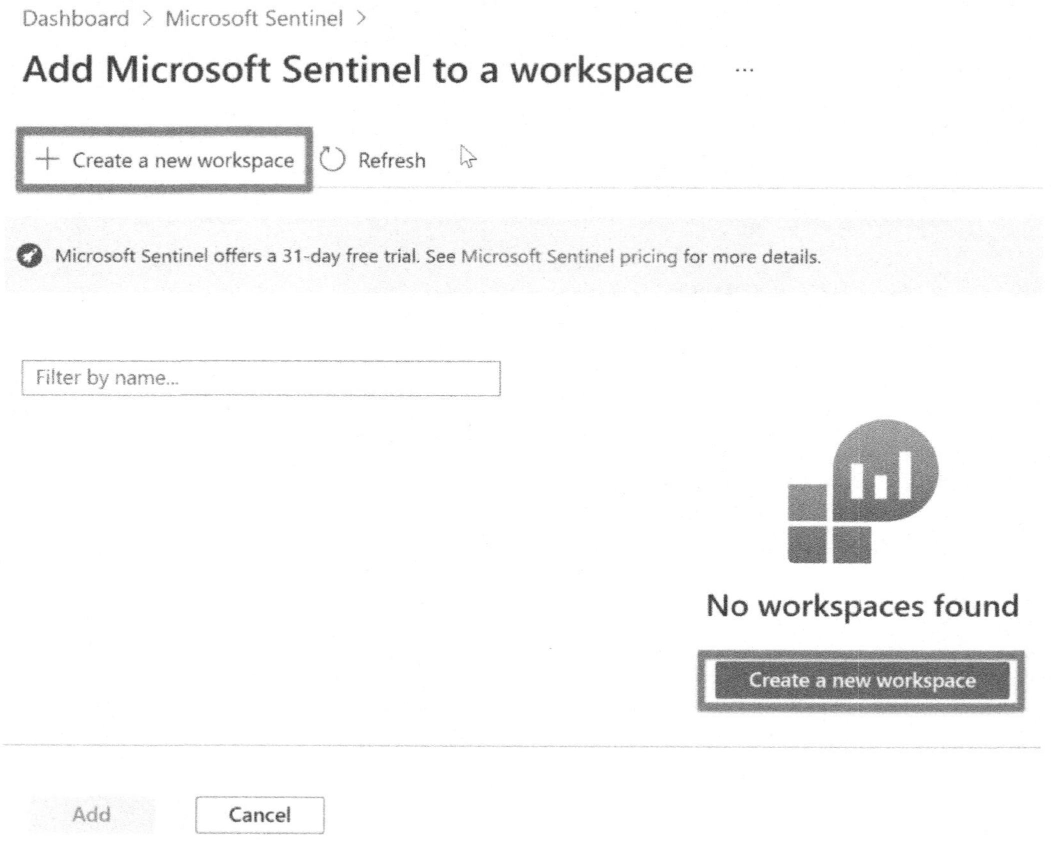

Figure 11.6 – Create a new Log Analytics workspace

4. Enter the information for the resource group and a name for Microsoft Sentinel. Select **Review + Create**:

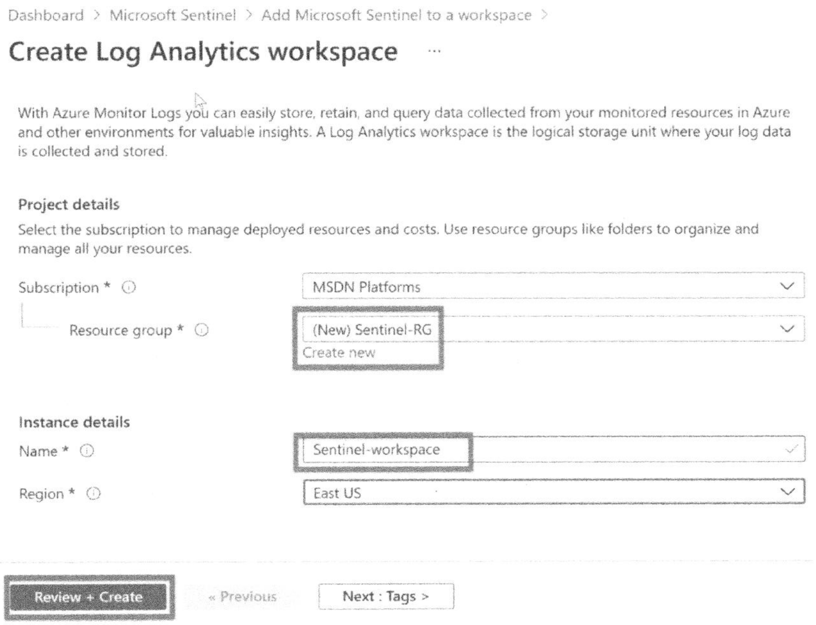

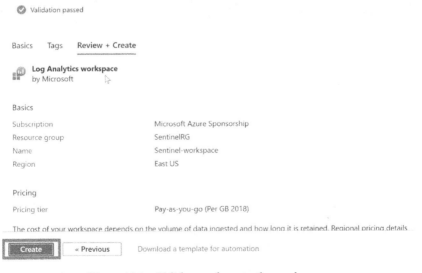

Figure 11.7 – Create the Log Analytics workspace

5. After the validation completes, select **Review + Create** to create the workspace:

Figure 11.8 – Validate and create the workspace

6. After the Log Analytics workspace is created, return to the **Add Microsoft Sentinel to a workspace** creation page. If you receive notification of the Log Analytics workspace being created and it does not appear, select **Refresh**. Select the Log Analytics workspace that was created and click **Add**:

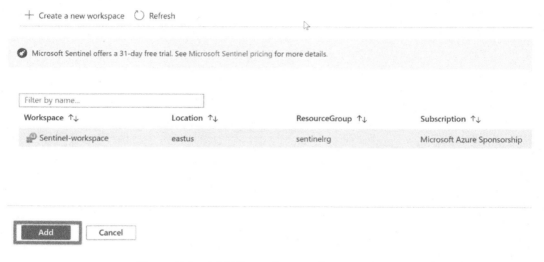

Figure 11.9 – Add Microsoft Sentinel to a workspace

7. After selecting **Add**, you will be taken to Microsoft Sentinel, and a 30-day trial of it will be activated. Select **OK** to begin using Microsoft Sentinel:

Figure 11.10 – The Microsoft Sentinel trial activated

8. The **Microsoft Sentinel** Getting Started page will open. This page provides the steps to configure Microsoft Sentinel. The first step is to collect data. Select **Connect** to go to the data connectors, as shown in *Figure 11.11*:

Figure 11.11 – Connect data to collect data

9. Connecting data can also be accessed through the **Data connectors** page under the **Configuration** menu:

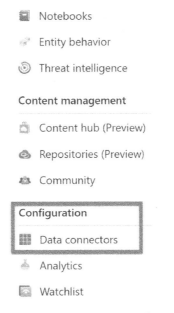

Figure 11.12 – Data connectors configuration

10. In this exercise, we are connecting Azure AD as the data connector. On the **Data connectors** page, use the search bar and type `Azure Active Directory`:

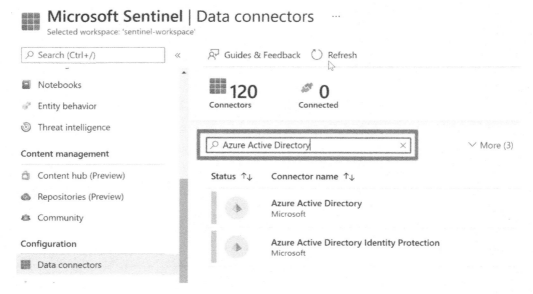

Figure 11.13 – Search for Azure Active Directory

11. Select **Azure Active Directory**. A new tile will open on the right, showing information about the **Azure Active Directory** connector:

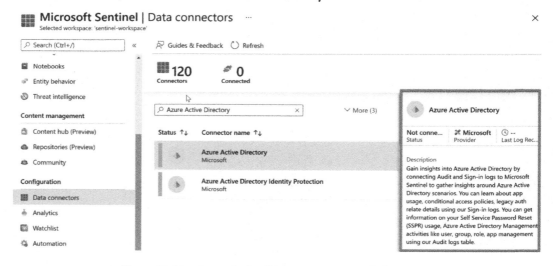

Figure 11.14 – Azure Active Directory connector information

12. Scroll down on this tile and select **Open connector page**:

Data types

〜∥ᐟ SigninLogs   --

〜∥ᐟ AuditLogs   --

〜∥ᐟ AADNonInteractiveUserSignInLogs   --

〜∥ᐟ AADServicePrincipalSignInLogs   --

〜∥ᐟ AADManagedIdentitySignInLogs   --

〜∥ᐟ AADProvisioningLogs   --

〜∥ᐟ ADFSSignInLogs   --

〜∥ᐟ AADUserRiskEvents   --

〜∥ᐟ AADRiskyUsers   --

Open connector page

Figure 11.15 – Open the Azure AD connector page

13. The connector page provides the prerequisites and the configuration to connect this data source. *Figure 11.16* shows that the prerequisites for connecting this data source have been met:

Azure Active Directory   ⋯

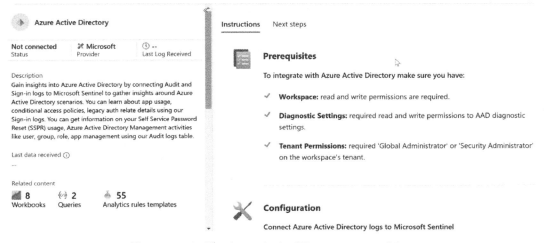

Figure 11.16 – The Azure Active Directory prerequisites

14. Next, select all of the **Sign-In Logs** and **Audit Logs** checkboxes, and click **Apply Changes** to save:

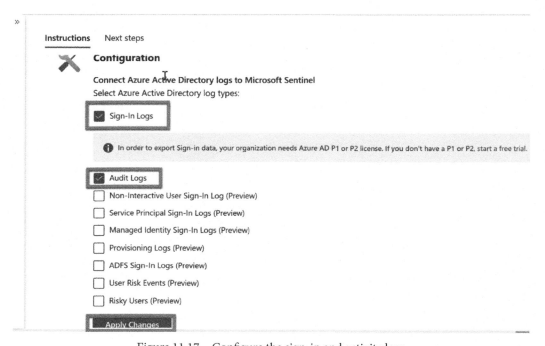

Figure 11.17 – Configure the sign-in and activity logs

15. On the **Data connectors** page, **Azure Active Directory** will show as connected. This process may take some time. *Figure 11.18* shows the connector for **Azure Active Directory** has been successfully connected with the green bar:

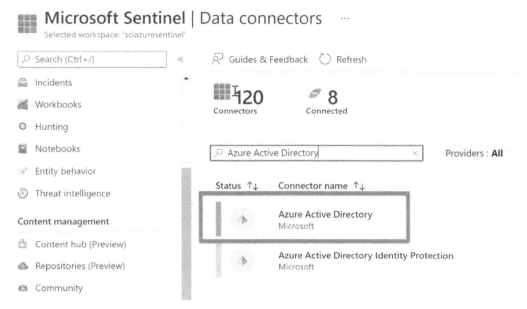

Figure 11.18 – The successful Azure AD data connected

16. You have now completed the creation of a Log Analytics workspace, connecting that workspace and creating Microsoft Sentinel, and connecting Azure AD data to Microsoft Sentinel. In the *Reviewing Azure AD activity by using Log Analytics and Microsoft Sentinel* section of this chapter, we will go through the steps to review this activity through queries in Log Analytics and Microsoft Sentinel workbooks.

Repeat steps *10* through *16* for each of the Microsoft Defender solutions to connect these data sources to Microsoft Sentinel.

The next section will discuss how Microsoft Sentinel provides the path for your company to establish a modern SOC.

Describe Microsoft Sentinel in a modern SOC

Microsoft Sentinel prepares a company to build a SOC that can focus on rapidly detecting, prioritizing, and triaging potential attacks. Companies that have a dedicated operations team that reviews events to identify and eliminate incidents that are false positives and be able to focus on real attacks. When you have a centralized security operations team, this team can monitor security-related data and investigate security breaches and threats. These teams work with other teams within an organization to communicate, investigate, and hunt activities that are aligned with the specific infrastructure or application teams.

Figure 11.19 provides a diagram of how an SOC team would respond to an incident:

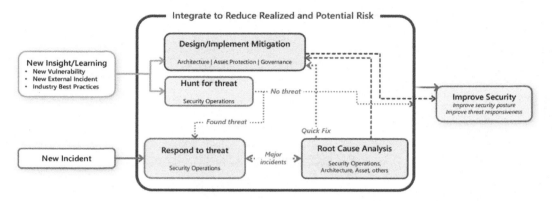

Figure 11.19 – The SOC incident response workflow

The NIST Cybersecurity Framework provides guidance and best practices for aligning security functions within your operations. For information on the NIST Cybersecurity Framework, you can visit this link: `https://www.nist.gov/cyberframework`.

Some of these best practices include the following:

- Detect, respond, and recover to restore confidentiality, integrity, and availability of workloads before and after an attack.

- Acknowledge an alert quickly.

- Reduce the time to remediate a detected adversary.

- Prioritize security investments into systems that have high intrinsic value.

- Proactively hunt for adversaries as your system matures.

Additional information about security operations within Microsoft can be found at this link: `https://docs.microsoft.com/en-us/azure/architecture/framework/security/monitor-security-operations`.

As part of building a modern SOC, you should understand the responsibilities and task structure of a security operations team. The following is a sample list of tasks, broken down into daily, weekly, and monthly tasks.

Daily tasks

The following are the daily tasks:

- Triage and investigate incidents.
- Explore hunting queries and bookmarks.
- Automatically create incidents from Microsoft security alerts.
- Hunt for threats with Microsoft Sentinel.
- Keep track of data during hunting with Microsoft Sentinel.
- Review and enable analytic rules.
- Review and enable data connectors.
- Verify resource connections to the Log Analytics agent.
- Check and address any playbook failures.

Weekly tasks

The following are the weekly tasks:

- Workbook updates
- Microsoft Sentinel GitHub repository review
- Microsoft Sentinel auditing

Monthly tasks

The following are the monthly tasks:

- Review user access.
- A Log Analytics workspace review.

More information on these tasks can be found at this link: `https://docs.microsoft.com/en-us/azure/sentinel/best-practices`.

The next section will provide a summary of what you have learned in this chapter.

Summary

In this chapter, we discussed Microsoft Sentinel and the capabilities to connect to data sources within Microsoft 365 Defender, Microsoft Defender for Cloud, multi-cloud resources, and third-party security solutions for a complete SIEM and SOAR solution for your company. We also discussed that using Microsoft Sentinel can establish a foundation to build a modern SOC for your company to detect, respond, and recover from threats and attacks. The next chapter will describe the security management and endpoint management capabilities within Microsoft 365.

12

Describing Security Management and the Endpoint Security Capabilities of Microsoft 365

The previous chapter covered the security capabilities of Microsoft Sentinel for SIEM and SOAR, and the creation of a modern **Security Operations Center** (**SOC**). In this chapter, we will describe the various security management capabilities of Microsoft 365 through the use of the Microsoft 365 Defender portal to increase your security posture, review reports, and manage incidents.

In this chapter, we're going to cover the following main topics:

- Describing the Microsoft 365 Defender portal
- Describing the use of Microsoft Secure Score
- Describing the security reports and dashboards
- Describing incidents and incident management capabilities
- Describing endpoint security with Microsoft Intune

Technical requirements

In this chapter, we will continue to explore configuring a tenant for use of solutions within Azure. There will be exercises that will require access to Azure. If you have not yet created the trial licenses for Microsoft 365 and a free trial of Azure, please follow the directions provided within *Chapter 1, Preparing for Your Microsoft Exam.*

Describe the Microsoft 365 Defender portal

In *Chapter 11, Describing the Security Capabilities of Microsoft Sentinel,* we described the various solutions that create Microsoft's **Extended Detection and Response (XDR)** capabilities within Microsoft 365 Defender. This chapter will describe how the Microsoft 365 Defender portal is used to manage security posture, review the various reports and dashboards, and respond to incidents. Let's start by reviewing the various areas of the Microsoft 365 Defender portal and accessing the Microsoft Defender solutions.

To access the Microsoft 365 Defender portal, navigate to `https://security.microsoft.com`.

When the Microsoft 365 Defender portal opens, you may be prompted for a quick guided tour of the portal, as shown in *Figure 12.1*:

Figure 12.1 – The Microsoft 365 Defender quick tour

Entering the home screen, there are tiles that you can use to begin to understand the security posture of your company. This includes Secure Score (which we will review in the next section), users at risk, potential threats, and enabling the **Microsoft 365 Defender** connector to Microsoft Sentinel:

Figure 12.2 – The Microsoft 365 Defender home screen

Figure 12.3 shows more of the tiles as you scroll down through the home screen with **Secure Score**, user risk, and noncompliant devices:

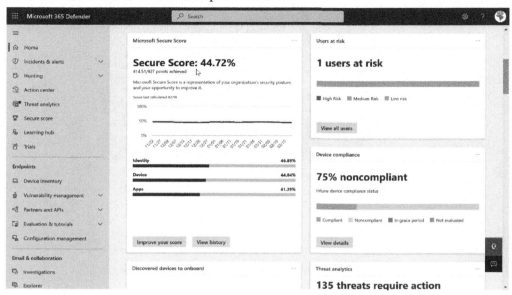

Figure 12.3 – Microsoft 365 Defender Secure Score and noncompliant devices

Figure 12.4 shows the threat detections and the Microsoft Sentinel connector tile:

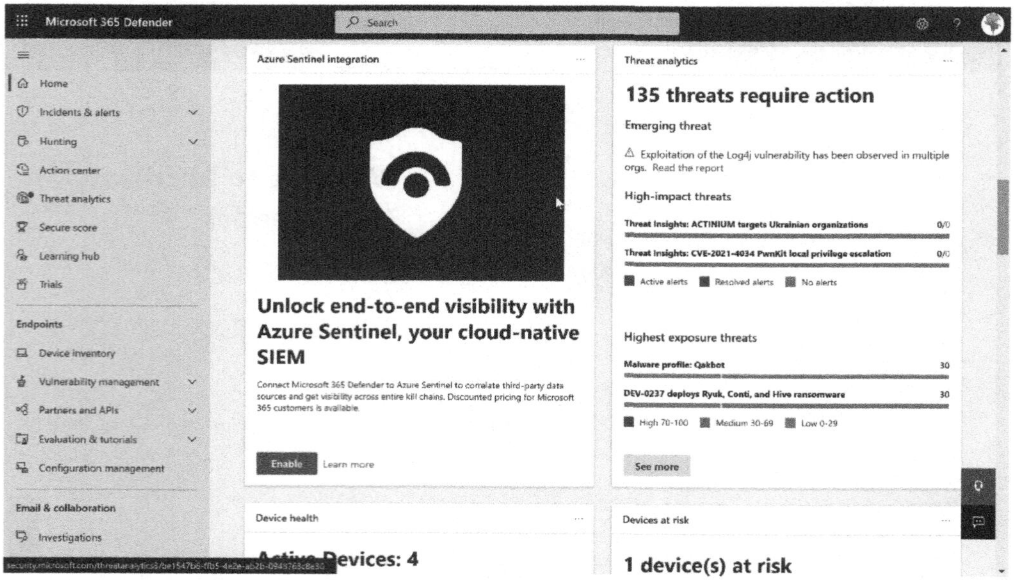

Figure 12.4 – The Microsoft Sentinel connection and active threats

For users of Microsoft 365, the **Microsoft 365 Defender** portal can be used as the central point to manage your company's security posture. The menu on the left provides direct access to manage **Endpoints**, **Email & collaboration**, service health, and activity and audit management.

The **Email & collaboration** menu provides helpful tools to trace messages, create campaigns, and provide attack simulation training, as shown in *Figure 12.5*:

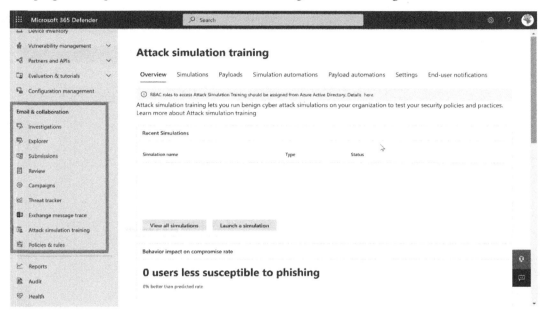

Figure 12.5 – The Email & collaboration menu in Microsoft 365 Defender

Email & collaboration can be very helpful to understand whether users are in additional need of training to understand the threats of unknown attachments and links in emails, shared drives (SharePoint Online and OneDrive for Business), and Teams channels and chats.

In the next section, we will describe using Microsoft Secure Score for Microsoft 365 security posture management.

Describe the use of Microsoft Secure Score

In *Chapter 9, Describing Security Management and Capabilities of Azure*, there was a section that described **Cloud Security Posture Management** (**CSPM**). In Azure, this is accomplished using Microsoft Defender for Cloud. For Microsoft 365 resources, the same can be accomplished within the Microsoft 365 Defender portal. As Microsoft Defender for Cloud provides a secure score for Azure AD and Azure resources, Microsoft 365 Defender provides Secure Score for Azure AD and Microsoft 365 resources, including identity, devices, and applications. *Figure 12.6* shows the **Secure Score** tile:

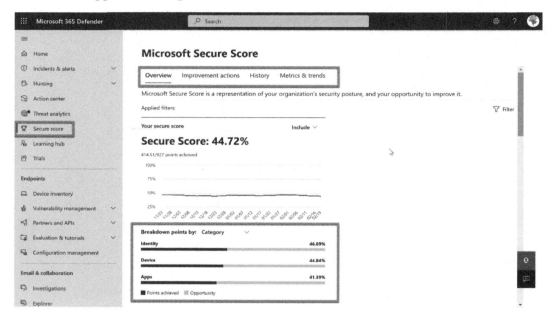

Figure 12.6 – Microsoft 365 Defender Secure Score

Microsoft 365 Defender Secure Score is made up of the following areas to manage your security posture:

- **Secure Score** is the adapted score based on best practices and controls in place for **Identity**, **Devices**, and **Applications**. *Figure 12.6* shows an example of the Secure Score.

- **Improvement actions** provides best practice guidance for controls that you can put in place to improve your Secure Score. These actions can be sorted by score impact and category to provide additional focus. The improvement actions can also be exported to review and report to others without access to the portal. *Figure 12.7* shows some improvement actions that you may see in your portal:

Microsoft Secure Score

Overview   **Improvement actions**   History   Metrics & trends

Actions you can take to improve your Microsoft Secure Score. Score updates may take up to 24 hours.

Applied filters:

↓ Export   146 items   🔍 Search   ▽ Filter   ☰ Group by ⌄

Rank	Improvement action	Score impact	Points achieved	Status	Regressed	Have license?	Cate
1	Block credential stealing from the Windows local security aut...	+0.97%	0/9	○ To address	No	Yes	Devi
2	Use advanced protection against ransomware	+0.97%	0/9	○ To address	No	Yes	Devi
3	Block Win32 API calls from Office macros	+0.97%	0/9	○ To address	No	Yes	Devi
4	Block execution of potentially obfuscated scripts	+0.97%	0/9	○ To address	No	Yes	Devi
5	Block Office applications from injecting code into other proc...	+0.97%	0/9	○ To address	No	Yes	Devi
6	Block executable content from email client and webmail	+0.97%	0/9	○ To address	No	Yes	Devi
7	Block process creations originating from PSExec and WMI co...	+0.97%	0/9	○ To address	No	Yes	Devi
8	Block Office applications from creating executable content	+0.97%	0/9	○ To address	No	Yes	Devi
9	Block persistence through WMI event subscription	+0.97%	0/9	○ To address	No	Yes	Devi

Figure 12.7 – Secure Score – Improvement actions

- **History** shows the trends of your secure score over the recent timeline. This can provide you with insights into areas where changes may have been made to improve or decrease your current Secure Score. *Figure 12.8* shows the **History** section:

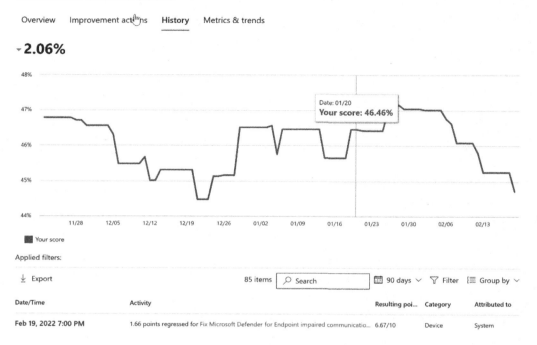

Figure 12.8 – Secure Score – History

- **Metrics & trends** shows the Secure Score trend against similar organizations. This includes any improvement or downward trends within your tenant and similar tenants. *Figure 12.9* shows the metrics and trends reporting:

Microsoft Secure Score

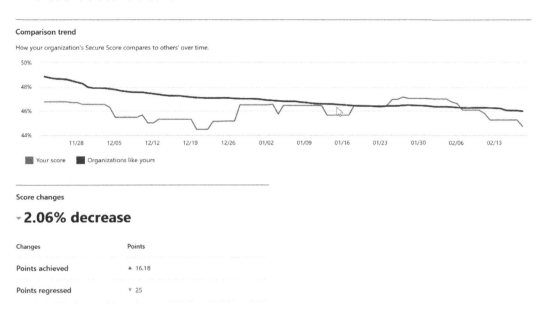

Figure 12.9 – Secure Score metrics and trends against other organizations

Additional information on Microsoft 365 Defender Secure Score can be found at this link: https://docs.microsoft.com/en-us/microsoft-365/security/defender/microsoft-secure-score?view=o365-worldwide.

The next section will describe how to use the Microsoft 365 Defender portal security reports and dashboards.

Describe the security reports and dashboards

As stated at the beginning of the previous section, the Microsoft 365 Defender portal is used for security posture management. This includes security reports and helpful dashboards for managing identity, devices, and applications. These dashboards include the ability to access the full solutions of the Microsoft 365 Defender XDR suite:

- Microsoft Defender for Office 365
- Microsoft Defender for Cloud Apps
- Microsoft Defender for Identity
- Microsoft Defender for Endpoint

Microsoft Defender for Office 365 and Microsoft Defender for Endpoint can be accessed through the **Microsoft 365 Defender** portal menu, as shown in *Figure 12.10*:

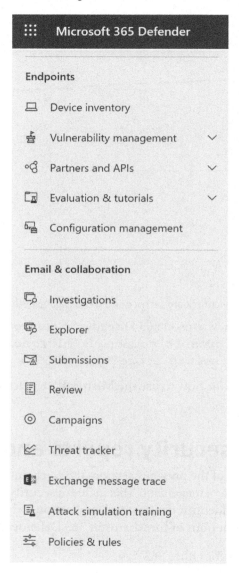

Figure 12.10 – The Endpoints and Email & collaboration menus

Other Microsoft Defender solutions can be found by scrolling down on the **Microsoft 365 Defender** menu to **More resources**. This tile includes access to the Microsoft Defender for Cloud Apps portal, Azure AD, Device Management, Office 365 security, and others. Some of these are shown in *Figure 12.11*:

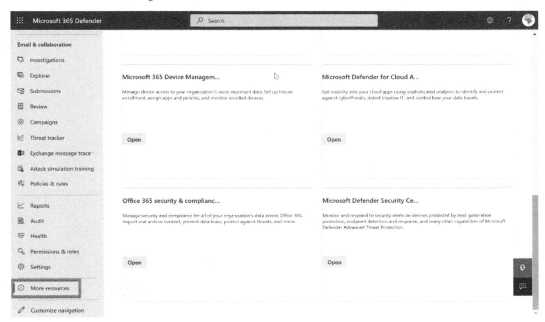

Figure 12.11 – Microsoft 365 Defender – More resources

At the bottom of the **Microsoft 365 Defender** portal menu, you will find the section to review reports, health reports, audit reports, permissions and roles, and settings, as shown in *Figure 12.12*:

Figure 12.12 – Reporting menu

The first section of this menu that we will review is **Reports**. Within the **Reports** tile, you have access to various reports based on general security reporting, endpoints, and email and collaboration. Each of these reports will take you to a separate dashboard with graphics to analyze any potential threats or vulnerabilities within your tenant:

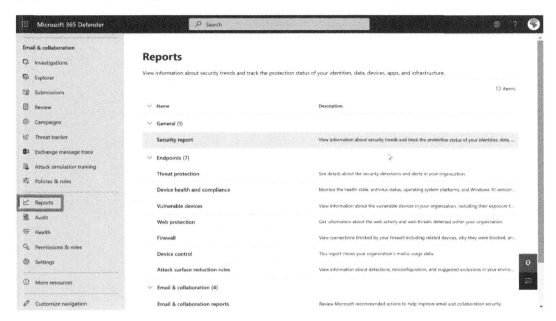

Figure 12.13 – Microsoft 365 Defender – Reports

The next selection is **Audit**. Within the **Audit** tile, you can search for specific activities that have taken place on files, folders, or sites. These searches can be used to investigate the activity of specific users. The **Audit** tile also allows us to set specific retention policies for our audits so that we can review these at a later date:

Figure 12.14 – Microsoft 365 Defender – Audits

Health allows you to review the service health of the Microsoft 365 solutions. This area is helpful if you are seeing an outage of a particular solution or service. You can review whether there is a regional or global service outage within Microsoft, or whether it is isolated to your tenant:

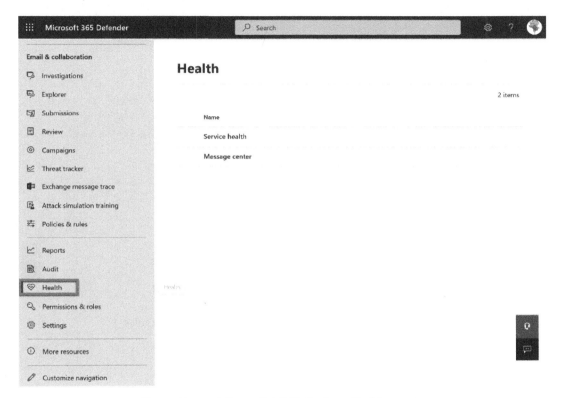

Figure 12.15 – Microsoft 365 Defender – Health reports

Permissions & roles allows you to manage specific roles within the Microsoft 365 Defender portal. These are role-based access controls for the specific capabilities within the portal and not the overall Azure AD tenant:

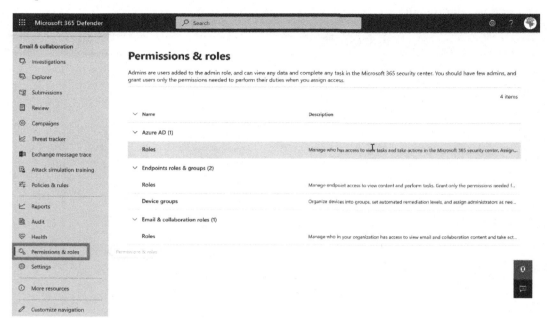

Figure 12.16 – Microsoft 365 Defender – Permissions & roles

The final section of this menu is **Settings**. This allows you to customize some of the settings within the Microsoft 365 Defender portal, as shown in *Figure 12.17*:

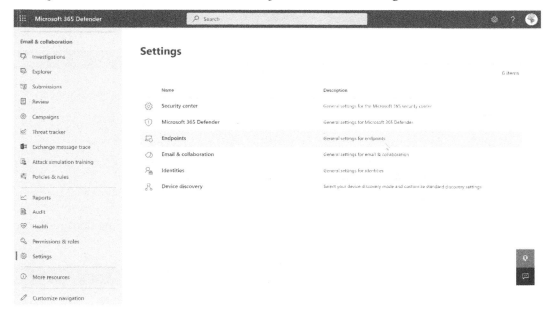

Figure 12.17 – Microsoft 365 Defender – Settings

You should now understand the different reports, audits, and settings that are provided within the Microsoft 365 Defender portal.

The next section will describe how to use the Microsoft 365 Defender portal for incident management.

Describe incidents and incident management capabilities

As stated at the beginning of the section describing Secure Score, the Microsoft 365 Defender portal can be used for security posture management within your entire Microsoft 365 tenant for identity, devices, and applications. This includes incidents created based on potential threats and vulnerabilities and the management of those incidents.

Within the Microsoft 365 Defender portal, there is an **Incidents & alerts** menu that will assign incidents on potential threats that need further investigation. You can manage these incidents through the incident response process within the portal, as shown in *Figure 12.18*:

Figure 12.18 – Microsoft 365 Defender – Incidents

You can also configure alerts based on incidents to assign to the specific incident response teams. The dashboard for **Alerts** is shown in *Figure 12.19*:

Figure 12.19 – Microsoft 365 Defender – Alerts

If your company is not using Microsoft Sentinel for security operations, Microsoft 365 Defender provides an **Advanced hunting** menu to run Kusto queries to review activity and find potential threats:

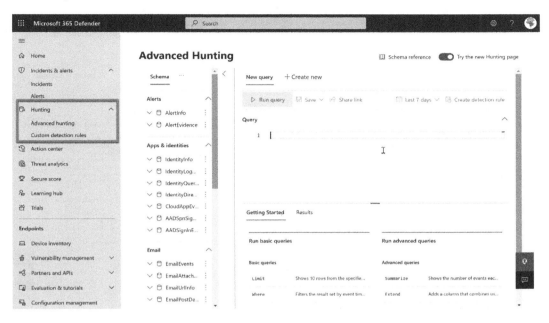

Figure 12.20 – Microsoft 365 Defender – Advanced Hunting

The **Threat analytics** menu provides a dashboard of known global threats found through Microsoft's threat intelligence team. This dashboard can help you identify potential threats and the possible impact on your tenant:

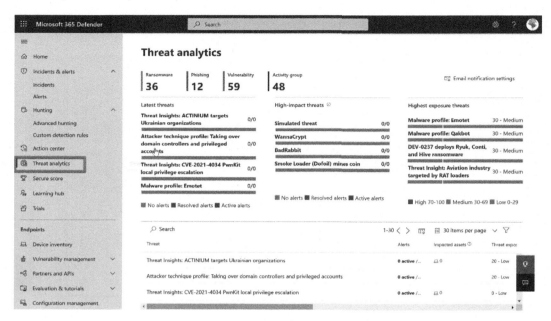

Figure 12.21 – Microsoft 365 Defender – Threat analytics

You should now have a fundamental understanding of how you can use Microsoft 365 Defender for incident management.

In the next section, we will describe endpoint security with Microsoft Endpoint Manager and Intune.

Describe endpoint security with Microsoft Intune

The Microsoft 365 Defender portal has a menu section for reviewing and managing security for endpoints. For full configuration and management of endpoints, you should be using Microsoft Defender for Endpoint and configure the management through Endpoint Manager with Microsoft Intune.

Figure 12.22 shows the device inventory list that is found within the Microsoft 365 Defender portal. This provides a list of devices that have been found within your tenant. This can be virtual machines or endpoint devices:

Figure 12.22 – Microsoft 365 Defender for Endpoint – Device inventory

Navigating to **Configuration management** shows further detail on devices that are being monitored with Microsoft Defender for Endpoint and provides you with an **Onboard more devices** link, as shown in *Figure 12.23*:

Figure 12.23 – Microsoft 365 Defender for Endpoint – Configuration management

Selecting **Onboard more devices** will take you directly to the Microsoft Endpoint Manager admin center and the Microsoft Defender for Endpoint portal. Within this portal, you can configure the security profile for devices and the **MDM** and **App Protection Policy** settings for devices that are registered on the Azure AD tenant. This is where you decide whether you are using Microsoft Intune for **Mobile Device Management** (MDM) or **Mobile Application Management** (MAM). More information on Microsoft Endpoint Manager can be found at this link: `https://docs.microsoft.com/en-us/mem/endpoint-manager-overview`.

Figure 12.24 shows some of these settings:

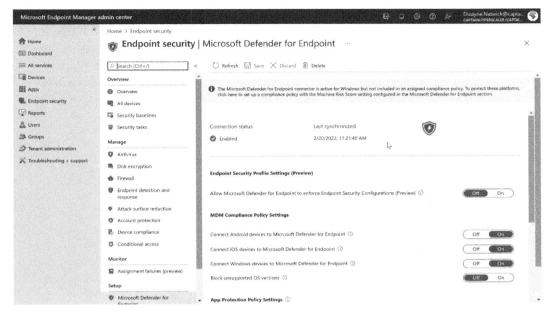

Figure 12.24 – Endpoint security in Microsoft Endpoint Manager for Intune

MDM is most widely used when a company supplies employees with company-owned devices or has very high compliance requirements. MDM manages the entire device and has full control; this is not always welcomed by users with personal devices. If companies want a level of protection for company data, MAM can manage company-specific resources without taking full control of a personal device.

More information on Microsoft Intune can be found at this link: `https://docs.microsoft.com/en-us/mem/intune/fundamentals/what-is-intune`.

The next section will provide a summary of what you have learned in this chapter.

Summary

In this chapter, we discussed the security management and endpoint management capabilities within Microsoft 365. This included reviewing the Microsoft 365 Defender portal. Within the Microsoft 365 Defender portal, we can manage our security posture using Secure Score to identify improvements and controls that we can put in place to protect identities, devices, and applications. We can also view reports, audit activities, manage and alert on incidents, and do threat analysis. In the next chapter, we will discuss the compliance capabilities within Microsoft.

Section 5:
The Microsoft Compliance Monitoring Capabilities within Microsoft 365 and Azure

This section will focus on the governance, compliance, and information protection solutions that are available within Azure and Microsoft 365.

This part of the book comprises the following chapters:

13
Compliance Management Capabilities in Microsoft

The previous chapter covered the various security management capabilities of Microsoft 365 through the use of the Microsoft 365 Defender portal to increase your security posture, review reports, and manage incidents. In this chapter, we will describe how to use the Microsoft compliance center to access and manage security best practices and regulatory compliance with your Microsoft 365 connected applications.

In this chapter, we're going to cover the following main topics:

- Describing the compliance center
- Describing Microsoft Compliance Manager
- Describing the use and benefits of the compliance score

Technical requirements

In this chapter, we continue to explore configuring a tenant for the use of solutions within Azure. There will be exercises that will require access to Azure. If you have not yet created the trial licenses for Microsoft 365 and a free trial of Azure, please follow the directions provided within *Chapter 1, Preparing for Your Microsoft Exam*.

Describe the compliance center

In *Chapter 12, Describing Security Management and Endpoint Security Capabilities of Microsoft 365*, we described how the Microsoft 365 Defender portal is used to manage security postures by reviewing various reports and dashboards, including Secure Score. The Microsoft 365 compliance center provides similar guidance for governance and compliance of Microsoft 365 solutions.

To access the Microsoft 365 compliance center, navigate to `https://compliance.microsoft.com`.

When the Microsoft 365 compliance center portal opens, you may be prompted for a quick guided tour of the portal, as shown in *Figure 13.1*:

Figure 13.1 – The Microsoft 365 compliance center

Entering the home screen, there are tiles that you can use to begin to understand the security posture of your company. This includes the compliance score, which we will review in the *Describe Compliance Manager* section, enabling Microsoft Priva, retention label usage, active alerts, communication compliance, pending disposition reviews, and the solution catalog:

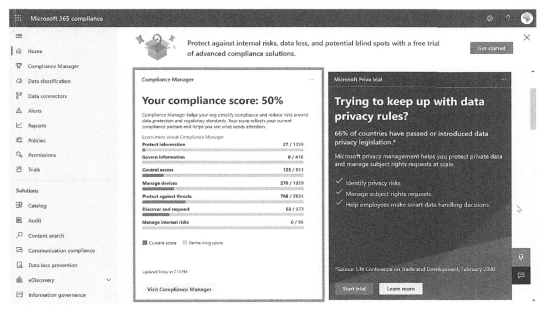

Figure 13.2 – The Microsoft 365 Defender home screen

Figure 13.3 shows the **Solution catalog** tile; selecting **View all solutions in the catalog** will take you to a catalog of the solutions:

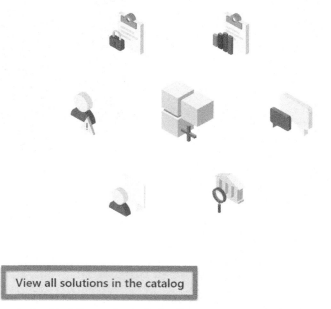

Figure 13.3 – The Microsoft 365 Defender Secure Score and non-compliant devices

Figure 13.4 shows the solutions available in the catalog's information protection and governance – privacy, insider risk management, and discovery and response:

Figure 13.4 – The Microsoft Sentinel connection and active threats

For users of Microsoft 365, the Microsoft 365 compliance center provides solutions to govern data, groups, sites, and collaboration. These solutions maintain a level of company control to classify information, recognize and report on communications that may be detrimental to the company, and protect against data being shared with unauthorized users inside or outside of the company.

Chapter 14, Describing Information Protection and Governance Capabilities of Microsoft 365, will provide further details describing these solutions with sensitivity label policies, data loss prevention policies, and retention label policies.

Chapter 15, Describing Insider Risk, eDiscovery, and Audit Capabilities in Microsoft 365, will provide further information on insider risk and the discovery and response solutions.

In the next section, we will describe Compliance Manager.

Describing Compliance Manager

As Microsoft Defender for Cloud provides a regulatory compliance section for reviewing company compliance to the Azure security baseline, ISO 27001:2013, and other standards, Microsoft 365 Compliance Manager does the same for Microsoft 365.

Compliance Manager provides a compliance score for the level of compliance against the Microsoft data protection baseline and regulatory standards. The data protection baseline is the default standard, much like the Azure security baseline is the default within Microsoft Defender for Cloud. Compliance Manager provides a compliance score based on the shared responsibility model, with a score for your responsibility and a score for Microsoft's responsibility. *Figure 13.5* shows the compliance score:

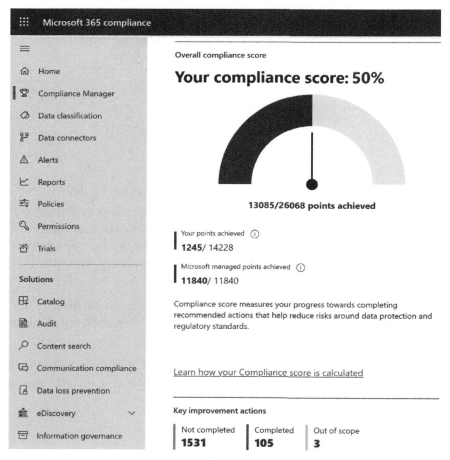

Figure 13.5 – The Microsoft 365 compliance score

For more information on calculations of the compliance score, go to this link: `https://docs.microsoft.com/en-us/microsoft-365/compliance/compliance-score-calculation?view=o365-worldwide`.

Microsoft 365 compliance is made up of the following areas to manage your governance and compliance of resources; the headings are shown in *Figure 13.6*:

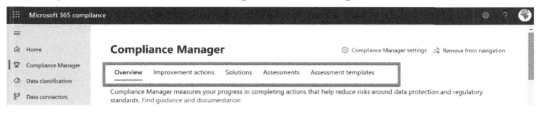

Figure 13.6 – The Compliance Manager sections

- **Overview** provides a summary of the compliance score for the data protection baseline, along with a summary list of improvement actions, solutions, and a breakdown based on the various solution areas.

- **Improvement actions** provides best practice guidance for controls that you can put in place to improve your compliance score. These actions can be sorted by score, impact, and category to provide additional focus. The improvement actions can also be exported to review and report to others without access to the portal. *Figure 13.7* shows some improvement actions that you may see in your portal:

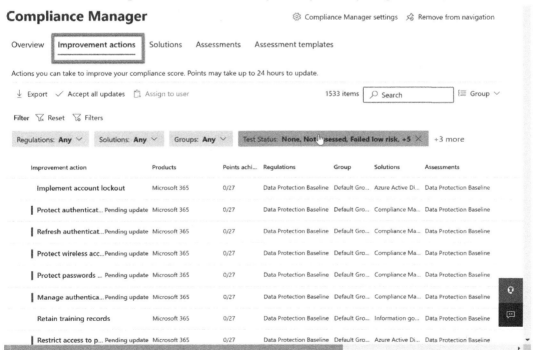

Figure 13.7 – Improvement actions

- **Solutions** provides information on how solutions contribute to your score and their remaining opportunity for improvement. This is provided in a list with the impact of enabling solutions. *Figure 13.8* provides a view of solution recommendations:

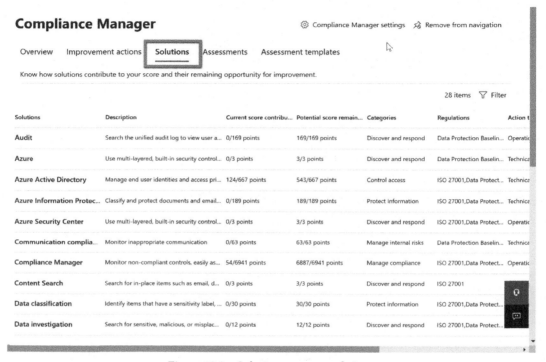

Figure 13.8 – Solution recommendations

- **Assessments** provides a view of the compliance score based on assessment templates that have been enabled on your Microsoft 365 tenant. *Figure 13.9* shows the results of the active assessments:

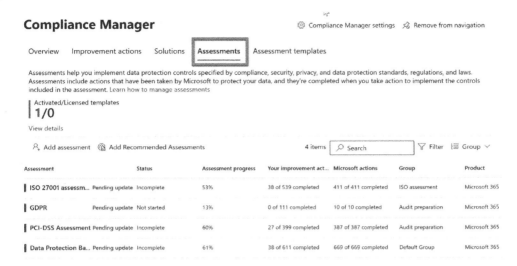

Figure 13.9 – Assessment results

- **Assessment templates** shows the various regulatory compliance standards that you can enable on your tenant or workloads for evaluating compliance. *Figure 13.10* shows where you can choose the various assessment templates for compliance and regulatory standards. Some of these templates require additional licensing:

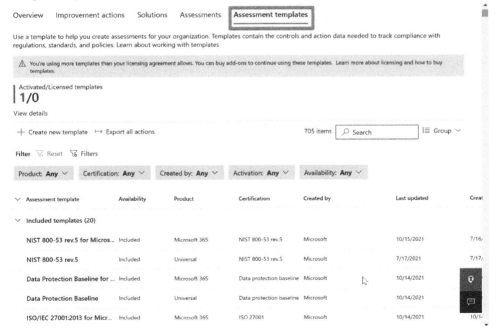

Figure 13.10 – The Compliance Manager sections

Additional information on Microsoft 365 Compliance Manager can be found at this link: `https://docs.microsoft.com/en-us/microsoft-365/compliance/compliance-manager?view=o365-worldwide`.

The next section describes the use and benefits of the compliance score.

Describe the use and benefits of the compliance score

As stated at the beginning of the previous section, we discussed the sections of Compliance Manager. The main focus of the Microsoft 365 compliance center and, specifically, Compliance Manager is the compliance score. In this section, we will break down the compliance score and how we can use it to increase company compliance.

There are three areas that make up the compliance score:

- The improvement action score provides a score based on the impact of implementing a recommended improvement. Each action has a different impact on your score, depending on the potential risk involved from not implementing the control.

- The control score is the sum of points earned by completing improvement actions within the control and is applied to your overall compliance score when the control meets an implemented status and a test result of passed.

- The assessment score is the sum of your control scores using each of the action scores, and Microsoft and your improvement actions.

Figure 13.11 shows this overall compliance score:

Overall compliance score

Your compliance score: 50%

13084/26068 points achieved

Your points achieved ⓘ
1244/ 14228

Microsoft managed points achieved ⓘ
11840/ 11840

Compliance score measures your progress towards completing
recommended actions that help reduce risks around data protection and
regulatory standards.

Figure 13.11 – Overall compliance score

The compliance score provides a snapshot of your company's governance and compliance
in relation to the protection of data and solutions within Microsoft 365.

Reviewing the improvement actions provides you with an idea of the impact that a control will make on decreasing vulnerabilities and risk within your company. Note that implementing an improvement action will take approximately 24 hours before the score will be impacted. *Figure 13.12* shows the improvement action list:

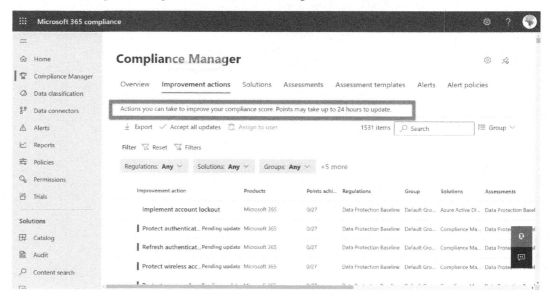

Figure 13.12 – The improvement action list

Selecting a specific improvement action will open a tile that provides directions and guidance for implementing the control. You also have the option to assign these actions and add details for possible implementation of a control that is not native to Microsoft, uploading the documentation for audit collateral.

Figure 13.13 shows this action tile and the various options:

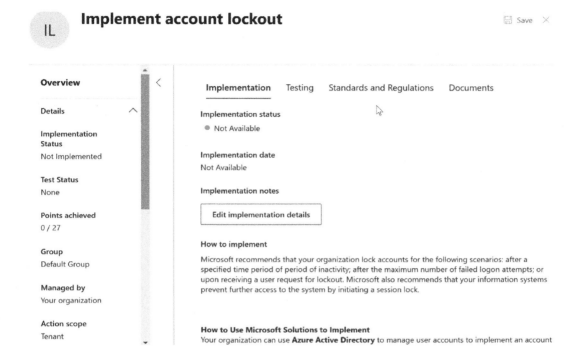

Figure 13.13 – The Improvement Action tile

In addition to improvement actions, the compliance score can be impacted by solution implementation. *Figure 13.14* shows the list of solutions and their contribution to the compliance score:

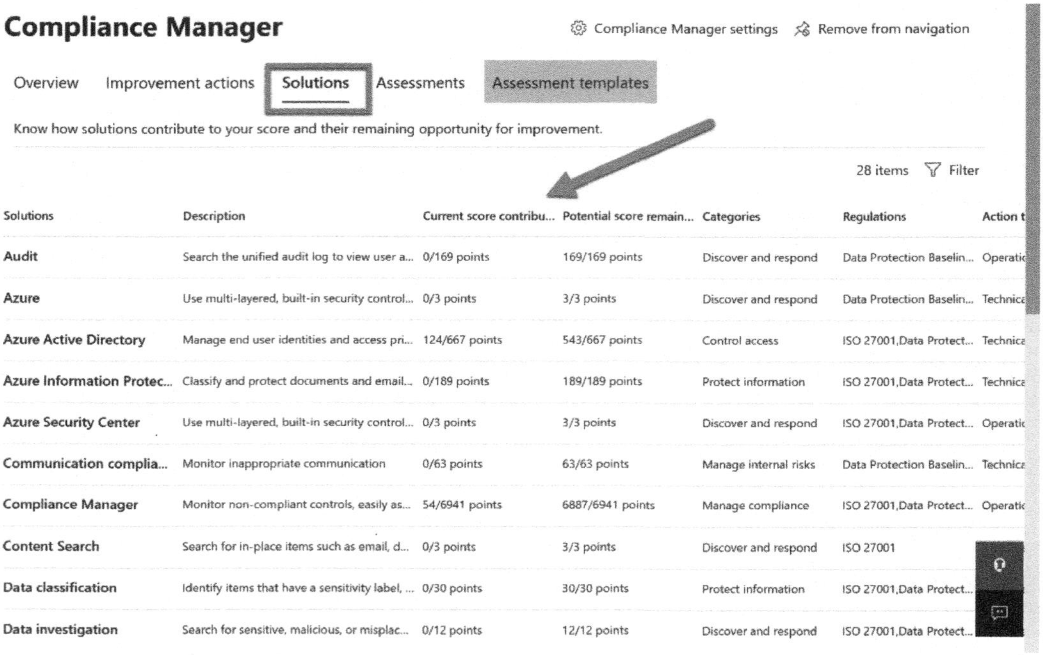

Solutions	Description	Current score contribu...	Potential score remain...	Categories	Regulations	Action t
Audit	Search the unified audit log to view user a...	0/169 points	169/169 points	Discover and respond	Data Protection Baselin...	Operati
Azure	Use multi-layered, built-in security control...	0/3 points	3/3 points	Discover and respond	Data Protection Baselin...	Technic
Azure Active Directory	Manage end user identities and access pri...	124/667 points	543/667 points	Control access	ISO 27001,Data Protect...	Technic
Azure Information Protec...	Classify and protect documents and email...	0/189 points	189/189 points	Protect information	ISO 27001,Data Protect...	Technic
Azure Security Center	Use multi-layered, built-in security control...	0/3 points	3/3 points	Discover and respond	ISO 27001,Data Protect...	Operati
Communication complia...	Monitor inappropriate communication	0/63 points	63/63 points	Manage internal risks	Data Protection Baselin...	Technic
Compliance Manager	Monitor non-compliant controls, easily as...	54/6941 points	6887/6941 points	Manage compliance	ISO 27001,Data Protect...	Operati
Content Search	Search for in-place items such as email, d...	0/3 points	3/3 points	Discover and respond	ISO 27001	
Data classification	Identify items that have a sensitivity label, ...	0/30 points	30/30 points	Protect information	ISO 27001,Data Protect...	
Data investigation	Search for sensitive, malicious, or misplac...	0/12 points	12/12 points	Discover and respond	ISO 27001,Data Protect...	

Figure 13.14 – Solutions' contribution to compliance score

Scrolling to the far right of the solutions list will show the remaining number of actions that you can take to improve your score and a link to open the solution, as shown in *Figure 13.15*:

Current score contribu...	Potential score remain...	Categories	Regulations	Action types	Groups	Remaining actions	Open solution
0/169 points	169/169 points	Discover and respond	Data Protection Baselin...	Operational,Technical	Default Group,Audit pr...	26	Open
0/3 points	3/3 points	Discover and respond	Data Protection Baselin...	Technical	Default Group,Audit pr...	2	Open
124/667 points	543/667 points	Control access	ISO 27001,Data Protect...	Technical,Operational	Default Group,Audit pr...	71	Open

Figure 13.15 – Remaining actions and Open solution

Selecting **Open** within the **Open solution** column will take you directly to that solution within Microsoft 365 or Azure. For example, selecting **Open** for Azure Active Directory will take you to the Azure AD portal, and selecting **Azure** will take you to the Azure portal. Solutions that are within the Microsoft 365 compliance center will take you to that menu tile.

The next section will provide a summary of what you have learned in this chapter.

Summary

In this chapter, we discussed the compliance capabilities within Microsoft 365. This included the list of solutions available within the compliance center and how to use Compliance Manager to monitor and manage your compliance score to govern Microsoft 365. In the next chapter, we will further discuss the information governance and protection capabilities within Microsoft 365, with data classification, sensitivity label policies, data loss prevention, and retention policies.

14

Describing Information Protection and Governance Capabilities of Microsoft 365

The previous chapter covered how to use the Microsoft 365 compliance center to access and manage security best practices and regulatory compliance with your Microsoft 365 connected applications. In this chapter, we will describe some of the specific areas of the Microsoft compliance center capabilities for information protection and information governance within Microsoft 365.

In this chapter, we're going to cover the following main topics:

- Describing data classification capabilities
- Describing sensitivity labels
- Describing data loss prevention
- Describing records management
- Describing retention policies and retention labels

Technical requirements

In this chapter, we will continue to explore configuring a tenant for use of solutions within Azure. There will be exercises that will require access to Azure. If you have not yet created the trial licenses for Microsoft 365 and a free trial of Azure, please follow the directions provided within *Chapter 1, Preparing for Your Microsoft Exam*.

Describe data classification capabilities

In *Chapter 13, Compliance Management Capabilities in Microsoft*, we described how the Microsoft 365 compliance center provides guidance for governance and compliance of Microsoft 365 solutions. This included walking through Microsoft Compliance Manager and how implementing solutions can impact and improve your company's compliance score. This chapter will describe some of those solutions, starting with data classification.

To access the solutions for the Microsoft 365 compliance center, navigate to `https://compliance.microsoft.com`. In the menu on the left, you will see the solutions. **Data classification** is directly below **Microsoft Compliance Manager** on the list. Select **Data classification** to explore your options.

When the **Microsoft 365 compliance center** portal opens, you may be prompted for a quick guided tour of the portal, as shown in *Figure 14.1*:

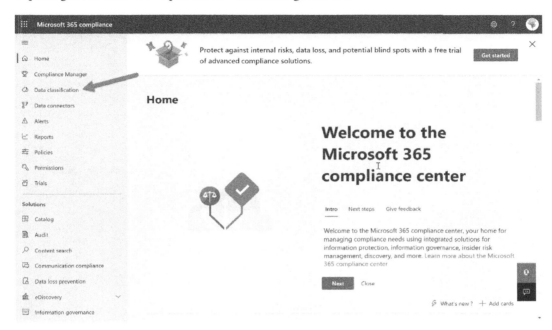

Figure 14.1 – Microsoft 365 compliance center data classification

Entering the **Data classification** tile will initially take you through a quick tour of the capabilities of data classification. The following screenshots highlight these capabilities. More information can be found at this link: `https://docs.microsoft.com/en-us/microsoft-365/compliance/data-classification-overview?view=o365-worldwide`.

Figure 14.2 explains what is described by data classification and how we can use these features to gain insight into what we are classifying to set up the correct policies to protect and govern data:

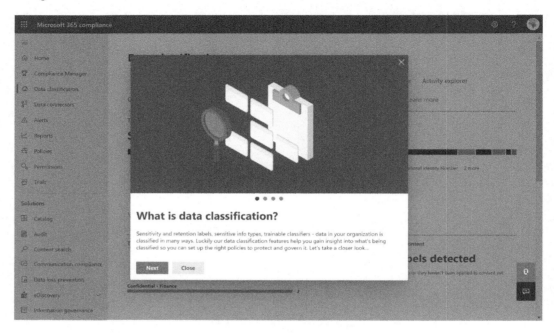

Figure 14.2 – What is data classification?

Selecting **Next** will take you to the description of the overview dashboard to understand where sensitive information may reside in Exchange, OneDrive, SharePoint, and other locations in your tenant. *Figure 14.3* shows the description:

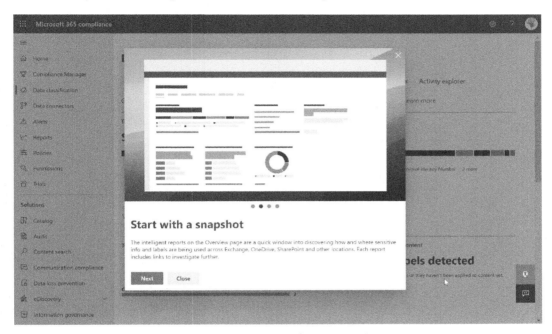

Figure 14.3 – Data classification snapshot

Selecting **Next** explains the capabilities to explore your content and find what may be found and identified as classified within your tenant locations, as shown in *Figure 14.4*. This is accomplished using the content explorer within **Data classification**:

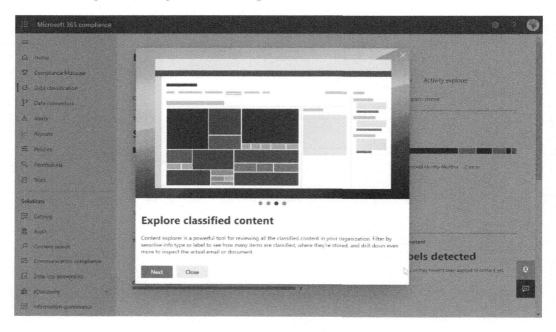

Figure 14.4 – Explore classified content

Selecting **Next** takes you to the final tutorial tile and how activity explorer monitors and reviews the activities that are taking place on data that has been classified. This is a daily-updated graphic that highlights the different activities and allows you to investigate further whether a suspicious activity is taking place, as shown in *Figure 14.5*:

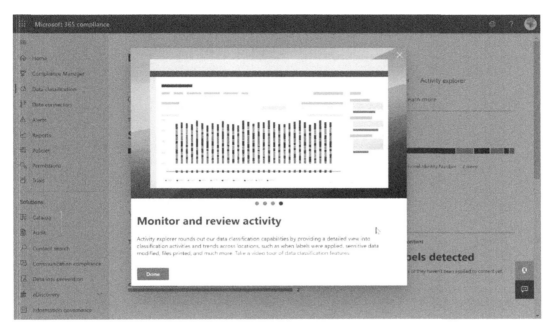

Figure 14.5 – Monitor and review activity

Once you have gone through the tutorial tiles, you will be taken to the **Data classification** overview, as shown in *Figure 14.6*. The top of this tile has additional tabs to further discover data within your tenant locations. The **Overview** tab provides a snapshot of the status of sensitive data within your tenant:

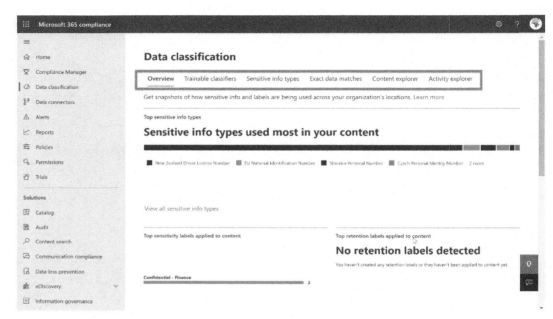

Figure 14.6 – The Data classification overview

The **Trainable classifiers** tab allows you to establish the types of data that you want to classify within your tenant locations. There is a list of built-in classifiers, and you can create your own classifiers. You can then scan your locations to find the data that matches these classifiers, as shown in *Figure 14.7*. Note that this process can take 1 to 2 weeks to complete:

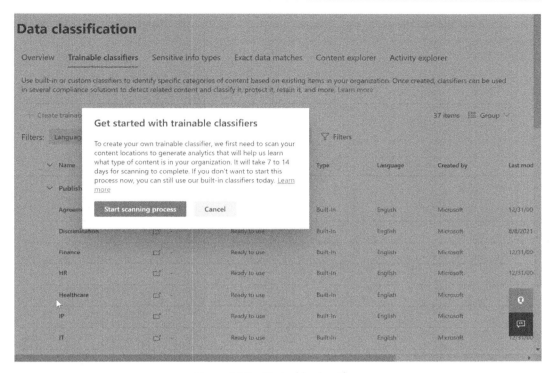

Figure 14.7 – Trainable classifiers

Something to note about trainable classifiers is that they do not include finding information such as **Personally Identifiable Information (PII)**, **Personal Health Information (PHI)**, or financial information. These trainable classifiers can identify possible intellectual property, IT information, discriminating language, harassment, and profanity that would have more of a litigious or reputational impact on the company. More information on trainable classifiers can be found at this link: `https://docs. microsoft.com/en-us/microsoft-365/compliance/classifier-learn- about?view=o365-worldwide`.

The next tab, **Sensitive info types**, focuses more on regulatory information, including PII, PHI, and financial information. This list is shown in *Figure 14.8*:

Data classification

Sensitive info types

Overview   Trainable classifiers   **Sensitive info types**   Exact data matches   Content explorer   Activity explorer

The sensitive info types here are available to use in your security and compliance policies. These include a large collection of types we provide, spanning regions around the globe, as well as any custom types you have created.

+ Create sensitive info type   ↻ Refresh   263 items   🔎 Search

Name ↑	Type	Publisher
○ ABA Routing Number	Entity	Microsoft Corporation
All Full Names	BundledEntity	Microsoft Corporation
All Medical Terms And Conditions	BundledEntity	Microsoft Corporation
All Physical Addresses	BundledEntity	Microsoft Corporation
Argentina National Identity (DNI) Number	Entity	Microsoft Corporation
Argentina Unique Tax Identification Key (CUIT/CUIL)	Entity	Microsoft Corporation
Australia Bank Account Number	Entity	Microsoft Corporation
Australia Driver's License Number	Entity	Microsoft Corporation
Australia Medical Account Number	Entity	Microsoft Corporation

Figure 14.8 – Sensitive information types

More information on sensitive information types can be found at this link: `https://docs.microsoft.com/en-us/microsoft-365/compliance/sensitive-information-type-learn-about?view=o365-worldwide`.

If you have specific information that you are attempting to identify and classify, such as invoice numbers or customer identification numbers, you can use exact data matches to do these searches, as shown in *Figure 14.9*:

Data classification

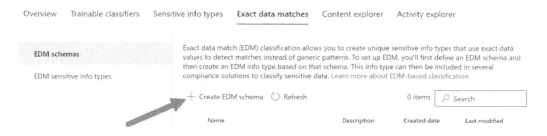

Figure 14.9 – Exact data matches

More information on how to use exact data matches can be found at this link: `https://docs.microsoft.com/en-us/microsoft-365/compliance/sit-learn-about-exact-data-match-based-sits?view=o365-worldwide#learn-about-exact-data-match-based-sensitive-information-types`.

Once you have these three identification types customized for your requirements, you can then complete a content search to determine the data and its location, which may contain these types in **Content explorer**, as shown in *Figure 14.10*:

Data classification

| Overview | Trainable classifiers | Sensitive info types | Exact data matches | Content explorer | Activity explorer |

Explore the email and docs in your organization that contain sensitive info or have labels applied. You drill down further by reviewing the source content that's currently stored in Exchange, SharePoint, and OneDrive. Support for more locations is coming soon. Learn more

ⓘ Support for exploring content in OneDrive is currently in preview. Depending on what preview capabilities are available for your organization, you might not see OneDrive listed as a location. If it is available, the experience and accuracy might be inconsistent as we work to improve the functionality.   ✕

🔍 Filter on labels, info types, or categories

All locations

Sensitive info types			↓ Export		4 items
New Zealand Driver License Number	**241**		Name	Files	
EU National Identification Number	13		Exchange	241	>
Slovakia Personal Number	12		OneDrive	0	>
Czech Personal Identity Number	10		SharePoint	0	>
IP Address	4		Teams	0	>

Figure 14.10 – Content explorer

More information on content explorer can be found at this link: `https://docs.microsoft.com/en-us/microsoft-365/compliance/data-classification-content-explorer?view=o365-worldwide`.

The final tab, **Activity explorer**, provides a summary of activities taking place on sensitive data, based on labels that have been applied to the data and locations. If you have not enabled any label policies within your company tenant locations, no information will be presented in this tab. The sensitivity label policies that we will apply will be described in the next section:

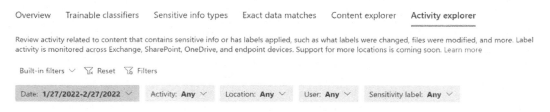

Figure 14.11 – Activity explorer

More information on the activity explorer can be found at this link: `https://docs.microsoft.com/en-us/microsoft-365/compliance/data-classification-activity-explorer?view=o365-worldwide`.

In the next section, we will describe how we can get activity in the activity explorer through the creation of sensitivity labels and policies.

Describe sensitivity labels

Sensitivity labels and label policies are an important part of a data governance strategy within your Microsoft 365 tenant. As stated in the previous section, without defining and implementing sensitivity labels for data and location, no activity will be monitored to identify misuse of information. Creating a sensitivity label to identify specific types of data from within your trainable classifiers, sensitive information types, and exact data matches will allow you to put policies in place to monitor activity. An important note here is that in order to monitor and govern activity on sensitive data, you will need to create a label and a policy for it.

More information on sensitivity labels and policies can be found at this link: `https://docs.microsoft.com/en-us/microsoft-365/compliance/sensitivity-labels?view=o365-worldwide`.

The following steps need to be completed to create a sensitivity label and policy:

1.   Go to `https://compliance.microsoft.com`.

2.   Select **Information protection** in the menu, as shown in *Figure 14.12*:

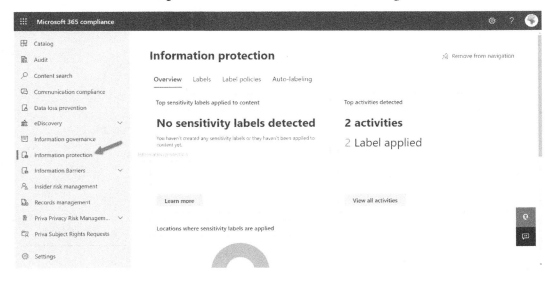

Figure 14.12 – Information protection

3. Select the **Labels** tab to create a sensitivity label. Select **+ Create a label**, as shown in *Figure 14.13*:

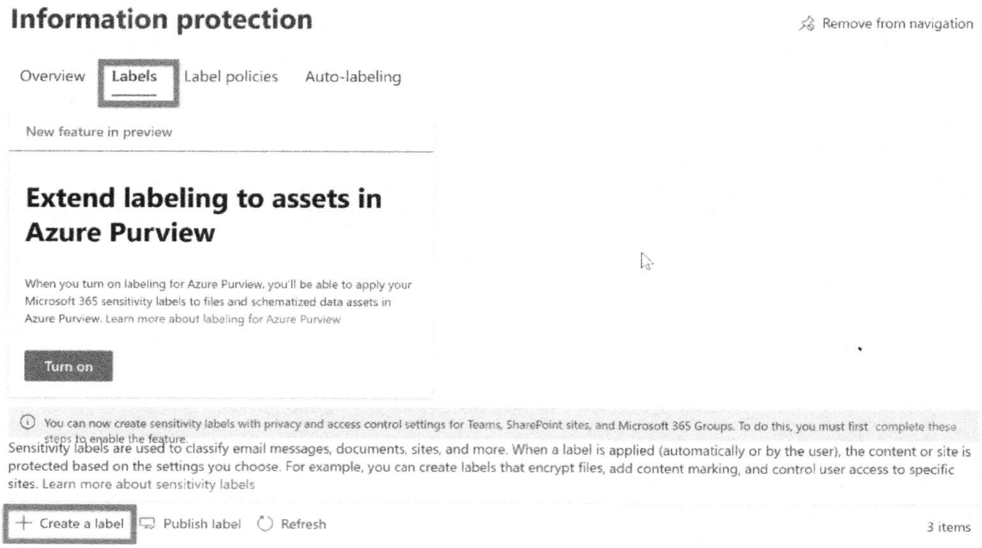

Figure 14.13 – Create a label

4. Complete the **Name & description** fields, as shown in *Figure 14.14*. Click **Next**:

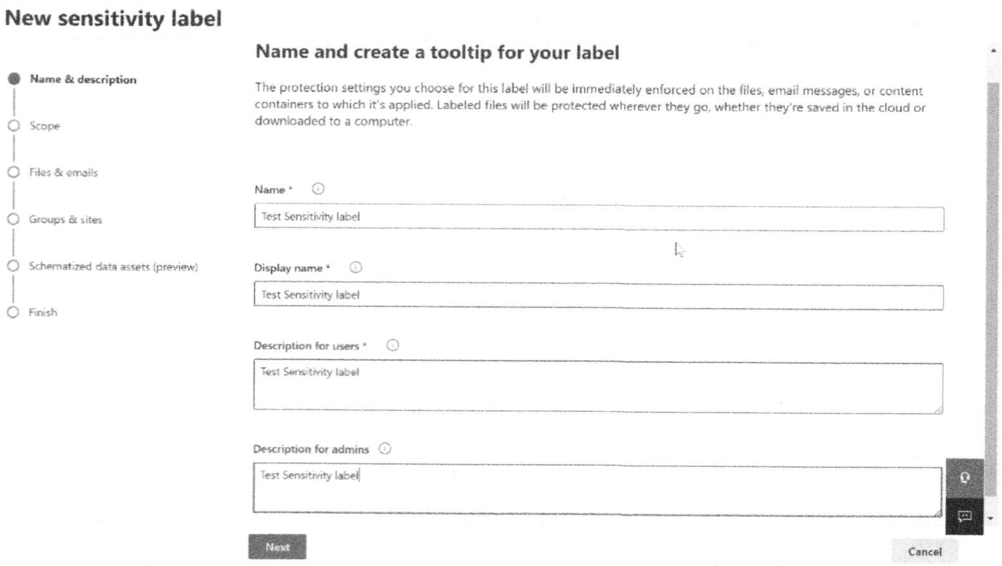

Figure 14.14 – The name and description of the label

5. Select the scope for the sensitivity label, as shown in *Figure 14.15*. For groups and sites, you may need to enable this feature using the link below the description. The same may be the case for schematized data assets, which require Azure Purview to be enabled. For this exercise, select **Files & emails** and then click **Next**:

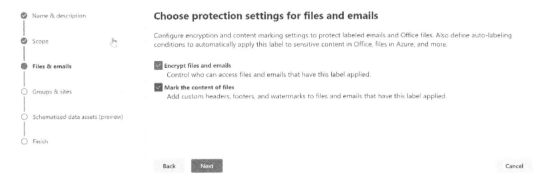

Figure 14.15 – The scope of the label

6. The next tile will provide you with choices for the protection actions that will be enforced by the label when the policy is created. Select both options to review the settings for each, as shown in *Figure 14.16*. Click **Next**:

New sensitivity label

- Name & description
- Scope
- **Files & emails**
- Groups & sites
- Schematized data assets (preview)
- Finish

Choose protection settings for files and emails

Configure encryption and content marking settings to protect labeled emails and Office files. Also define auto-labeling conditions to automatically apply this label to sensitive content in Office, files in Azure, and more.

☑ **Encrypt files and emails**
   Control who can access files and emails that have this label applied.

☑ **Mark the content of files**
   Add custom headers, footers, and watermarks to files and emails that have this label applied.

Back   Next   Cancel

Figure 14.16 – The protection settings for files and emails

7. The next tile provides the encryption configuration and how permissions to the sensitive information will be assigned. Configure these settings to allow users to assign permissions in Outlook, as shown in *Figure 14.17*, and click **Next**. If we want to assign permissions to specific users or groups and have these settings assigned immediately, we can do that here as well:

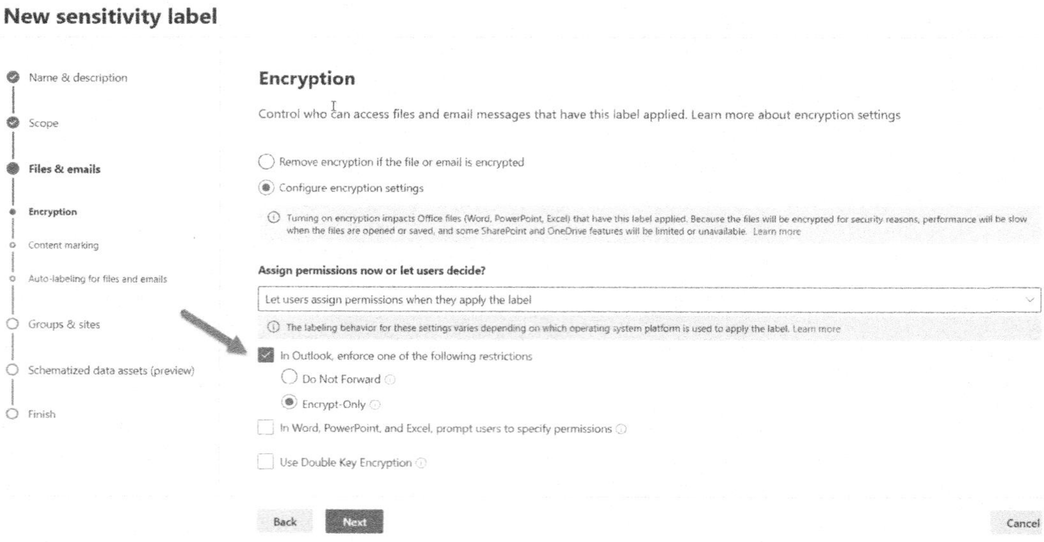

Figure 14.17 – Assign the encryption settings

8. In **Content marking**, set the slider to *on* and add customized header text for emails and files, as shown in *Figure 14.18*. Once you have completed the steps, click **Next**:

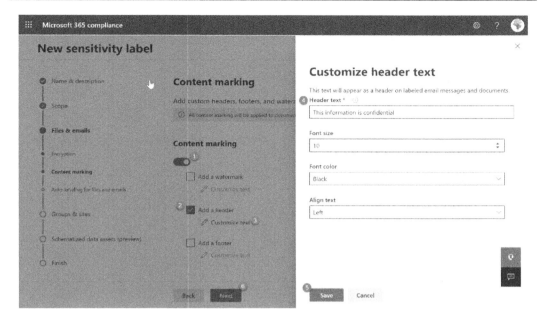

Figure 14.18 – Content markings

9. The next tile allows you to configure the label to be applied automatically to sensitive data or provide a recommendation to users when sensitive information is detected. Turn this on to automatically apply the label, as shown in *Figure 14.19*, and click **Next**:

Figure 14.19 – Auto-labeling

10. Click **Next** for **Groups & sites** and **Schematized data assets**; you are not using these as part of the label scope. Review your settings and click **Create label**, as shown in *Figure 14.20*:

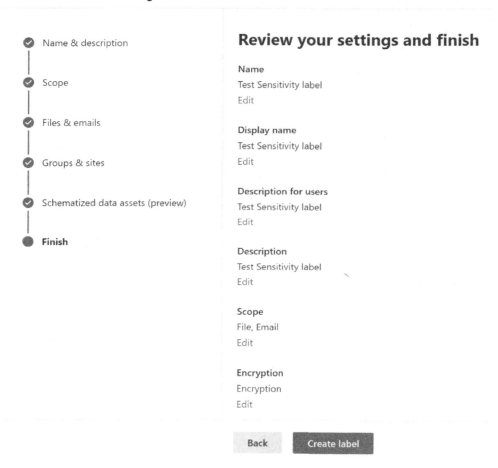

Figure 14.20 – Create label

11. *Figure 14.21* shows that the label was created successfully and provides some links for the next steps. Click **Done**:

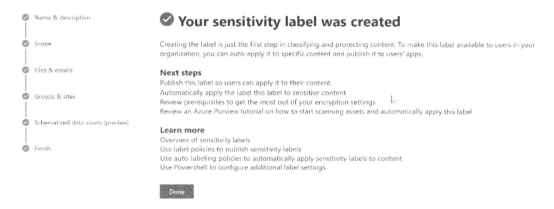

Figure 14.21 – The sensitivity label created

12. Your new label will be created with the highest priority within the list of labels that you have already created. You have the ability to reorder these labels within the list. The priority order will determine which label will take priority when sensitive information is found within multiple labels. The higher priority takes precedence over the lower-priority labels:

Figure 14.22 – The label priority list

13. Select **Publish label** to create a label policy:

Name		Order	Scope	Created by	Last modified
sc900 label	:	0 - lowest	File, Email		
Confidential All employees	:	1	File, Email		
Confidential - Finance	:	2	File, Email		
Test Sensitivity label	:	3 - highest	File, Email		

+ Create a label   □ Publish label   ○ Refresh   4 items

Figure 14.23 – Publish label

14. Select the link to choose the sensitivity label to publish, select the label that you created, click **Add**, and then click **Next**, as shown in *Figure 14.24*:

Figure 14.24 – Choose the sensitivity label

15. In the next tile, you can select specific users and groups to whom this policy will apply. If you select **All** and other labels are applied to all users and groups, the priority order will be used to determine how the label policy is handled. For this exercise, leave the default of **All** and click **Next**, as shown in *Figure 14.25*:

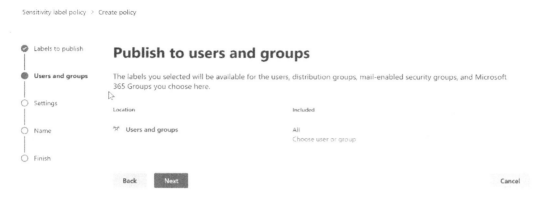

Figure 14.25 – Publish to all users and groups

16. In the **Policy settings** tile, select the checkboxes for **Users must provide a justification to remove a label or lower its classification** and **Require users to apply a label to their emails and documents**, as shown in *Figure 14.26*. Click **Next** to continue:

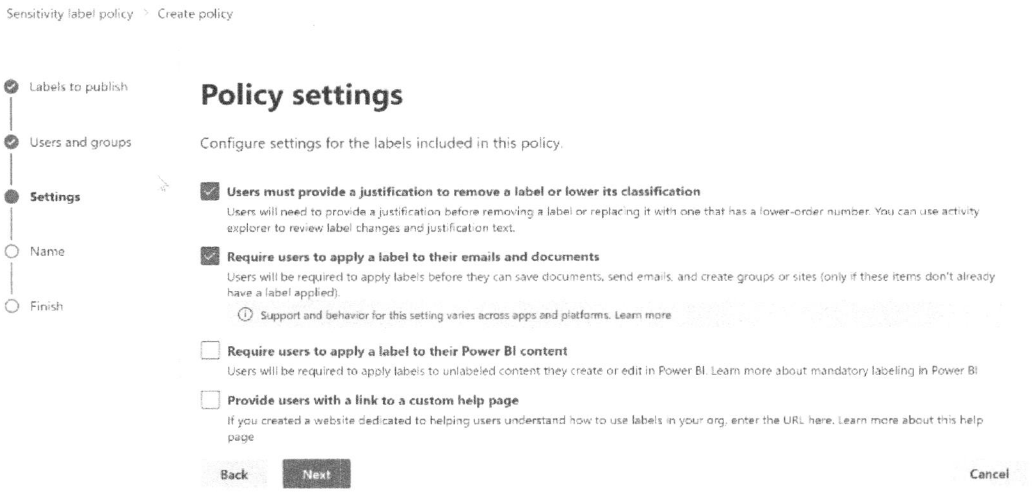

Figure 14.26 – Policy settings

17. Provide a name for your label policy. Click **Next** to continue:

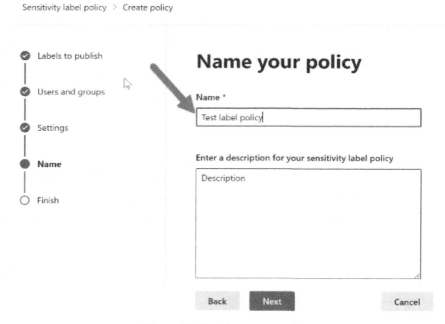

Figure 14.27 – Name your policy

18. The **Finish** tile allows you to review the settings. Click **Submit** to complete:

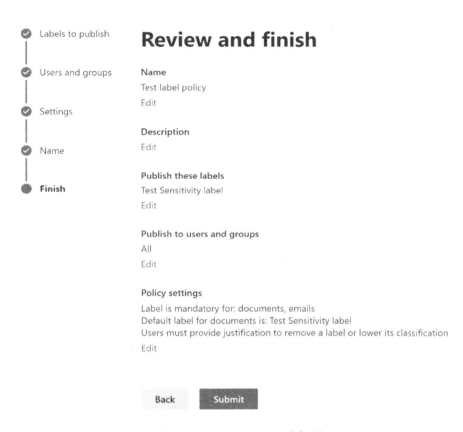

Figure 14.28 – Review and finish

19. The new policy has been created. Note the message on the tile that explains that this may take 24 hours to be applied and published to users for enforcement:

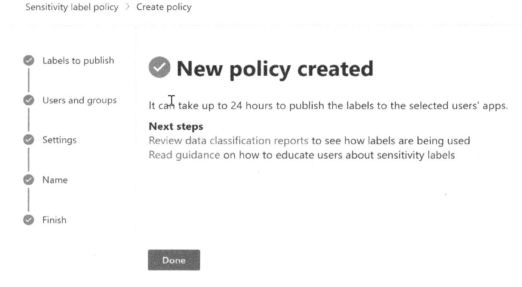

Figure 14.29 – New policy created

You have now created a sensitivity label and published it to a policy. This will now monitor the activity and use of sensitive data types for these users and groups when they are handling data in emails and files.

Next, we will describe data loss prevention.

Describe data loss prevention

As discussed in the previous section, sensitivity labels and sensitivity policies are used to identify sensitive data within files, emails, sites, and collaboration groups. The policies then determine an action that can take place to label or encrypt that data, as identified by an administrator or the user. The activity on this sensitive information is then monitored to identify misuse of this information. A key feature that is missing from sensitivity labels and sensitivity policies is the ability to block this information from being shared. For this, a data loss prevention policy must be in place.

Data loss prevention policies are used to prevent data loss and avoid sensitive data from being leaked to unauthorized users inside or outside of a company. The ability to avoid this data loss relies on a policy to be put in place against the types of sensitive data, using either a sensitivity label that has been created or built-in data types that are selected when creating a data loss prevention policy.

Figure 14.30 shows the **Data loss prevention** overview dashboard. Within this dashboard are additional tabs to create policies, review and manage alerts, set up endpoint data loss prevention settings for Microsoft Defender for Endpoint, and review activity with the activity explorer:

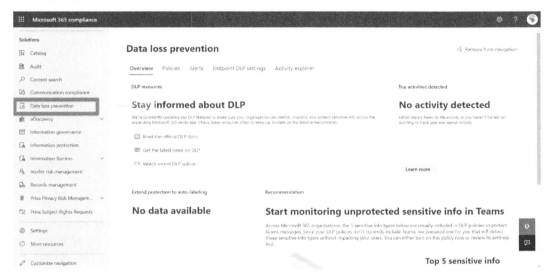

Figure 14.30 – The Data loss prevention overview

When you go to the **Policies** tab, you will see a list of policies that may have been created previously. Note that in *Figure 14.31*, there is a priority order assigned to these policies in a similar way to how they are within the sensitivity policies. Within this tab, you can create a new policy. The steps for creating a data loss prevention policy are based in a wizard in a similar manner as sensitivity labels. For more information on the process, please visit this link: `https://docs.microsoft.com/en-us/microsoft-365/compliance/protect-documents-that-have-fci-or-other-properties?view=o365-worldwide`:

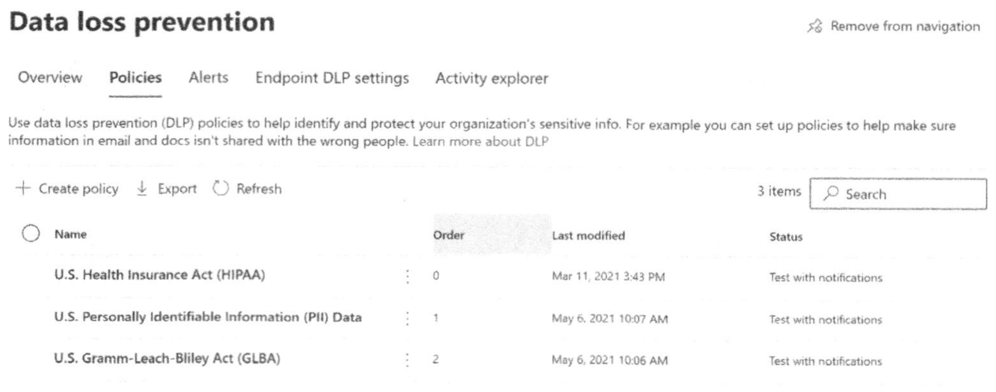

Figure 14.31 – Data loss prevention policies

Data loss prevention policies will alert administrators when information within the scope of a policy has been shared. They can also block information being shared with users outside of the organization or users and groups that are not authorized to view the information within the policy. If sensitive information within the scope of the data loss prevention policy is being shared, tips can be provided to the user on how to handle the information.

Additional information on planning data loss prevention policies can be found at this link: `https://docs.microsoft.com/en-us/microsoft-365/compliance/dlp-learn-about-dlp?view=o365-worldwide`.

A final point is that data loss prevention policies provide preventative measures to avoid data from being overshared across emails, files, SharePoint sites, and Teams collaboration.

Next, we will describe records management and how to use retention policies to govern documents for legal, government, and regulatory requirements.

Describe records management

The previous sections of this chapter described solutions that provide information protection in our governance strategy. This is important to make sure that information is not being shared or communication is not being sent that could affect a company in terms of compliance, including financial and reputational.

Records management is governing how our documents are managed and retained to comply with governmental, legal, and regulatory standards that are within a company's jurisdiction. As a company, we have requirements in our company policies and within the governmental borders in which our documents reside to manage and maintain them for set periods of time. The process of marking these documents as records and setting the proper retention periods is records management.

More information on getting started with records management can be found at this link: `https://docs.microsoft.com/en-us/microsoft-365/compliance/get-started-with-records-management?view=o365-worldwide`.

In the Microsoft 365 compliance center, the **Records management** overview dashboard looks like *Figure 14.32*:

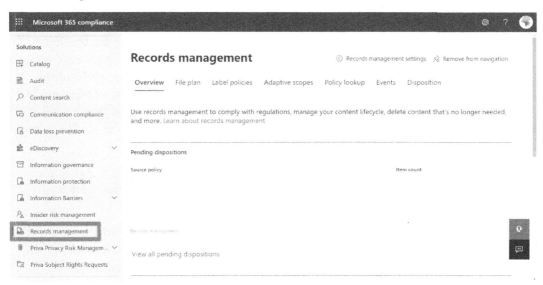

Figure 14.32 – The Records management overview

Within **Records management**, there are tabs for **File plan**, **Label policies**, **Adaptive scopes**, **Policy lookup**, **Events**, and **Disposition**. These tabs go through a records management life cycle. The record starts with a file plan and then is removed (deleted or archived) as part of the disposition.

More details on records management can be found here: `https://docs.microsoft.com/en-us/microsoft-365/compliance/records-management?view=o365-worldwide`.

Figure 14.33 shows how the file plan starts with the creation of a retention label and then continues to a retention label policy:

Figure 14.33 – A records management file plan

Previously, we saw that no action takes place on a sensitivity label without a sensitivity label policy; a similar process applies to records management. File plans are the first step to records management. The file plan and the scope of it determine how a record is handled during the retention period. This includes tracking, monitoring, and auditing anyone that accesses the record, and whether any changes or revisions have been made to it. This is extremely important for legal documents or documents that may be called as evidence for litigation. The use of eDiscovery will be described in *Chapter 15, Describing Insider Risk, eDiscovery, and Audit Capabilities in Microsoft 365.*

Additional information on creating and managing a file plan can be found at this link: `https://docs.microsoft.com/en-us/microsoft-365/compliance/file-plan-manager?view=o365-worldwide`.

For the scoping of a record policy to prevent or audit the use of the record, please see this link: `https://docs.microsoft.com/en-us/microsoft-365/compliance/retention?view=o365-worldwide#adaptive-or-static-policy-scopes-for-retention`.

Now that you understand records and records management, the next section will describe in more detail retention labels and retention policies.

Describe retention policies and retention labels

As stated in the previous section, a key feature in managing records is the file plan and how we manage the retention and disposition of records. The ability to manage records within Microsoft 365 is accomplished with retention labels and policies. The labels identify and mark documents as records, and the policies then ensure that these records are not disposed of by users before the scope of the policy has been met.

More information on the scope of records retention can be found at this link: `https://docs.microsoft.com/en-us/microsoft-365/compliance/retention?view=o365-worldwide`.

Figure 14.34 shows the **Information governance** dashboard where you can manage retention labels and retention policies:

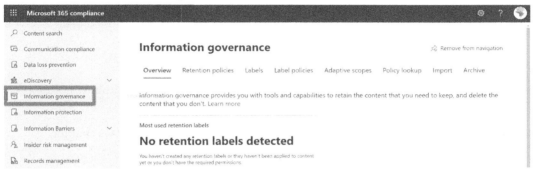

Figure 14.34 – The Information governance dashboard

Retention labels and policies can be created to be driven by events on a document. These events could be when the document was created or when it was last modified. Keep in mind that retention labels can be used for documents that are not considered records. Additional information on these event-driven retention policies can be found at this link: `https://docs.microsoft.com/en-us/microsoft-365/compliance/event-driven-retention?view=o365-worldwide`.

Creating a retention label and retention policy is another wizard-driven graphical interface, similar to sensitivity labels. You can start by selecting **+ Create a label** from the **Labels** tab, as shown in *Figure 14.34*.

One tab to point out within **Information governance** is the **Archive** tab. This tab provides a list of users with mailboxes, and you can enforce archiving of these Exchange Online mailboxes from this tab. Additional information on how to manage this in **Information governance** can be found at this link: https://docs.microsoft.com/en-us/ microsoft-365/compliance/enable-archive-mailboxes?view=o365- worldwide.

Figure 14.35 shows this tab for archiving mailboxes:

Figure 14.35 – The Information governance archive

You now understand the information protection and information governance solutions within the Microsoft 365 compliance center.

The next section will provide a summary of what you have learned in this chapter.

Summary

In this chapter, we discussed the information governance and protection capabilities within Microsoft 365 with data classification, sensitivity label policies, data loss prevention, and retention policies. In the next chapter, we will describe additional governance capabilities within the Microsoft 365 compliance center. These will include insider risk management, eDiscovery, and the audit capabilities to monitor activity within the Microsoft 365 compliance center.

15
Describing Insider Risk, eDiscovery, and Audit Capabilities in Microsoft 365

In the previous chapter, you learned how to use some of the specific areas of the **Microsoft compliance center** for information protection and information governance purposes within Microsoft 365. In this chapter, we will describe the additional governance capabilities in Microsoft 365 – that is, **insider risk**, **eDiscovery**, and **audit capabilities**.

In this chapter, we're going to cover the following main topics:

- The insider risk management solution
- Information barriers and Customer Lockbox

- The core eDiscovery workflow
- The core audit capabilities of Microsoft 365

Technical requirements

In this chapter, we will continue learning how to configure a tenant so that we can use solutions within Azure. There will be exercises where you will require access to Azure. If you have not created the trial licenses for Microsoft 365 and do not have a free Azure trial, please follow the instructions provided in *Chapter 1, Preparing for Your Microsoft Exam.*

The insider risk management solution

In *Chapter 14, Describing Information Protection and Governance Capabilities of Microsoft 365*, we described the information protection, loss prevention, and information governance solutions that Microsoft 365 provides through sensitivity policies, data loss prevention policies, and retention policies. We also explored record management for marking documents for proper retention and disposition. In this chapter, you will learn about additional solutions within the Microsoft 365 Compliance portal to help you govern your data and communication within the company. These solutions include **insider risk management**, **communication compliance**, **information barriers**, and **eDiscovery**. Let's start by describing insider risk management.

Insider risk management

To access the insider risk management solution for the Microsoft 365 compliance center, navigate to `https://compliance.microsoft.com`. In the left-hand side menu, you will see the solutions. **Insider risk management** is located under the **Solutions** section.

Insider risk management detects and monitors possible malicious or inadvertent activities that are being performed by users. These activities are found through Microsoft's machine learning capabilities, which detect anomalous behavior by users, including high volume downloads from OneDrive for Business or documents being printed suddenly. Insider risk management policies are used to alert and remediate these data leaks and the theft of intellectual property threats. When an insider risk policy is triggered, it can initiate a case to triage, investigate, and take action while coordinating with the compliance, human resources, legal, and security departments within the company. The following diagram shows the workflow of an insider risk case:

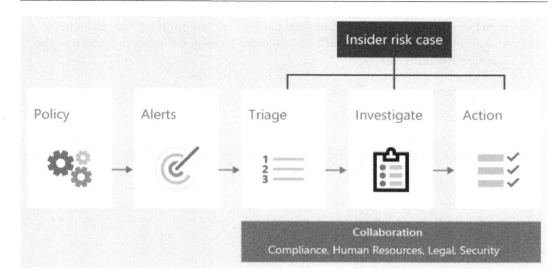

Figure 15.1 – Insider risk case workflow

More information on insider risk management can be found at `https://docs.microsoft.com/en-us/microsoft-365/compliance/insider-risk-management?view=o365-worldwide`.

Next, we will discuss communication compliance.

Communication compliance

When you go to `https://compliance.microsoft.com` and go to the left-hand menu, you will see **Communication compliance** located under the **Solutions** section.

Communication compliance is used to protect the company from potential communication by users who could harm the company's reputation and possibly lead to legal cases being brought against the company. Communication compliance detects, captures, monitors, and alerts you to communications across channels, such as email, Teams chat and channels, Skype for Business, and Yammer, for inappropriate communication. Inappropriate communication could include profanities, racism, harassment, threats, and pornography found in text and images.

Communication policies are created to detect and alert you to this content to identify violations and handle them with users. The different types of policies can be seen in the following screenshot:

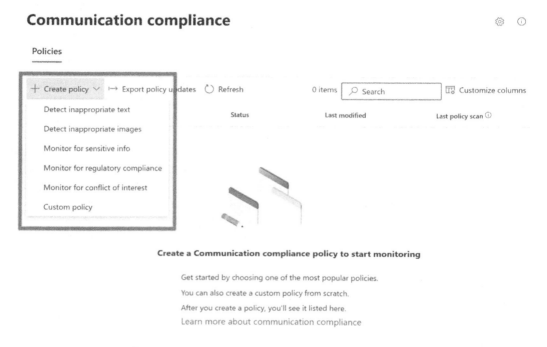

Figure 15.2 – Communication compliance policy types

These policies can be created through templates that have been provided for popular information types. Alternatively, you can create a custom communication compliance policy if your company wishes to detect information that's being shared that is specific to the company. More information on communication compliance can be found at https://docs.microsoft.com/en-us/microsoft-365/compliance/ communication-compliance?view=o365-worldwide.

Insider risk management and communication compliance are governance solutions that monitor, detect, investigate, and remediate against potential information or communication within the company that may result in theft or legal damage. In practice, both of these solutions are detective and corrective. Proper education and company acceptable use policies should be in place if you want more preventative measures to proactively avoid potential insider risk and communication compliance issues from inadvertent users. Unfortunately, malicious activities still may be detected and need further investigation.

In the next section, we will describe information barriers and Customer Lockbox.

Information barriers and Customer Lockbox

The next two solutions we will describe provide more preventative activities to help protect information and avoid improper communication. These are information barriers and Customer Lockbox. Let's start by describing information barriers.

Information barriers

Information barriers are used to avoid communication between users who may cause a potential conflict of interest within the company. These conflicts of interest could cause legal or reputational damage to the company. Information barriers block communication between users or groups through voice, text, and email channels and monitor those attempts to communicate.

Information barriers is another solution that can be found within `https://compliance.microsoft.com` under the **Solutions** section on the left. The following screenshot shows the **Information Barriers** tile. To configure the information barrier, you must create a **Segment**:

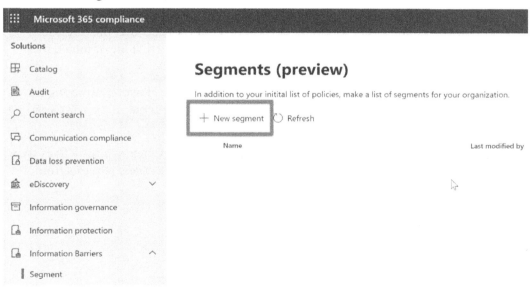

Figure 15.3 – Information barrier segment

An example of a use case for creating an information barrier segment would be within a law firm. A law firm consists of many different lawyers; some of them may handle defense cases, while others may handle prosecution cases. There may be a situation where a defense attorney and a prosecution attorney within the same law firm may be representing both sides of a legal case. To avoid any conflicts of interest between the two parties that may affect the case, information barriers can be placed on these attorneys and their teams to block them from communicating with each other unless it's through a third-party mediator.

More information on information barriers can be found at `https://docs.microsoft.com/en-us/microsoft-365/compliance/information-barriers?view=o365-worldwide`.

Next, let's learn about Customer Lockbox.

Customer Lockbox

Customer Lockbox is used as a preventative solution to monitor and prevent a Microsoft support engineer from accessing sensitive information when providing support to a user within your company. By using Customer Lockbox, you can identify files and folders that will be blocked from Microsoft engineer access if they need to access a company device for support. If the support issue involves the locked files or folders, then the Microsoft engineers will need to request access through the user. If they approve, the Microsoft engineer will be provided with access. While they are accessing that file or folder, the activity is monitored and a report is provided to the company.

Customer Lockbox is a compliance solution for Microsoft 365. However, to configure Customer Lockbox, you must use the Microsoft 365 admin center at `https://admin.microsoft.com`.

Customer Lockbox Requests can be found under the **Support** menu on the left, as shown in the following screenshot. This is where you will find the data access requests from Microsoft when an engineer is responding to a support ticket.

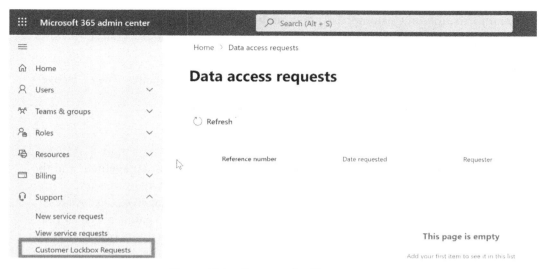

Figure 15.4 – Customer Lockbox request

To set up **Customer Lockbox Requests** and configure the locations that you want to protect, go to the **Settings** menu and click on **Org settings**. Within that tile, go to the **Security & privacy** tab and find **Customer lockbox**. This is where you will configure Customer Lockbox for service requests, as shown in the following screenshot:

Figure 15.5 – Customer Lockbox settings

More information on Customer Lockbox can be found at `https://docs.microsoft.com/en-us/microsoft-365/compliance/customer-lockbox-requests?view=o365-worldwide`.

Next, we will describe eDiscovery and the workflow for core and advanced eDiscovery cases.

The Core eDiscovery workflow

In the first section of this chapter, you learned about insider risk management and the workflow of an insider risk case. Similar to an insider risk case, where we want to triage and investigate activity that may create a legal issue for your company, eDiscovery is used to gather evidence that will possibly be used in a legal case against a user or users within your company. When an eDiscovery case is created, the activity of that user across Microsoft 365 services is suspended and documented so that it can be held for legal investigations. Note that when an eDiscovery case is created, the documents have a 24-hour delay in terms of being legally held. Therefore, you should not make the user or users aware that they are under any type of investigation to avoid loss of evidence. As a company, you should already have tools in place, such as insider risk management, to monitor and detect this malicious activity.

For an additional overview of eDiscovery within the Microsoft 365 compliance center, go to `https://docs.microsoft.com/en-us/microsoft-365/compliance/ediscovery?view=o365-worldwide`.

Now, let's discuss the Core eDiscovery service.

Core eDiscovery

Core eDiscovery is available with Microsoft 365 E3 licenses. Core eDiscovery allows a company to put a legal hold on a user's content across Exchange Online, OneDrive for Business, SharePoint Online, Microsoft Teams, Microsoft 365 Groups, and Yammer teams. This will include their documents and communication within these locations for the legal teams to investigate what is pertinent to the case.

Core eDiscovery consists of three steps – **Create eDiscovery holds**, **Search for content**, and **Export and download search results**, as shown in the following screenshot:

Figure 15.6 – Core eDiscovery workflow

Core eDiscovery is located in the **Microsoft 365 compliance** center under the **Solutions** menu, as shown in the following screenshot. You can select **Create a case** to configure a new case.

Figure 15.7 – Core eDiscovery

Once a case has been created, you can review the status of the case by selecting the case from the Core eDiscovery list. When you open the case, you can review or change its status from the home tab, as well as review the searches, holds, exports, and settings of the case.

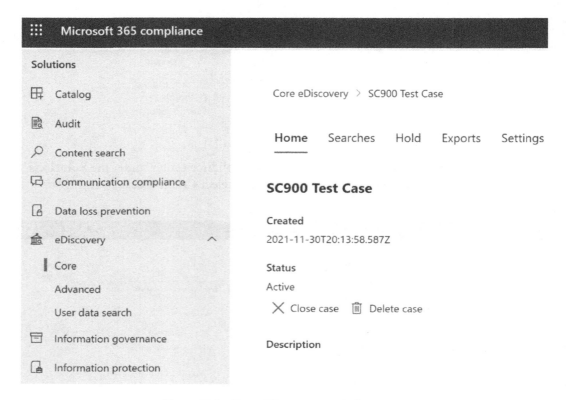

Figure 15.8 – Core eDiscovery case information

The **Settings** tab allows you to configure the specific information for the case, as well as delegate any permissions that are needed to let others access the case, as shown in the following screenshot:

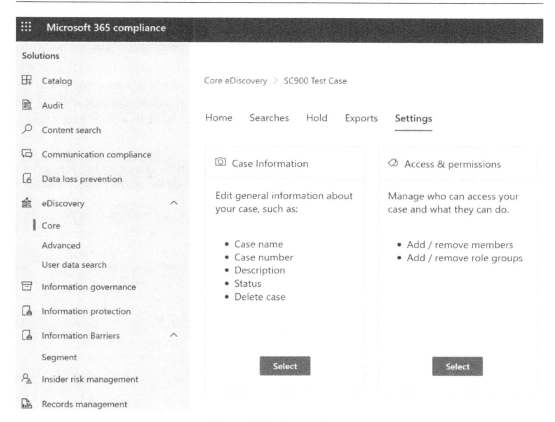

Figure 15.9 – Case settings

More information on Core eDiscovery can be found at `https://docs.microsoft.com/en-us/microsoft-365/compliance/get-started-core-ediscovery?view=o365-worldwide`.

Next, let's learn about advanced eDiscovery cases.

Advanced eDiscovery

Advanced eDiscovery has an expanded workflow from Core eDiscovery. Advanced eDiscovery is available with Microsoft 365 E5 licenses. Compared to the Core eDiscovery workflow, which only consists of three steps, Advanced eDiscovery has more steps and the ability to do a more detailed content search. This capability allows the custodian of the case to search for content that is relevant to the investigation rather than fully exporting all user content. The following screenshot shows this workflow:

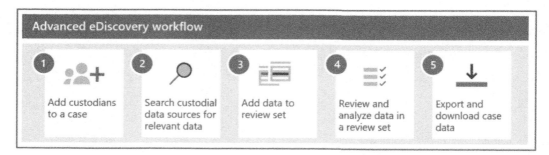

Figure 15.10 – Advanced eDiscovery workflow

More information on Advanced eDiscovery can be found at `https://docs.microsoft.com/en-us/microsoft-365/compliance/overview-ediscovery-20?view=o365-worldwide`.

Since these are more advanced searches that are used to gather documents and communication information for a case, the custodian of the case becomes an important part of the workflow. This custodian will be assigned to search through sources and review that the information that's been collected is appropriate for the case that's being investigated. Once this takes place, the case data is then exported so that it can be provided to the investigative team.

The following screenshot shows a case and the additional tabs you can use to review the case within the **Microsoft 365 compliance** portal. You have a greater ability to review the content search data for Advanced eDiscovery than what you have available with a Core eDiscovery case.

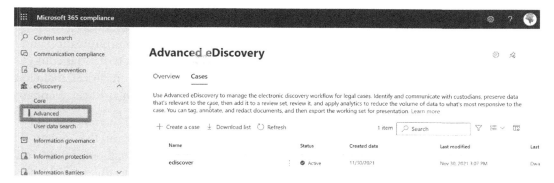

Figure 15.11 – Advanced eDiscovery case details

In addition to the eDiscovery cases within the Microsoft 365 compliance center, you can create a **User data search** and create a case. This is like eDiscovery, but is not necessarily coming from any legal case. A user data search, formerly a data subject request, is based on some country's privacy requirements, such as the **General Data Protection Regulation** (**GDPR**), which states that a person's privacy is their human right and that there's a right for their information to be forgotten. This privacy right allows users to request information about their data from the company, have it collected, and request for it to be removed. The **User data search** area within the **Microsoft 365 compliance** center can create this case, complete the search, and execute the request by the user. This can be seen in the following screenshot:

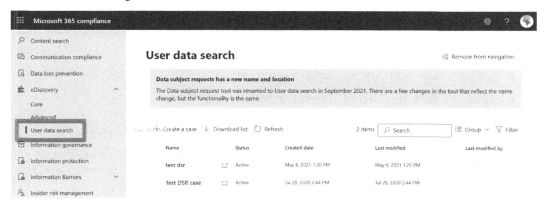

Figure 15.12 – User data search

More information on **User data search** can be found at https://docs.microsoft.com/en-us/compliance/regulatory/gdpr-data-subject-requests.

Next, we will describe the core audit capabilities within Microsoft 365.

The core audit capabilities of Microsoft 365

Previously in this chapter, we described solutions for governing our communication and content within Microsoft 365 services to prevent, detect, and correct activity that could cause harm to our company. This can be through inappropriate communication, malicious theft of company information, and legal actions that have been taken against the company.

These solutions performed searches and audits of user activity through the policies and cases that were created. There are times when you may want to understand the activity that is taking place without it being a part of a legal case or a detected malicious user. You may just want to review activities taking place on the tenant. You can do this with the core and advanced audit activities that are available within Microsoft 365. These capabilities are divided into core and advanced audits.

The core audit has the following features:

- Companies can view user and administrator activity.

- An audited activity creates an audit record that is stored within the audit log.

- When you're searching the audit log, you must turn on the search capability and have the correct role assigned.

- After performing a search, the results can be exported to a CSV file that you can provide to others who do not have access to the admin centers.

The advanced audit has all of the core audit features, plus the following:

- The ability to set up the long-term retention of the audit logs

- Customizable audit retention policies

- Access to the Office 365 Management Activity API

- Access to crucial events for investigation through search queries

More information about these auditing capabilities can be found at `https://docs.microsoft.com/en-us/microsoft-365/compliance/search-the-audit-log-in-security-and-compliance?view=o365-worldwide`.

To learn how to use the advanced audit, go to `https://docs.microsoft.com/en-us/microsoft-365/compliance/advanced-audit?view=o365-worldwide`.

The following screenshot shows the **Audit** tile, where you can create the search. You can access the **Audit retention policies** tab to find the customizable retention policies that are available with advanced audit:

Figure 15.13 – Audit search

You can also complete a content search using the **Content search** section of the **Solutions** menu, as shown in the following screenshot. This search is done in the same way that it is done from within an eDiscovery case.

Figure 15.14 – Content search

At the time of writing, a new solution has been introduced by Microsoft 365 for privacy and rights management. This service is **Priva Privacy Risk management**. This solution is located under the **Solutions** section in the Microsoft 365 compliance center. Priva can be used to identify, detect, and protect sensitive data and create subject rights requests about, for example, insider risk management and a user data search. Priva is not currently within the scope of this exam, but it is important to know that it is a solution for governance and compliance for Microsoft 365. The following screenshot shows the **Privacy management: Overview** page:

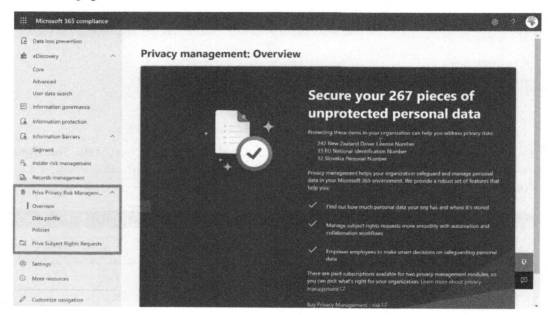

Figure 15.15 – Priva management

For more information on Priva, please go to https://docs.microsoft.com/en-us/privacy/priva/priva-overview.

Now, let's summarize what we learned in this chapter.

Summary

In this chapter, we discussed additional governance and compliance solutions within Microsoft 365, including insider risk management, communication compliance, information barriers, Customer Lockbox, eDiscovery, and audit and content searches. In the next chapter, we will describe the compliance and governance capabilities within Azure, including Policy, Blueprints, and Purview.

16

Describing Resource Governance Capabilities in Azure

In the previous chapter, you learned how to use some of the additional governance capabilities that are provided in Microsoft 365 – that is, insider risk, eDiscovery, and audit capabilities. In this chapter, we will describe the compliance and governance capabilities within Azure with Policy, Blueprints, and Purview.

In this chapter, we're going to cover the following main topics:

- Azure Policy and its use cases
- Azure Blueprints
- Azure Purview

Technical requirements

In this chapter, we will continue to explore how to configure a tenant that can be used for solutions within Azure. There will be exercises where you will require access to Azure. If you have not created the trial licenses for Microsoft 365 and do not have a free Azure trial, then please follow the instructions provided in *Chapter 1, Preparing for Your Microsoft Exam.*

Azure Policy and its use cases

In *Chapter 9*, *Describing Security Management and Capabilities of Azure*, we discussed Microsoft Defender for Cloud and how it is used to manage security posture. In the *Describing the security baselines for Azure* section, we provided an exercise that steps through the various tiles within Microsoft Defender for Cloud, including the regulatory compliance tile. The ability to manage the Azure Security baseline and the various regulatory compliance standards that are available within Microsoft Defender for Cloud is done through Azure Policy. Azure Policy is a tool that monitors compliance based on the definitions that have been assigned to the resources that are governed by that policy or initiative.

A policy is a single definition that is assigned to a subscription or resource group. The policy looks at all the resources within the assigned group, checks for compliance on existing resources, and verifies compliance when creating resources. A policy definition can be used for cost, security, location, monitoring, and other requirements that the company sets for governing resources. The following screenshot shows some of the built-in policy definitions within Azure Policy:

Figure 16.1 – Policy definitions

An initiative is a group of policies that are assigned to a subscription or resource group. This group of policies is then used to audit for compliance on Azure resources for multiple policies. The following screenshot shows some of the built-in initiative definitions within Azure Policy. Note the **Policies** column, which shows the number of policies that are within the initiative.

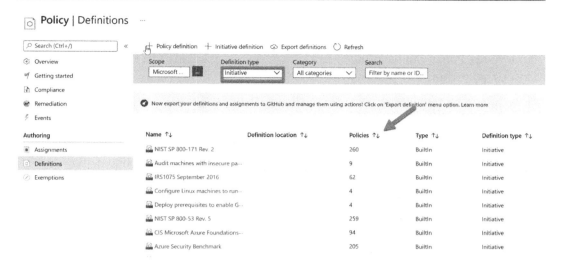

Figure 16.2 – Initiative definitions

When creating an Azure subscription, the Azure Security Baseline initiative is assigned to the subscription as the ASC default initiative. This is the initiative that audits resources for the Secure score, which we discussed in *Chapter 9, Describing Security Management and Capabilities of Azure*. The following screenshot shows the overview tile of Azure Policy, where you can review your compliance with active policies and initiatives. You can access Azure Policy by going to `https://portal.azure.com` and searching for `Policy`.

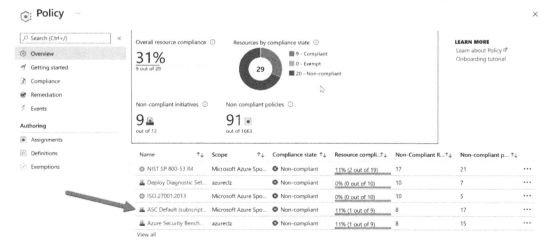

Figure 16.3 – Policy overview

Resources that are governed by Azure Policy are audited every 24 hours. If anything changes within that time frame, the compliance percentage will change. More information about Azure Policy can be found at `https://docs.microsoft.com/en-us/azure/governance/policy/overview`.

As we mentioned previously, you can use Azure Policy to govern resource costs by setting ceilings on subscription levels for Azure App Services or virtual machine types to avoid expensive resources from being created.

Azure Policy can be used to define the regions where you will be allowed to deploy resources. You can do this for both cost and data governance reasons. Some regions have a higher cost for resources, so using the lower-cost regions can help you control your costs. If you require data to be on resources within certain countries, you can set the resource groups for resources within that country to only select that country's Azure regions.

Azure Policy can also be used for regulatory and standards compliance. There are built-in initiatives that can be assigned to your subscription or specific resource groups to audit and monitor compliance with these standards.

Resources that are found to be non-compliant can be reviewed by selecting the specific policy or initiative within the **Compliance** menu, as shown in the following screenshot:

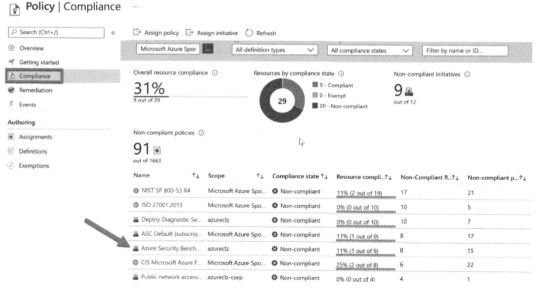

Figure 16.4 – Policy compliance

Then, you can review compliance with the specific initiative, as shown in the following screenshot:

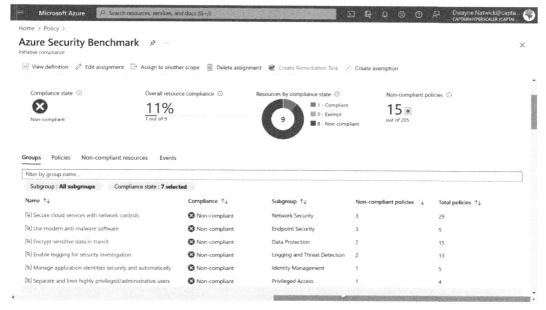

Figure 16.5 – Initiative compliance

You can go to the **Remediation** menu to determine the steps to remediate and gain compliance, as shown in the following screenshot:

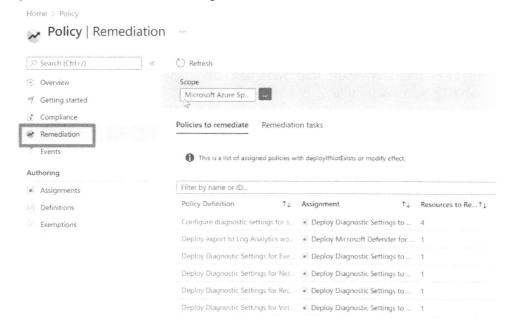

Figure 16.6 – Policy remediation

By selecting a Policy definition, you can start creating a **Remediation task** for the resources to gain compliance with the policy.

Let's assign a built-in policy to a resource group:

1. Log in to `https://portal.azure.com`.

2. Enter `policy` in the search bar to get to Azure Policy.

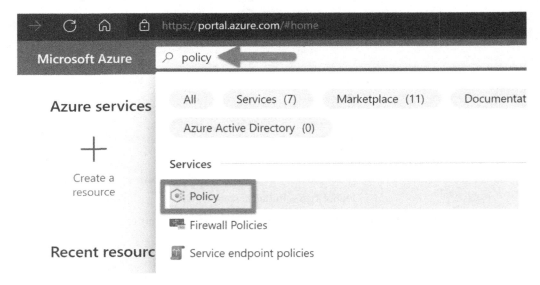

Figure 16.7 – The Policy service

3. In the **Policy** overview tile, find **Definitions** in the left menu. Select this option to view the policy definitions.

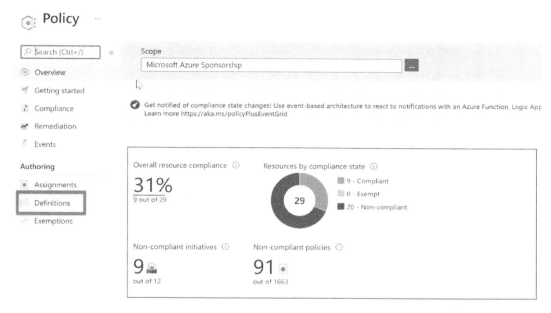

Figure 16.8 – Locating and selecting Definitions

4. Within the policy definitions, set **Definition type** to **Policy** and find **Windows machines should meet requirements for "Security Options – System settings"**. Select this policy, as follows:

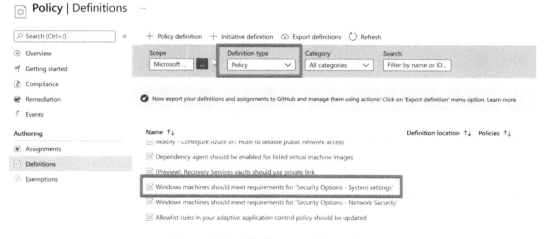

Figure 16.9 – Windows machines policy

5. In the **Policy definition** tile, select **Assign**.

Figure 16.10 – Assigning a policy

6. Select a **Scope** for the policy assignment and specify a **Subscription** and **Resource Group**. Choose **Select** and then **Review + create**, as shown in the following screenshot:

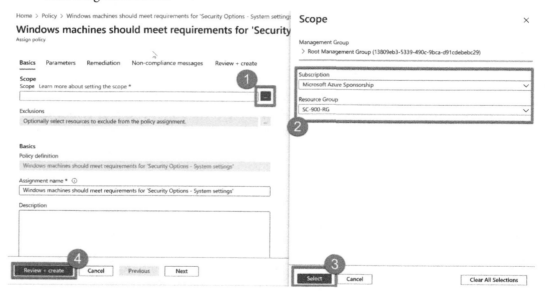

Figure 16.11 – Configuring the policy assignment

7.   Review the policy settings and select **Create**.

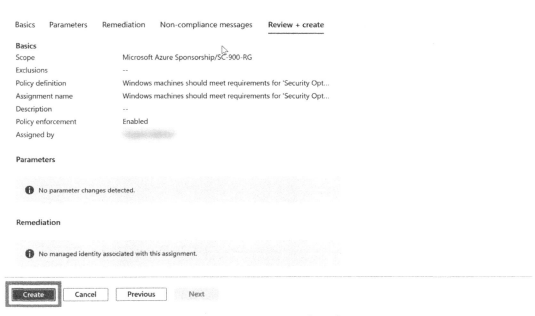

Windows machines should meet requirements for 'Security Options - System settings'
Assign policy

| Basics | Parameters | Remediation | Non-compliance messages | Review + create |

Basics
Scope   Microsoft Azure Sponsorship/SC-900-RG
Exclusions   --
Policy definition   Windows machines should meet requirements for 'Security Opt...
Assignment name   Windows machines should meet requirements for 'Security Opt...
Description   --
Policy enforcement   Enabled
Assigned by

Parameters

ℹ No parameter changes detected.

Remediation

ℹ No managed identity associated with this assignment.

| Create | Cancel | Previous | Next |

Figure 16.12 – Creating the policy

8.   Once the policy has been assigned, you will receive a notification stating that the policy assignment succeeded, as shown in the following screenshot:

✅ **Creating policy assignment succeeded**   ✕

Creating policy assignment 'Windows machines should meet requirements for 'Security Options - System settings'' in 'Microsoft Azure Sponsorship/SC-900-RG' was successful. Please note that the assignment takes around 30 minutes to take effect.

a few seconds ago

Figure 16.13 – Policy assignment succeeded

9.   Congratulations – you have successfully assigned a policy within Azure!

When you first assign the policy and go to the **Compliance** dashboard, you will see that the auditing process has not started, as shown in the following screenshot. Within the next 24 hours, you will be able to monitor the compliance of Windows virtual machines on your network and whether they meet the requirements of this policy.

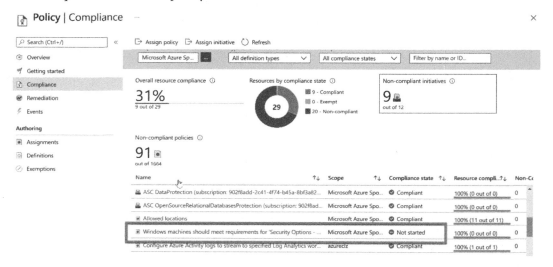

Figure 16.14 – Compliance and policy audit not started

Now, you should know how policies and initiatives are used to manage Azure resources. You should also know how to assign a policy definition to resources. Planning the policies that will work best for your company will help you manage and monitor compliance and governance over your resources.

In the next section, we will describe Azure Blueprints.

Azure Blueprints

Azure Blueprints allows you to create templates so that you can deploy resources in a standardized manner. As an example, a builder has standard blueprints that establish the foundation of each of the houses within the neighborhood they are building. Azure Blueprints governs how resources are created within Azure in the same way.

Azure Blueprints allows you to set the foundation for resources, including their size, network configuration, security controls, baselines, and policies that will be deployed with the Azure resources. This includes the **Azure Resource Manager** (**ARM**) templates you wish to deploy.

To access Blueprints, go to `https://portal.azure.com` and search for **Blueprints**, as shown in the following screenshot:

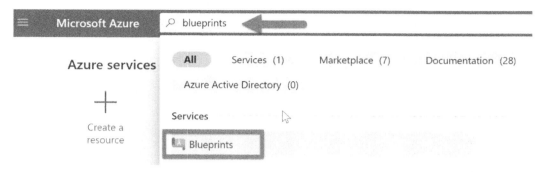

Figure 16.15 – Searching for Blueprints

The first time that you go to Blueprints, you will find a **Getting started** guide for creating a blueprint.

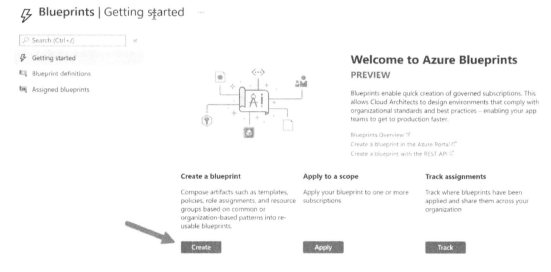

Figure 16.16 – Blueprints – Getting started

Click the **Create** button to create your first Blueprint.

When you select **Create**, you will be taken to a list of Blueprint templates that you can use, as shown in the following screenshot. Here, you will see templates for Azure Security Benchmark, **Cloud Adoption Framework** (**CAF**), Landing Zones, and many others. You also have the option to create a custom blueprint using the **Blank Blueprint** option.

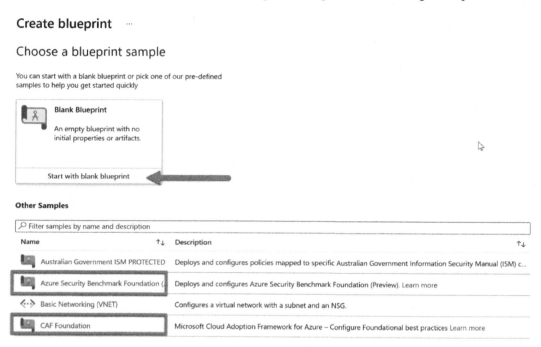

Figure 16.17 – The Create blueprint page

When you create a blueprint, you must select the subscription and save artifacts for your deployment requirements. In the following screenshot, you can see that you must specify a name for the blueprint and describe the subscription that it was assigned.

Create blueprint   ···

Basics   Artifacts

Blueprint name *   ⓘ

> SC900Blueprint

Blueprint description

> Deploys and configures Azure Security Benchmark Foundation (Preview).

Definition location *   ⓘ

> Microsoft Azure Sponsorship   ···

The management group or subscription where the blueprint is saved. The definition location determines the scope that the blueprint may be assigned to. Learn more at aka.ms/BlueLocation.

Save Draft   Discard   Next : Artifacts »

Figure 16.18 – Blueprint name and subscription

After naming the blueprint and assigning a subscription, click **Next : Artifacts** >>. Here, you can start adding artifacts. If you are using a template blueprint, then these artifacts will be populated with ARM templates and policies. You must add these yourself if you're using a blank template. You can also add additional artifacts to resources if you need additional policies or ARM templates beyond what is in the template. This can be seen in the following screenshot:

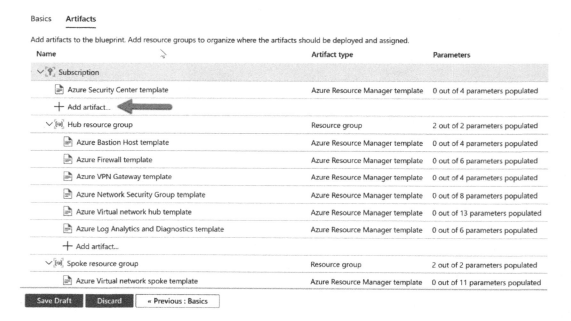

Figure 16.19 – Artifacts

Blueprints can be used to govern the resources with Azure and create a standard for deployment. For more information on Blueprints, go to `https://docs.microsoft.com/en-us/azure/governance/blueprints/overview`.

Next, we will describe Azure Purview.

Azure Purview

Azure Purview is a service that can be used for unified data governance across all of your company's data, whether it's on-premises, in Azure, Microsoft 365, or other **Software-as-a-Service (SaaS)** or cloud provider services, such as Amazon S3 storage.

Azure Purview can create a holistic data map of the entire hybrid data landscape through automated data discovery. Azure Purview can use sensitivity policies and data loss prevention policies for information protection and governance. The following screenshot shows how Azure Purview brings these data sources together:

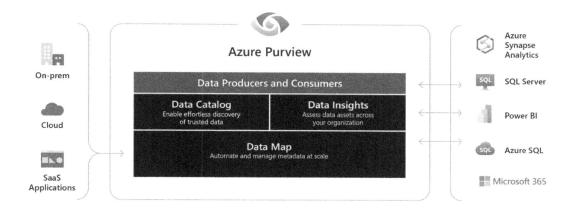

Figure 16.20 – Azure Purview data sources

For more information on Azure Purview, go to `https://docs.microsoft.com/en-us/azure/purview/overview`.

To access Azure Purview, go to `https://portal.azure.com` and search for `Purview`. Select **Azure Purview accounts** to go to the **Azure Purview** tile, as shown in the following screenshot:

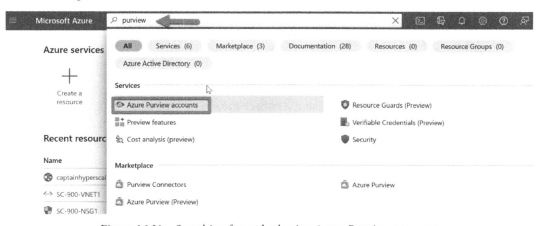

Figure 16.21 – Searching for and selecting Azure Purview accounts

In the **Azure Purview** tile, you will need to create an Azure Purview account. Select **Create Azure Purview account** to open the **Create Azure Purview account** tile, as shown in the following screenshot:

Create Azure Purview account ...

Provide Azure Purview account info

*Basics   *Networking   Tags   Review + Create

Create an Azure Purview account to develop a data governance solution in just a few clicks. A storage account and eventhub will be created in a managed resource group in your subscription for catalog ingestion scenarios. Learn more ☐

Project details

Subscription * | Microsoft Azure Sponsorship   ∨ |

    Resource group * | ∨ |
                          Create new

Instance details

Azure Purview account name * ⓘ | Enter a name for your Azure Purview account |

Location * | South Central US   ∨ |

> ❶ 1 Capacity unit (CU) = 25 ops/sec and 10 GB of metadata storage. Any new Azure Purview account will be provisioned with 1 CU with auto scale capabilities. Learn more ☐

Managed resources

A resource group, a storage account, and an Eventhub will be created in the selected subscription for catalog ingestion scenarios. The Microsoft.Storage and Microsoft.EventHub resource providers will get registered. Learn more ☐

[Review + Create]   [Previous]   [Next: Networking >]

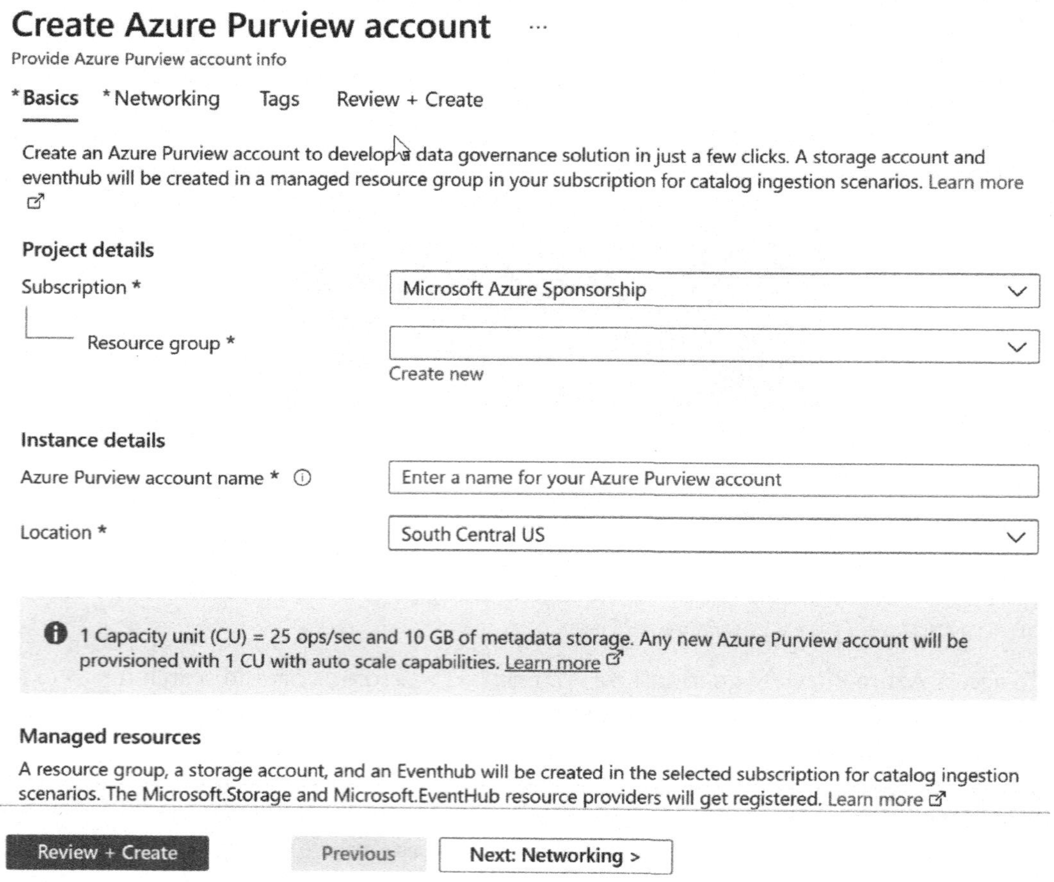

Figure 16.22 – Create Azure Purview account

The **Basics** tab will require you to assign a subscription and resource group, name the Azure Purview account, as shown in the preceding screenshot, and also create a **Managed resource group name**, as shown in the following screenshot. Once you've entered this information, select **Next: Networking**.

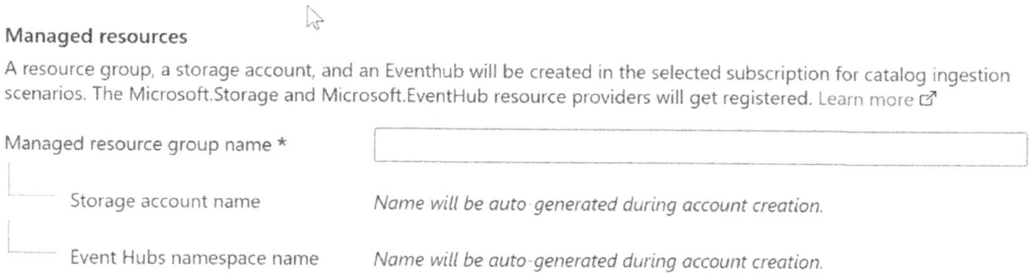

Managed resources

A resource group, a storage account, and an Eventhub will be created in the selected subscription for catalog ingestion scenarios. The Microsoft.Storage and Microsoft.EventHub resource providers will get registered. Learn more ☐

Managed resource group name *

Storage account name — *Name will be auto-generated during account creation.*

Event Hubs namespace name — *Name will be auto-generated during account creation.*

Figure 16.23 – Managed resources

Within the **Networking** tab, set the connectivity method to **All networks** or **Private endpoint**, as shown in the following screenshot. Select **Review + Create** to set up the Azure Purview account.

Create Azure Purview account   ...

Provide Azure Purview account info

* Basics   * **Networking**   Tags   Review + Create

Network connectivity

You can connect to your Azure Purview account either publically, via public IP addresses or service endpoints, or privately, using a private endpoint.

Connectivity method *   ● All networks

○ Private endpoint

All networks will be able to access this Azure Purview account.

[Review + Create]   [Previous]   [Next: Tags >]

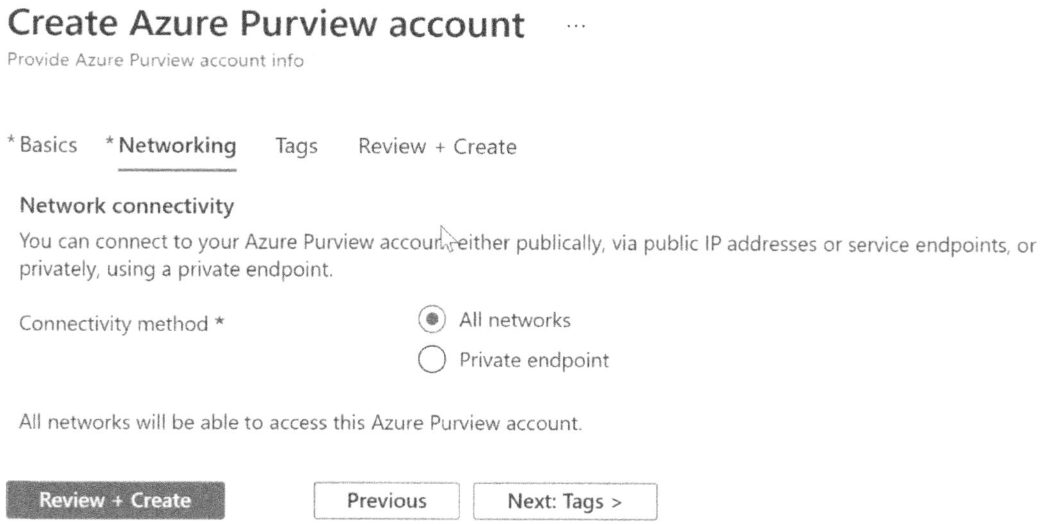

Figure 16.24 – Network connectivity

Once the account has been created, you will be taken to the Azure Purview dashboard, where you can configure your account with Azure Purview Studio, as shown in the following screenshot:

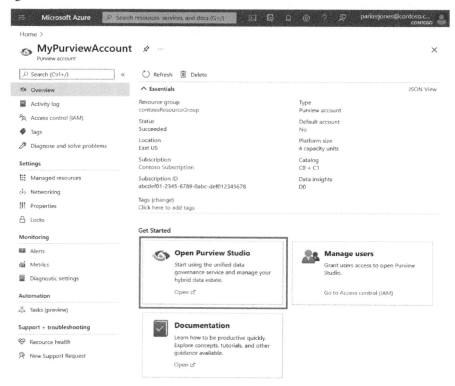

Figure 16.25 – Azure Purview account overview

For more information on configuring your Azure Purview account, go to `https://docs.microsoft.com/en-us/azure/purview/create-catalog-portal`.

Azure Purview Studio allows you to manage and govern your data sources and estate.

Now, let's summarize what we learned in this chapter.

Summary

In this chapter, we discussed the compliance and governance capabilities within Azure, including Policy, Blueprints, and Purview. At this point, you should understand where to go within the Azure portal to access these services and how to assign a policy to a subscription or resource group. With that, we have covered the content and objective areas for security, compliance, and identity for Microsoft 365 and Azure.

17
Final Assessment/ Mock Exam

Throughout this book, you have learned about the objectives that you need to master in order to pass the *Microsoft Security, Compliance, and Identity Fundamentals exam (SC-900)*. The exercises have provided you with hands-on practice for preparation and reference to understand the security, compliance, and identity solutions available within Microsoft 365 and Microsoft Azure. This final assessment can be used as additional preparation for passing the SC-900 exam. For information regarding the exam structure and content, please review *Chapter 1, Preparing for Your Microsoft Exam*. In this assessment, you can expect the following:

- A number of questions – 65 in total
- Multiple-choice and true or false questions

Questions

For a true exam experience, attempt this assessment as a closed book and give yourself 190 minutes to take the assessment. Use a notepad to answer the questions, and then review the answers so that you can grade your exam and determine any areas that require additional review. The recommendation for practice assessments is that you should be able to score 90% or better. Once you have attained this score, you should be ready to sit and pass the SC-300 exam. So, let's begin:

1. When thinking about **Identity and Access Management (IAM)**, which of the following is the most accurate statement?

   a. Identity is your password, and access is your application.

   b. Identity is who you are, and access is the permission that is granted.

   c. Identity is the permission that is granted, and access is who you are.

   d. Identity is your username, and access is your administrative privileges.

2. The principle of least privilege is defined as _____.

   a. The concept where a user or resource only has access to the applications and information required to perform their specific duties.

   b. The concept where a user has global administrator privileges to access all applications within the company.

   c. The concept where a user must request access to applications and information every time they need to complete their duties.

   d. The concept where a user has no administrator access regardless of their job role.

3. There are three levels of IAM: traditional, advanced, and optimal. Which of the following characteristics is not included in optimal IAM?

   a. Password-less authentication.

   b. Multifactor authentication is enforced.

   c. Single sign-on is not present.

   d. User behavior is analyzed in real time for possible risks.

   e. None of the above.

4. Which built-in AAD role has full control over the tenant and should be assigned to a limited number of select users?

   a. Billing administrator

   b. Security administrator

   c. Global administrator

   d. User administrator

   e. None of the above

5. Which device registration option is commonly used for personal devices (BYOD)?

   a. Hybrid AD-joined

   b. Azure AD-joined

   c. Azure AD-registered

   d. None of the above

6. Which of the following is **NOT** a function of security defaults when enabled?

   a. Requiring all users to register for Azure AD MFA

   b. Enforcing and requiring the use of Azure AD MFA for all administrators

   c. Allowing legacy authentication methods

   d. Protecting privileged access activities

   e. Requiring MFA for accessing sensitive information

7. A partner relationship between two companies within Azure AD is known as _____.

   a. B2C

   b. A2B

   c. B2B

   d. C2B

8. When you visit a shopping website and it gives you the option to use your Microsoft account to log in, this is an example of a _____ relationship.

   a. B2C

   b. A2B

   c. B2B

   d. C2B

9. You have created an Azure AD tenant. You also have an on-premises Windows Active Directory that includes users and groups. What can you use to bring together a hybrid infrastructure for the Azure AD cloud applications and synchronize on-premises users and groups for IAM?

   a. Application proxy

   b. **AD Federation Services (AD FS)**

   c. Azure AD Connect

   d. External identities

10. There are three Azure AD Connect synchronization options. Which is the least complex and can be configured with the Express settings?

    a. Password hash synchronization

    b. Pass-through authentication

    c. AD FS

11. Which Azure AD Connect synchronization option would you choose if you have a third-party **multi-factor authentication (MFA)** solution?

    a. Password hash synchronization

    b. Pass-through authentication

    c. AD FS

12. Which of the following is **NOT** a factor that is part of MFA?

    a. Something you know

    b. Something you have

    c. Something you are

    d. Something you belong to

13. You have entered your username and password to log in to the company intranet site. You are prompted to provide an additional form of verification. Which of the following would **NOT** be a proper second form of verification with MFA?

    a. A fingerprint

    b. Code from an authenticator app

    c. A PIN number

    d. A phone call to a cell phone

14. **Self-service password reset (SSPR)** uses many of the same forms of verification as MFA. Which of the following is used by SSPR but **NOT** MFA?

    a. A mobile phone

    b. An authenticator app

    c. A security question

    d. An app code

15. Which of the following is **NOT** configured in Azure AD Password Protection?

    a. Lockout threshold

    b. Lockout duration

    c. Global banned passwords

    d. Custom banned passwords

    e. Windows AD password protection

16. True or false: Password-less authentication, such as Windows Hello, is considered an authentication method with MFA.

    a. True

    b. False

17. The verification workflow of a zero-trust identity model includes which of the following? Select all that apply.

    a. A signal

    b. A trigger

    c. A decision

    d. An enforcement

18. What is the service that implements zero trust for identity within Azure AD?

    a. Azure AD Identity Protection

    b. Privileged Identity Management (PIM)

    c. Identity Governance

    d. Conditional Access

19. Smart lockout in Azure AD Identity Protection can protect users against what type of attack?

    a. SQL injections

    b. Cross-site scripting

    c. Phishing

    d. Brute-force dictionaries

20. An alert in Azure AD Identity Protection based on atypical travel is a form of what type of risk?

    a. User risk

    b. Sign-in risk

    c. Device risk

    d. None of the above

21. An alert in Azure Identity Protection regarding potentially leaked credentials is what type of risk?

    a. User risk

    b. Sign-in risk

    c. Device risk

    d. None of the above

22. What is the primary use of Microsoft Defender for Cloud Apps?

    a. Discovery apps to monitor for shadow IT

    b. To assign cloud apps to users

    c. To register for cloud app licensing

    d. All of the above

23. Which service provides just-in-time administrator access that is time-bound to decrease the attack surface of elevated privileges?

    a. Identity Protection

    b. Access Packages

    c. PIM

    d. Microsoft Defender for Cloud

24. True or false: Microsoft Sentinel is a scalable, cloud-native, **security information event management (SIEM)**, **extended detection and response (XDR)**, and **security orchestration automated response (SOAR)** solution.

    a. True

    b. False

25. What order does Microsoft Sentinel's workflow provide the following in?

    a. Respond, collect, detect, and investigate

    b. Collect, detect, investigate, and respond

    c. Investigate, detect, collect, and respond

    d. Detect, collect, investigate, and respond

26. In reference to a cyber attack, what is exfiltration?

    a. When an attacker cuts off access to resources.

    b. When an attacker has gained access to a system and is ready to exploit it. They will want to gain administrator-level access.

    c. When an attacker has gained access to sensitive information and they are able to remove that information to do harm in some way.

    d. When an attacker attempts to keep their access anonymous.

27. In a shared responsibility model for cloud services, the customer is *ALWAYS* responsible for protecting which of the following?

    a. Information, data, accounts, and identities

    b. Operating systems and network controls

    c. Applications and directory infrastructure

    d. Physical hosts, networks, and data centers

28. True or false: Shadow IT is a common internal threat to a company's security and compliance.

    a. True

    b. False

29. In a cloud defense-in-depth strategy, what is the "new perimeter?"

    a. Physical

    b. Identity and access

    c. Network

    d. Compute

30. True or false: Modern authentication uses an identity provider for authentication, whereas legacy authentication relies on the application to have a directory.

    a. True

    b. False

31. Advanced Azure AD security features, such as PIM and Identity Protection, are available with which of the following?

    a. An Azure AD free license

    b. An Office 365 Apps license

    c. Azure AD Premium P1

    d. Azure AD Premium P2

32. Which of the following is *NOT* a hybrid identity configuration with Azure AD?

    a. Legacy authentication

    b. Password hash synchronization

    c. Pass-through authentication

    d. AD FS

33. True or false: Windows Hello authentication is regarded as MFA.

    a. True

    b. False

34. For MFA, you have a password and require a second form of verification. Which of the following is NOT a valid second verification source?

    a. Facial recognition

    b. PIN

    c. Text code

    d. Authenticator app

35. True or false: A risky user refers to the likelihood that a user's credentials have been hacked.

    a. True

    b. False

36. Protection against traffic being flooded to the network perimeter is provided with which of the following?

    a. Azure Firewall

    b. Network Security Groups (NSGs)

    c. Web application firewall

    d. DDoS protection

37. Which of the following is NOT a connection that you can associate with an NSG?

    a. A virtual network

    b. A Bastion subnet

    c. A virtual network subnet

    d. A virtual machine virtual network interface

38. Which of the following does Azure Key Vault not provide customer management to?

    a. Administrator passwords

    b. Secrets

    c. Keys

    d. Certificates

39. In Microsoft Defender for Cloud, what information can be used to find improvement actions that will create a better security posture based on the Azure Security Baseline?

    a. Compliance dashboard

    b. Secure Score

    c. Vulnerability scanning

    d. Just-in-time virtual machine access

40. True or false: Microsoft Sentinel is Microsoft's cloud-based SIEM, SOAR, and XDR solution for security operations management.

    a. True

    b. False

41. In Microsoft's Cloud Adoption Framework for Azure, which step comes after *Define Strategy*?

    a. Govern

    b. Manage

    c. Ready

    d. Plan

42. What are the two components of responsibility as they pertain to regulatory compliance?

    a. Microsoft and customer responsibilities

    b. Microsoft and ISP responsibilities

    c. Customer and ISP responsibilities

    d. Auditor and customer responsibilities

43. Which of the following does resource locks not provide?

    a. Prevention against accidental changes or deletion.

    b. They allow for the deletion of resources within the scope of the lock.

    c. ReadOnly locks prevent all changes and deletions within the lock scope.

    d. Delete locks prevent any deletion of resources within the lock scope.

44. Which of the following does Azure Blueprints not include?

    a. Role assignments

    b. Resource audits

    c. Policy assignments

    d. ARM templates

45. True or false: An initiative is a group of policies used to govern resources and subscriptions.

    a. True

    b. False

46. Which of the following is not a Microsoft 365 Defender service?

    a. Microsoft Defender for Identity

    b. Microsoft Defender for Cloud Apps

    c. Microsoft Defender for Cloud

    d. Microsoft Defender for Office 365

47. Microsoft Defender for Identity is very similar to which Azure AD security service?

    a. Identity Protection

    b. Conditional Access

    c. PIM

    d. Cloud App Security

48. True or false: Microsoft Defender for Cloud Apps allows a company to discover and manage shadow IT cloud apps for security and compliance.

    a. True

    b. False

49. Which service does Microsoft Defender for Office 365 NOT protect?

    a. Exchange Online

    b. OneDrive Personal

    c. Microsoft Teams

    d. SharePoint Online

50. True or false: Microsoft 365 Security Center provides a secure score that is similar to what Microsoft Defender for Cloud does within Azure.

    a. True

    b. False

51. Which of the following is the best option for managing company-owned devices with Microsoft Intune?

    a. Conditional Access policies

    b. Identity Protection

    c. Mobile Application Management

    d. Mobile Device Management

52. Which of the following is NOT an area of securing devices with Microsoft Intune?

    a. Feature updates

    b. Security baselines

    c. Conditional Access for compliance

    d. Microsoft Defender for Endpoint integration

53. True or False: Incidents are a collection of alerts that are created when suspicious activity is found.

    a. True

    b. False

54. Which of the following services is used for Security Incident Management and automated response?

    a. Microsoft Defender for Cloud

    b. Microsoft Sentinel

    c. Microsoft 365 Defender

    d. Microsoft Defender for Cloud Apps

55. True or False: Incident management is critical to ensure that any incident alerts are properly contained and addressed.

    a. True

    b. False

56. Which of the following is not a Microsoft Privacy principle?

    a. Transparency

    b. Strong legal protections

    c. Security

    d. Content-based marketing

57. When you search and find documentation pertaining to Microsoft's compliance audit, which of the following is the best option for you to place that document for quick access later?

    a. Save it to your online library.

    b. Download the document.

    c. Bookmark the browser location.

    d. Do nothing; leave it as it is.

58. Which of the following does Microsoft 365 Compliance Center not provide?

    a. A customer-only list of controls

    b. A compliance score

    c. Compliance assessments and templates

    d. Improvement actions and alerts

59. There are two eDiscovery workflows, Core and Advanced. Which of the following is *ONLY* part of an Advanced workflow?

    a. Creating a case and holding

    b. Adding data to the review set

    c. Searching for content

    d. Exporting and downloading case data

60. True or false: When searching audit log data, you can filter and export the data to a CSV file.

    a. True

    b. False

61. Which of the following is *NOT* a component of data protection and governance?

    a. Knowing your data

    b. Protecting your data

    c. Preventing data loss

    d. Deleting your data

62. Data classification is governed by which Microsoft 365 service?

    a. Sensitivity labels and policies

    b. Retention labels and policies

    c. Data loss prevention policies

    d. Records management

63. True or false: Data loss prevention can recognize the types of PII and PHI and can protect against any accidental sharing of this data.

    a. True

    b. False

64. True or false: A record is a document that has a plan for retention and disposition and should have all activities logged.

    a. True

    b. False

65. True or false: Communication barriers protect against potential conflicts of interest.

    a. True

    b. False

Answers

We recommend that you review the following answers after attempting to answer the preceding questions. Check your answers and review the sections within the recommended chapters for additional clarificatio:.

1. The answer is b. The most accurate statement is that identity is who you are, and access is the permission that is granted. Your identity might include your password and username, and access might include your authorized applications and administrative privileges, but these are not the most accurate statements in the responses. For additional details, see *Chapter 5, Defining Identity Principles/Concepts and the Identity Services within Azure AD*.

2. The answer is a. The principle of least privilege is the concept that a user or resource only has access to the applications and information required to perform their specific duties. For additional details, see *Chapter 5, Defining Identity Principles/ Concepts and the Identity Services within Azure AD*.

3. The answer is c. Within an optimal IAM infrastructure, single sign-on should be present for all cloud and on-premises applications. For additional details, see *Chapter 6, Describing the Authentication and Access Management Capabilities of Azure AD*.

4. The answer is c. The global administrator has full administrative control over the tenant and subscription and should only be assigned to 3–5 select users. For additional details, see *Chapter 5, Defining Identity Principles/Concepts and the Identity Services within Azure AD*.

5. The answer is c. The most common way to manage a personal device within Azure AD is to register the device in Azure AD. This allows the device to be managed with Microsoft Intune when requiring a full Azure AD join. For additional details, see *Chapter 5, Defining Identity Principles/Concepts and the Identity Services within Azure AD*.

6. The answer is c. One feature of security defaults is to block legacy authentication, not allow it. All of the other choices are features of security defaults. For additional details, see *Chapter 5, Defining Identity Principles/Concepts and the Identity Services within Azure AD*.

7. The answer is c. When a partner relationship is established between two companies within Azure AD, this is a B2B or business-to-business relationship. For additional details, see *Chapter 6, Describing the Authentication and Access Management Capabilities of Azure AD*.

8. The answer is a. This is an example of a B2C, or business-to-consumer, relationship. For additional details, see *Chapter 6, Describing the Authentication and Access Management Capabilities of Azure AD*.

9. The answer is c. Azure AD Connect is used to synchronize on-premises users and groups with Azure AD. Application Proxy can be used for hybrid infrastructures, but it utilizes Azure AD for identity and access, not on-premises directly. For additional details, see *Chapter 6, Describing the Authentication and Access Management Capabilities of Azure AD*.

10. The answer is a. Password hash synchronization is the least complex and the only option that would be configured with the Express settings. For additional details, see *Chapter 6, Describing the Authentication and Access Management Capabilities of Azure AD*.

11. The answer is c. AD FS is required to synchronize with Azure AD when using a third-party MFA solution. For additional details, see *Chapter 6, Describing the Authentication and Access Management Capabilities of Azure AD*.

12. The answer is d. MFA consists of using two forms to verify a person's identity. These can be a combination of something you know, something you have, and something you are. For additional details, see *Chapter 6, Describing the Authentication and Access Management Capabilities of Azure AD*.

13. The answer is c. A PIN is something that you know, and so is a password. Therefore, it does not meet the requirements for MFA. For additional details, see *Chapter 6, Describing the Authentication and Access Management Capabilities of Azure AD*.

14. The answer is c. MFA does not use security questions as a valid factor for verification, but they can be used for SSPR. For additional details, see *Chapter 6, Describing the Authentication and Access Management Capabilities of Azure AD*.

15. The answer is c. Global banned passwords are included by default within your Azure AD tenant, and there is no need to configure this list. For additional details, see *Chapter 6, Describing the Authentication and Access Management Capabilities of Azure AD*.

16. The answer is b. This statement is false. Using password-less authentication provides a high level of usability and security without additional complexity. For additional details, see *Chapter 6, Describing the Authentication and Access Management Capabilities of Azure AD.*

17. The answer is a, c, and d. The zero-trust model for identity has a workflow that includes a signal that initiates a decision, which enforces the final result of authorizing or denying access. For additional details, see *Chapter 2, Describing Security Methodologies.*

18. The answer is d. Conditional Access policies follow the zero-trust workflow to enforce the zero-trust verification of identities. For additional details, see *Chapter 6, Describing the Authentication and Access Management Capabilities of Azure AD.*

19. The answer is d. Configuring Smart Lockout in Azure AD Identity Protection protects users against a brute-force dictionary attack where an attacker is attempting to guess the user password by running multiple attempts. For additional details, see *Chapter 7, Describing the Identity Protection and Governance Capabilities of Azure AD.*

20. The answer is b. Atypical travel identifies a potential sign-in risk. For additional details, see *Chapter 7, Describing the Identity Protection and Governance Capabilities of Azure AD.*

21. The answer is a. Leaked credentials identify a potential user risk. For additional details, see *Chapter 7, Describing the Identity Protection and Governance Capabilities of Azure AD.*

22. The answer is a. Microsoft Defender for Cloud Apps can discover apps that are being used on your network and help you monitor and protect against shadow IT. For additional details, see *Chapter 12, Describing Security Management and the Endpoint Security Capabilities of Microsoft 365.*

23. The answer is c. PIM provides just-in-time access to administrator roles. For additional details, see *Chapter 7, Describing the Identity Protection and Governance Capabilities of Azure AD.*

24. The answer is b. Microsoft Sentinel is not an XDR solution. Microsoft Defender provides the XDR solutions that can be used with Sentinel's SIEM and SOAR solutions. For additional details, see *Chapter 11, Describing the Security Capabilities of Microsoft Sentinel.*

25. The answer is b. Microsoft Sentinel's workflow is to collect, detect, investigate and respond. For additional details, see *Chapter 11, Describing the Security Capabilities of Microsoft Sentinel.*

26. The answer is c. This is an example of exfiltration within a cyber attack. For additional details, see *Chapter 3, Understanding Key Security Concepts.*

27. The answer is a. Whether on-premises, IaaS, PaaS, or SaaS, the customer is always responsible for these areas along with securing devices. For additional details, see *Chapter 3, Understanding Key Security Concepts.*

28. The answer is a. Shadow IT is the use of unapproved applications within a company network. These applications can cause potential security and compliance threats. For additional details, see *Chapter 12, Describing Security Management and the Endpoint Security Capabilities of Microsoft 365.*

29. The answer is b. Since the customer is no longer responsible for physical security, it becomes extremely important to protect identity and access as the first line of defense. For additional details, see *Chapter 5, Defining Identity Principles/Concepts and the Identity Services within Azure AD.*

30. The answer is a. This statement is true. For additional details, see *Chapter 5, Defining Identity Principles/Concepts and the Identity Services within Azure AD.*

31. The answer is d. The Premium P2 license is the only Azure AD license with PIM and Identity Protection services. For additional details, see *Chapter 7, Describing the Identity Protection and Governance Capabilities of Azure AD.*

32. The answer is a. Legacy authentication is when an application directory provides authentication. This cannot be used for a hybrid identity infrastructure. For additional details, see *Chapter 5, Defining Identity Principles/Concepts and the Identity Services within Azure AD.*

33. The answer is a. Windows Hello uses a PIN that is saved on the hardware and facial recognition for MFA. For additional details, see *Chapter 6, Describing the Authentication and Access Management Capabilities of Azure AD.*

34. The answer is b. A PIN is considered something you know and, therefore, falls in the same category as a password. Therefore, it cannot be used alongside a password for MFA. For additional details, see *Chapter 6, Describing the Authentication and Access Management Capabilities of Azure AD.*

35. The answer is b. This is the definition of a risky sign-in. A risky user is where there is a possibility that a user has been compromised and the person logging in is not who they say they are. For additional details, see *Chapter 7, Describing the Identity Protection and Governance Capabilities of Azure AD.*

36. The answer is d. DDoS provides protection against distributed denial-of-service attacks, which are flooded traffic requests to access the network. Basic DDoS protection is provided to Azure customers at no additional cost. For additional details, see *Chapter 9, Describing Security Management and Capabilities of Azure.*

37. The answer is a. An NSG cannot be associated directly with the virtual network. It must be associated with a subnet or network interface within the virtual network. For additional details, see *Chapter 9, Describing Security Management and Capabilities of Azure.*

38. The answer is a. Azure Key Vault does not manage passwords. For additional details, see *Chapter 9, Describing Security Management and Capabilities of Azure.*

39. The answer is b. The secure score provides improvement actions to increase the security posture based on Azure's Security Baseline and best practices. For additional details, see *Chapter 10, Describing Threat Protection with Microsoft 365 Defender.*

40. The answer is b. Microsoft Sentinel is a cloud-based SIEM and SOAR solution. XDR is provided through Microsoft Defender services. For additional details, see *Chapter 11, Describing the Security Capabilities of Microsoft Sentinel.*

41. The answer is d. After the business stakeholders have met and defined the strategy to move to the cloud, the planning process begins. For additional details, see *Chapter 3, Understanding Key Security Concepts.*

42. The answer is a. Any responsibility for compliance or security control has either a Microsoft and/or a customer responsibility. For additional details, see *Chapter 3, Understanding Key Security Concepts.*

43. The answer is b. When a lock is in place, deletion of that resource will not be allowed, whether it is a ReadOnly or Delete lock. For additional details, see *Chapter 16, Describing Resource Governance Capabilities in Azure.*

44. The answer is c. Azure Blueprints has nothing to do with auditing resources, but it can define the resource groups and policies that would be used for these audits after they have been created. For additional details, see *Chapter 16, Describing Resource Governance Capabilities in Azure.*

45. The answer is a. Initiatives are a group of policies. For additional details, see *Chapter 16, Describing Resource Governance Capabilities in Azure.*

46. The answer is c. Microsoft Defender for Cloud is an Azure service, not a Microsoft 365 service. For additional details, see *Chapter 8, Describing Basic Security Services and Management Capabilities in Azure.*

47. The answer is a. Microsoft Defender for Identity identifies risky users and risky sign-ins for an on-premises Active Directory infrastructure, much like Azure AD Identity Protection does for cloud identities. For additional details, see *Chapter 12, Describing Security Management and the Endpoint Security Capabilities of Microsoft 365.*

48. The answer is a. For additional details, see *Chapter 12, Describing Security Management and the Endpoint Security Capabilities of Microsoft 365*.

49. The answer is b. Microsoft Defender for Office 365 protects business services, so it would protect OneDrive for Business. For additional details, see *Chapter 12, Describing Security Management and the Endpoint Security Capabilities of Microsoft 365*.

50. The answer is a. For additional details, see *Chapter 10, Describing Threat Protection with Microsoft 365 Defender*.

51. The answer is d. If the company owns and provides the device, MDM is the best option for Intune management. For additional details, see *Chapter 12, Describing Security Management and the Endpoint Security Capabilities of Microsoft 365*.

52. The answer is a. Though feature updates can be managed with Microsoft Intune, these do not pertain to security. For additional details, see *Chapter 12, Describing Security Management and the Endpoint Security Capabilities of Microsoft 365*.

53. The answer is a. For additional details, see *Chapter 11, Describing the Security Capabilities of Microsoft Sentinel*.

54. The answer is b. Sentinel is Microsoft's cloud-based SIEM and SOAR solution. For additional details, see *Chapter 11, Describing the Security Capabilities of Microsoft Sentinel*.

55. The answer is a. For additional details, see *Chapter 11, Describing the Security Capabilities of Microsoft Sentinel*.

56. The answer is d. Microsoft has a principle of NO content-based marketing. For additional details, see *Chapter 4, Key Microsoft Security and Compliance Principles*.

57. The answer is a. This is the best option. If the documents are updated between the times that you need them, they will be updated at this location. For additional details, see *Chapter 4, Key Microsoft Security and Compliance Principles*.

58. The answer is a. Compliance Center provides *BOTH* a customer list and a Microsoft list of controls. For additional details, see *Chapter 13, Compliance Management Capabilities in Microsoft*.

59. The answer is b. Advanced eDiscovery allows for an additional step of creating a review set for more pertinent information to the case. For additional details, see *Chapter 15, Describing Insider Risk, eDiscovery, and Audit Capabilities in Microsoft 365*.

60. The answer is a. For additional details, see *Chapter 15, Describing Insider Risk, eDiscovery, and Audit Capabilities in Microsoft 365*.

61. The answer is d. This is NOT a component of data protection and governance. The fourth point in the workflow is governing your data. For additional details, see *Chapter 14, Describing Information Protection and Governance Capabilities of Microsoft 365.*

62. The answer is a. Sensitivity labels and policies govern classified data in Microsoft 365. For additional details, see *Chapter 14, Describing Information Protection and Governance Capabilities of Microsoft 365.*

63. The answer is a. For additional details, see *Chapter 14, Describing Information Protection and Governance Capabilities of Microsoft 365.*

64. The answer is a. For additional details, see *Chapter 14, Describing Information Protection and Governance Capabilities of Microsoft 365.*

65. The answer is a. This is a true statement. For additional details, see *Chapter 15, Describing Insider Risk, eDiscovery, and Audit Capabilities in Microsoft 365.*

Summary

This completes your assessment and preparation for the *SC-900 Microsoft Security, Compliance, and Identity Fundamentals* exam. Good luck! We wish you continued success in your certification and professional journey.

Index

Packt.com

Subscribe to our online digital library for full access to over 7,000 books and videos, as well as industry leading tools to help you plan your personal development and advance your career. For more information, please visit our website.

Why subscribe?

- Spend less time learning and more time coding with practical eBooks and Videos from over 4,000 industry professionals

- Improve your learning with Skill Plans built especially for you

- Get a free eBook or video every month

- Fully searchable for easy access to vital information

- Copy and paste, print, and bookmark content

Did you know that Packt offers eBook versions of every book published, with PDF and ePub files available? You can upgrade to the eBook version at packt.com and as a print book customer, you are entitled to a discount on the eBook copy. Get in touch with us at customercare@packtpub.com for more details.

At www.packt.com, you can also read a collection of free technical articles, sign up for a range of free newsletters, and receive exclusive discounts and offers on Packt books and eBooks.

Other Books You May Enjoy

If you enjoyed this book, you may be interested in these other books by Packt:

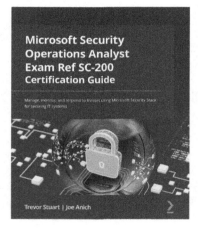

Microsoft Security Operations Analyst Exam Ref SC-200 Certification Guide

Trevor Stuart, Joe Anich

ISBN: 9781803231891

- Discover how to secure information technology systems for your organization
- Manage cross-domain investigations in the Microsoft 365 Defender portal
- Plan and implement the use of data connectors in Microsoft Defender for Cloud
- Get to grips with designing and configuring a Microsoft Sentinel workspace
- Configure SOAR (security orchestration, automation, and response) in Microsoft Sentinel
- Find out how to use Microsoft Sentinel workbooks to analyze and interpret data
- Solve mock tests at the end of the book to test your knowledge

Microsoft Identity and Access Administrator Exam Guide

Dwayne Natwick

ISBN: 9781801818049

- Understand core exam objectives to pass the SC-300 exam

- Implement an identity management solution with MS Azure AD

- Manage identity with multi-factor authentication (MFA), conditional access, and identity protection

- Design, implement, and monitor the integration of enterprise apps for Single Sign-On (SSO)

- Add apps to your identity and access solution with app registration

- Design and implement identity governance for your identity solution

Packt is searching for authors like you

If you're interested in becoming an author for Packt, please visit `authors.packtpub.com` and apply today. We have worked with thousands of developers and tech professionals, just like you, to help them share their insight with the global tech community. You can make a general application, apply for a specific hot topic that we are recruiting an author for, or submit your own idea.

Share Your Thoughts

Now you've finished *Microsoft Security, Compliance, and Identity Fundamentals Exam Ref SC-900*, we'd love to hear your thoughts! Scan the QR code below to go straight to the Amazon review page for this book and share your feedback or leave a review on the site that you purchased it from.

`https://packt.link/r/1801815992`

Your review is important to us and the tech community and will help us make sure we're delivering excellent quality content.

Made in United States
North Haven, CT
24 May 2023